D0216756

HD 6095 .G72 1980

Greenwald, Maurine Weiner

Women, war, and work

DATE DUE

MAY 0 6 2013			

WOMEN, WAR, AND WORK

Recent Titles in Contributions in Women's Studies

Women's Studies: An Interdisciplinary Collection
Kathleen O'Connor Blumhagen and Walter D. Johnson, editors

Latin American Women: Historical Perspectives
Asuncion Lavrin

Beyond Her Sphere: Women and the Professions in American History
Barbara J. Harris

Literary America, 1903-1934: The Mary Austin Letters
T. M. Pearce, editor

The American Woman in Transition: The Urban Influence, 1870-1920
Margaret Gibbons Wilson

Liberators of the Female Mind: The Shirreff Sisters, Educational
Reform, and the Women's Movement
Edward W. Ellsworth

The Jewish Feminist Movement in Germany: The Campaigns of the
Jüdischer Frauenbund, 1904-1938
Marion A. Kaplan

Silent Hattie Speaks: The Personal Journal of Senator Hattie Caraway
Diane D. Kincaid, editor

Women in Irish Society: The Historical Dimension
Margaret MacCurtain and Donncha O'Corrain

Margaret Fuller's **Woman in the Nineteenth Century:** A Literary Study
of Form and Content, of Sources and Influence
Marie Mitchell Olesen Urbanski

Sisters and Wives: The Past and Future of Sexual Equality
Karen Sacks

To Work and To Wed: Female Employment, Feminism, and the
Great Depression, 1929-1941
Lois Scharf

Unsung: A History of Women in American Music
Christine Ammer

WOMEN, WAR, AND WORK

The Impact of World War I on Women Workers in the United States

Maurine Weiner Greenwald

CONTRIBUTIONS IN WOMEN'S STUDIES, NUMBER 12

Greenwood Press

WESTPORT, CONNECTICUT • LONDON, ENGLAND

Library of Congress Cataloging in Publication Data

Greenwald, Maurine Weiner, 1944-
    Women, war, and work.

    (Contributions in women's studies ; no. 12
ISSN 0147-104X)
        Bibliography: p.
    Includes index.
        1. Women—Employment—United States—History.
    2. European War, 1914-1918—Economic aspects—United
    States. I. Title. II. Series.
    HD6095.G72   331.4'0973   80-540
    ISBN 0-313-21355-0 (lib. bdg.)

Library of Congress Catalog Card Number: 80-540
ISBN: 0-313-21355-0
ISSN: 0147-104X

First published in 1980

Greenwood Press
A division of Congressional Information Service, Inc.
88 Post Road West, Westport, Connecticut 06881

Printed in the United States of America

10 9 8 7 6 5 4 3 2 1

TO MICKEY

Contents

Illustrations   ix
Tables   xi
Acknowledgments   xiii
Introduction   xix
1. From Afar and Near: Patterns of Change in
   Women's Work   3
2. The Technical and the Human: Managing
   Women Workers   46
3. The Limits of Opportunity: Working for the Railroads   87
4. The Right to Wage Labor: Women as Streetcar
   Conductors   139
5. No Service, No Smile: Telephone Operators and the War   185
6. Conclusion   233
Abbreviations   245
Notes   247
Bibliography   285
Index   301

Illustrations

1. Vertical milling machine workers   16
2. Women tending a cutting press   17
3. Drill press operator   18
4. Tire finishers   19
5. Cannery operatives   28
6. Racial segregation in the garment industry   29
7. Black women at work in a brick yard   30
8. Patriotism in the factory   36
9. Women and patriotism   37
10. Mary van Kleeck, industrial sociologist   62
11. Mary Anderson, trade unionist and social reformer   63
12. Pauline Goldmark, social reformer   64
13. Clerical workers   95
14. Training of railroad dispatchers   96
15. Women car cleaners   108
16. Track walkers   109
17. Woman oiling a railroad engine   110
18. Railroad yard common labor   111
19. Women railroad workers and engine no. 940   112
20. Electric welder   121
21. "Another Military Expediency?"   122
22. Women streetcar conductors   140
23. Teenage boys operating an early telephone switchboard   191

24. Male and female operators in a New York City
    exchange in 1885   192
25. An all-female telephone operating staff   193
26. Julia O'Connor, trade union activist on behalf of
    telephone operators   206

Tables

1. Women Laborers and Operatives Employed in Selected
   Industries, 1870-1910   7

2. The Ascendancy of Women Office Workers, 1870-1910   9

3. Women in Sales Occupations, 1870-1910   11

4. Women Employed as Service Workers, 1870-1910   12

5. Increase and Decrease in the Number of Women
   Employed in the Principal Nonagricultural
   Occupations, 1910-1920   14

Acknowledgments

Beyond any question Martin A. Greenwald deserves my greatest gratitude for helping bring this book to completion. When the history of women began to come into its own as an area of scholarship, he encouraged me to pursue answers to my many questions about women's experience. From the inception of this particular project nearly a decade ago, he has provided unfailing support at every step of the way. As I became immersed in the complexities of the study, he frequently calmed my nagging doubts and reassured me of my ability to make sense of the historical puzzle. Successive drafts of every chapter received his most thorough, sensitive, and perceptive evaluation. His recommendations improved the structure and substance of my arguments as well as my writing style. His historical knowledge and professional rigor as well as his extensive editorial advice have contributed immeasurably to whatever value this study might have. Mickey's influence can be found on every page of this book and for these reasons, I have dedicated it to him.

I began my research on the American wartime domestic experience as a graduate student at Brown University and completed it as a faculty member at the University of Pittsburgh. Individuals at both institutions have aided my endeavor. When I first designed my research, only the vaguest notions informed my understanding of the history of women workers. As a result of my residence at the University of Pittsburgh, I learned to think about my project in new ways. David Montgomery deserves special thanks for introducing me to the study of labor history. As a result of his probing questions and avid interest in my research, I radically altered my original research design. His insightful lectures and publications on the collective experience of working people provided a framework for my interpretation of changes in women's work in the early twentieth century. Over the course of several years he discussed my study's problems and findings, critically evaluated my written work, and suggested useful sources. He taught me the meaning of collegiality. Thanks are also due to Samuel Hays, who convinced me of the importance of a social-historical perspective and who read and criticized my analyses of the railroad and telephone industries. This book has also benefited from Peter Karsten's commentary on an earlier version of the study.

At Brown University John L. Thomas offered sound professional counsel, honest evaluations, and useful editorial assistance. He diligently criticized numerous versions of this manuscript. Mari Jo Buhle applied her considerable knowledge of women's history to a careful assessment of this study. Her thoughtful questions sent me in pursuit of additional sources to test further and refine my arguments.

Other people came to my aid as well. Joan W. Scott suggested ways of clarifying my main arguments. Patrick Fridenson considered the entire manuscript in light of French scholarship in labor and women's history and made useful recommendations. Susan Porter Benson wrote an assessment of my work that was a model of detailed and constructive criticism. As I revised parts of the manuscript, I often referred to her perceptive and cogent advice. Barbara Rosen and Carolyn Accola read an entire draft of an earlier version of this work and raised excellent questions for my consideration. Students who took my graduate seminar on women's labor history in the summer of 1977 also contributed to revisions of the study. I wish to thank Rena Henderson, Penny Ricchio, Debra Walker, and Nora Wyse for their compelling questions about my work.

Throughout the course of my research many individuals suggested valuable primary and secondary sources. Susan Porter Benson's willingness to photocopy obscure journal articles and long-forgotten studies of women's work brought many unfamiliar sources to my attention. Patricia Cooper informed me of little-known strike investigations by the Department of Justice. From Cecelia Bucki I received several Ordnance Department reports that I had been unable to locate. Steven Sapolsky directed me to informative sources on the streetcar industry and shared his ideas about transit workers' militancy. I am also grateful to Keith Dix for sending me unusual information on women in the American coal industry during World War I. Marge Yeager kept my interests in mind during her frequent visits to the Carnegie Library of Pittsburgh. She kept me abreast of the latest books on the Bell Telephone System, but more importantly, she extended genuine moral support when and as needed. My bibliophile colleague, Robert Colodny, provided me with a steady stream of helpful references and kindly loaned me many books of interest from his extensive library. Robin Miller Jacoby combed her research notes for detailed biographical information about several women labor organizers.

The staffs of many libraries and archives provided helpful and efficient service. Joseph Howerton of the National Archives deserves special thanks for his exceptional assistance in locating primary sources for my work. William Lind, James Walker, Carmen delle Donne, John Taylor, Tim Nenninger, Rita Boyd, and Lane Moore helped to make my research trips to the National Archives more productive. Eleanor M. Lewis of the Sophia Smith Collection at Smith College helped me to make best use of the Mary van Kleeck Papers. At Hillman Library at the University of Pittsburgh, Adelaide Sukiennik and Oxanna S. Kaufman provided exceptional service in the acquisition of important sources for the study of women's labor history. Ingrid Glasco and Suzanne Crosby dealt very effectively with the many aggravations of acquiring resource materials through interlibrary loan. The staffs of the Library of Congress, Department of Labor Library, Schlesinger Library, and Brown University Library also provided excellent service.

Several individuals were very instrumental in tracking down information about telephone workers. Special thanks are due Mary Lyons for retrieving valuable documents and photos from the archives of the American Telephone and Telegraph Company. Roy Dickinson of the International Brotherhood of Electrical

Workers fulfilled my request for photographs and biographical information about Julia O'Connor. Bruce Crowther of the Southern New England Telephone Company helped me to locate retired telephone operators through the Telephone Pioneers of America.

My frequent research trips to Washington, D.C. were made easier and more pleasant thanks to the help of many friends. Barbara Kraft generously fed and housed me in Washington for weeks at a time over the course of several years, while Nora Faires thoughtfully tended plants and pets left in Pittsburgh. My colleagues in Women's Studies, Mary Louise Briscoe and Irene Frieze, shouldered some of my administrative burdens so that I could arrange my schedule for research travel and writing.

Janelle Greenberg and Linda Pritchard provided personal encouragement at numerous junctures as this work progressed. Martel Montgomery deserves my special gratitude for her gracious hospitality and her unfailing moral support. Bernard B. Greenwald, my father-in-law and also my friend, receives my thanks for saving me from egregious mathematical errors that only the trained eye of an accountant could see at first glance.

For their good cheer, efficiency, and willingness to meet my deadlines, I extend my appreciation to Mildred Baer, Gerry Katz, and Faye Schneider, who worked into their ordinarily demanding duties as secretaries at the University of Pittsburgh the typing of the final manuscript.

Permission was granted by the American Telephone and Telegraph Company, the International Brotherhood of Electrical Workers, and the National Archives for the reprinting of photographs for this book. The poems "The Reason Why" and "She Hands Him a Lemon" are reprinted with the permission of Eagle Publications of Claremont, New Hampshire, which owns the rights to the *Springfield Reporter*, in which the poems first appeared. Peter Stearns permitted the reprinting of information about women railroad workers from "Women Workers and World War I: The American Railroad Industry, A Case Study," *Journal of Social History* 9 (Winter 1975): 154-77. The poem "Keep the Girls Off the Cars" is reprinted with the permission of the Amalgamated Transit Union. Fabian Bachrach kindly allowed me to publish a photo of Mary van Kleeck taken by his firm.

Finally, I gratefully acknowledge the University of Pittsburgh for providing me with a generous research grant from the Provost's Development Fund which enabled me to complete revisions of this book.

MWG
November 1979
Pittsburgh

Introduction

This book studies American women wage earners in the era of the First World War. It explores the war's direct effects on female employment in the context of fundamental long-term social and economic changes in the nature and structure of work in the United States. The analysis is presented through a series of case studies which both exemplify the larger trends and indicate the war's specific impact on various work settings.

During the five-decade period beginning in 1870 dramatic changes occurred in the structure and scale of American business and finance and in the organization of work in factories, foundries, offices, retail stores, and many other workplaces. In those fifty years the corporation became the dominant form of business, while all manner of work underwent subdivision, routinization, and mechanization. Organizational and technological changes of this sort frequently permitted the dilution of skills formerly needed to perform standard work processes, and women often gained employment in such redefined jobs. As a part of this business revolution, white-collar work assumed increasing importance in the economy and women came to compose a major segment of this new working class. Business initiated new pay schemes and introduced innovative welfare measures to help stabilize the work force and encourage employees to increase their efficiency and maximize productivity. As a result of management innovations, workers had to contend now not only with traditional supervisors and bosses, but also with the instructions, standards, and intrusiveness of time-

and-motion experts. A steep price paid for this half century of increasing business rationalization was the frequent and lamentable regimentation of work.

The international crisis of 1914 and America's official entry into the Great War in April 1917 served to hasten the economic and social changes which for fifty years had been transforming American business and American labor, but the war also created new circumstances which directly affected the employment of women. The prewar dilution of labor skills had made it possible to interchange male and female workers who were performing increasingly specialized tasks. As the war induced demands for laboring men to serve in the military, on the one hand, and for increased domestic production, on the other hand, the practice of substituting one group of wage earners for another was vastly accelerated. In particular, white women took the places of white men, while black women filled the jobs left vacant by white women and black men.

The wartime labor shortage opened to women a host of new job opportunities at higher wages than women had been earning before the war. This unusual situation set in motion a whirl of job changes and raised expectations among women. When hopes were not realized and women failed to receive what they considered their just due, widespread militancy emerged among women workers. Wartime production pressures also prompted the introduction of women into nontraditional jobs that in turn brought these women into conflict with male co-workers. The altered gender composition of the work force in factories, offices, and elsewhere was viewed differently by male and female wage earners. Union men in particular looked at women's introduction into their fields of employment as a threat to their customary work practices, working conditions, and wages, while women perceived the new jobs as a distinct advance in their occupational status and earnings. In fact, wartime work changes affected these two groups so contrarily that intraclass tensions along gender lines began to flare at home while the military conflict raged abroad.

Another of the unusual wartime conditions involved the new role of the federal government in the operation of American industry. To increase production needed to prosecute the war effectively, the federal government took control of the nation's financially troubled railroads and its overburdened telephone service. The government's new economic function significantly affected the working conditions of women in these industries, though in very different ways. In the case of the railroads, federal control substantially improved women's chances for wages equal to men's and for job advancement, but government operation of the nationwide telephone network had the opposite effect of worsening women's pay scales and denying them adequate opportunities to air grievances. The government's wartime economic regime affected other industries in similarly important yet equally diverse ways, depending on a variety of circumstances.

To the historian, the crisis atmosphere of wartime and the government's economic involvement during the war permit an unusually sharp focus on the critical factors which affected women's employment. Participation in the war effort heightened the consciousness of women workers, male co-workers, managers, and government officials alike, as is evident in contemporary documents and subsequent wartime memoirs. A larger and more systematic documentary boon, however, resulted directly from the new federal economic role, which required detailed policy formulations, investigations, and administrative and judicial decisions, all of which generated many valuable records on the working conditions and attitudes of women wage earners at the time of the First World War.

This book takes advantage of the unique wartime data on women workers to suggest answers to the following questions: How did World War I affect the variety and structure of American women's employment? How did the unusual wartime conditions affect women wage earners' consciousness of themselves as workers and as women? What changes occurred in the particular work options and experiences of black women during the war? In what ways did women reformers attempt to make use of the war situation to promote the interests of working women? What was the nature of the government's policies and those of business toward women wage earners? How did men and women interact in those work settings in which women were introduced for the first time during the war?

There is at present no other book-length study of women workers' experience in the course of the First World War. Little has been written about American women wage earners and the war since the 1920s. In succeeding decades the war period has not received as sustained and careful an examination as other facets of women's history. Even the past ten years' surge of scholarship on women has largely bypassed this topic. A recent work on female reformers in the 1920s, a survey of women's political and economic roles between 1920 and 1970, an examination of male and female sex roles since 1900, and various textbooks on women's history provide passing commentaries on the situation of women workers in the era of the Great War.[1] Most of the available literature reflects the information and limited perspective offered in postwar publications of the Women's Bureau of the United States Department of Labor. Scholars have essentially been content to recapitulate the aggregate patterns of female wartime employment as determined by Women's Bureau statisticians. A typical treatment of the subject may refer briefly to the fact that women replaced men in some types of employment during the war, only to disappear from their new jobs with the war's termination, when wartime "progress" yielded to traditional economic discrimination against women. Although historians have observed the war's effects on women's employment to some extent, they have neglected to explore the phenomenon in any depth.

Studies on the general subject of women or the situation of labor at the time of the First World War have tended to avoid any extensive comment on women workers as such. In most previous treatments which focus directly on women during the war, the effort by suffragists to win the vote has assumed center stage.[2] These works also usually accord honorable mention to the women who provided social services to men in uniform, sold Liberty bonds, or attempted to promote international peace.[3] Scholarly studies of labor during the war have in turn been limited to several principal themes which generally exclude concern for women wage earners. Some authors have examined the presumed unholiness of the alliance between the Wilson administration and the American Federation of Labor. Other writers have studied the federal government's campaign to destroy radical dissident groups, such as the Industrial Workers of the World, during and just after the war. Some business-oriented studies have focused on the relative willingness of corporate leaders to cooperate with American labor as mandated by the federal government during the war.[4] In studies of the domestic effects of the war, scholars have devoted most attention to the leadership and policies of various government agencies, segments of the business world, and particular social movements.[5]

In the new field of women's history there have been some useful studies of women workers, though most of these studies have not paid particular attention to the period of World War I. The recent work on female labor has mostly been concerned with documenting patterns of gender segregation and gender discrimination.[6] Several historians have lately diverged from such descriptive investigations to pioneer in the analysis of work organization in relation to women wage earners' experience in the fields of office employment, sales, and nursing since the late nineteenth century.[7] Unlike these efforts, a preliminary study of three groups of women railroad workers does focus directly on the First World War.[8] The present study complements and expands upon insights in these works to provide perspective on the general situation of women workers in the period affected by the war.

There is, then, a dearth of published scholarship on women workers during World War I, although there is a handful of tangentially related books on women and on labor in the era of the war and a few useful pioneering studies on the historical experience of women as workers. In contrast to virtually ignoring women wartime workers, social and intellectual historians have carefully studied the contours and meaning of work in the late nineteenth and early twentieth centuries from a number of different points of view. Much attention has been focused on the effects of new business methods and organization on craftsmen's customary control over industrial production and on foremen's customary authority over hiring and shop-floor operations. Changing ideas about the organization and importance of work have been perceptively examined.[9] These works provide a useful framework for the present study, although they offer more hints than substance on the special relationship between women's wage labor and the rise of monopoly capitalism in the United States.

The current study departs from the usual administrative and organizational emphases in domestic studies of countries at war. It also rejects facile generalizations about women and particularly about women workers during World War I. This study is neither a record of social, economic, or racial discrimination per se, nor another rendition of compensatory history which recalls that "women were there too." The investigation presented here focuses rather on the ways in which the war accelerated long-term trends in the gender-segregated organization of work, how the war reinforced the separateness of men's and women's work lives, and how the international conflict temporarily brought some groups of men and women into direct competition and conflict for the first time. Such wartime phenomena are considered in their economic and social contexts.

The present work combines an interest in the labor movement, management policies, and patterns common to women's work with an exploration of job structures, the collective experiences of working people, and varying patterns of gender relations at work. This book recognizes the need to examine the formal and informal organization of workers, to survey the substance of day-to-day interactions at work no less than the impact of dramatic events and impersonal forces on workers' lives, and to evaluate the strategies of labor no less than those of business and government.

The varying experiences of women at work are not reducible solely to gender differences, male-female tensions, or "sexual" politics. As shown in this study, working women's experiences varied considerably from one economic and social setting to another. Male-female conflicts or cooperation arose in specific places at particular times and consequently any explanation for the diversity of male-female work relations must be multidimensional. To understand the situation faced by women workers in the war years, it is imperative to explore the interrelationships of the political economy of an industry, the organization of work processes within it, its traditional gender specific tasks, the recruitment of women into new jobs, and finally male workers' responses to women newly employed in their fields. The subject also requires a discussion of the state's role in the development of wartime labor-management policies and their effect on women workers. From a strictly social perspective, the study of women's work during the war demands a particular sensitivity to caste relations in the working class itself, both inside and outside the labor movement, between not only males and females, but also between black and white workers.

Women's employment is examined from the dual perspective of immediate wartime changes and the longer-term trends of the prewar and postwar decades. This pendular movement differentiates the changes which are ephemeral from those that are longer-lasting. As a way of sorting out the varied effects of the war on women's employment in diverse workplaces, this book employs a case study method. Separate analyses of several industries in a number of cities illuminate both the general situation faced by women and the significance of local circumstances and particular industrial conditions. In this way, the examination of women's work history focuses attention on a large time frame, diverse localities, and several distinct industries. This triangulation of the subject through time, place, and activity provides a perspective for assessing the unique qualities and the common patterns of women's wartime work experiences in the United States.

The book opens with an overview of women's employment patterns from 1870 to 1910 and moves from there to consider the effects of the First World War on women's job options and women's perceptions of new wartime labor conditions. Particular attention is paid to the efforts of white and black women to improve their respective economic status during the international crisis. Female wage earners played an important role in the massive wartime labor revolt in the United States. Women's job actions are placed within the context of wartime patriotism and workers' heightened animosity toward perceived capitalist exploitation.

To explore and compare the various effects of the war on women's employment in several occupations and locales, the investigation is divided into four case studies.

(1) Following the review of prewar economic trends and wartime changes in women's work patterns and attitudes, the study examines the war's contribution to the development of labor policy toward women on the part of corporations, the federal government, and female social reformers. The growing "tightness" of the

wartime labor market and the resulting increase in labor militancy not only provided a rationale for management's introduction of women into numerous occupations, but also stimulated a new interest in the field of labor management. The war prompted employers to contemplate more carefully the "human" as well as the technical side of production. The special meaning of labor management to female social reformers is well illustrated by the wartime practices of the Women's Branch of the Ordnance Department of the United States Army and the Women's Service Section of the United States Railroad Administration.

(2) A close analysis of the daily experience of women at work in the railroad offices, yards, and machine shops explores the enduring difficulties that women experienced under the favorable conditions provided by the federal government's assumption of direct control over private railroads from 1918 until 1920.

(3) The streetcar industry affords a look into the intraclass contest of power and principles which occurred when women became streetcar conductors in several cities for the first time during the war. A detailed examination of three local confrontations illustrates the range of responses among the parties involved and the fundamental importance of local economic and political conditions in shaping reactions to the introduction of women into male-dominated municipal transit.

(4) A study of the telephone industry relates the nationwide militancy of telephone operators in 1918 and 1919 to the development of the American Telephone and Telegraph Company; to the design of a rigid, hierarchical, routinized work program for women; and to the repressive wartime labor policies of the postmaster general, who controlled telephone traffic during the war and the immediate postwar period.

The conclusion brings together many facets of the national picture and aspects of the case studies to assess the war's short- and long-term effects on the nature of women's employment and male-female work relations in the United States. Three major topics that figure in the case studies at varying points are summarized and synthesized here. These questions concern women workers' attitudes towards their employment, the circumstances that resulted in cooperation or conflict between men and women wage earners, and an assessment of the roles of women reformers and the government in relation to labor during the war. A final remark considers the utility of studying a period of crisis such as the First World War to gain perspective on social, economic, and gender relations.

The book's perspective and its sources make it a unique study. Information comes from a host of individual, labor, and business manuscript collections. The records of the Women's Service Section of the Railroad Administration have been of particular importance. This source provides insight into the work experiences of 13,000 employees in twenty-three states and the District of Columbia. Verbatim transcripts of the National War Labor Board hearings of labor disputes in fields with women employees provide valuable information about women's backgrounds and their attitudes towards the government, their employers, and their co-workers. Post Office Department records on federal control of the telephone industry contain a wealth of data about telephone operators' wartime and postwar concerns. These materials have made it possible for women's own perceptions to form a vital part of the analysis. The manuscript sources have been supplemented with published census data and government documents, state and federal hearings and investigations, labor and urban newspapers, as well as trade and union journals. The careful combing of these sources for patterns of change and continuity has produced a collective portrait of women at work during the World War I era.

This study is based on a selective number of work settings, but its findings display the complexity and diversity of women's employment experiences. The approach it illustrates to the study of women's work, male-female relations, and women workers' consciousness can be tested in other workplaces and in other times.

WOMEN,
WAR, AND WORK

1 From afar and near: patterns of change in women's work

> [M]odern war casts its shadow long before it happens and . . .
> its social effects are felt for longer and longer periods after
> armed conflict has ceased.
>
> Richard Titmuss[1]

During the First World War a domestic servant left the isolated
environment of home labor for semiskilled work in a large modern
food factory. Attracted by high wages, a veteran garment maker
became an assembler of dangerous explosives. A New York typist
answered the call for labor and travelled to Washington, D.C. to
work in a federal government office. A young black southern
woman left her rural hometown in search of high-paying employment in a northern railroad yard. A middle-aged white woman, the
wife of an invalid and mother of several children, traded the security of her thirteen-year-old job as a head comptometer operator for
the challenge of a man's position as a skilled remittance clerk. A
woman who was sick and tired of waitressing for ten years, the wife
of a soldier fighting overseas, became one of the first female trolley
conductors in the United States. In such biographical fragments
can be found the patterns of women's wartime experience: job
changes within the female sector of the labor force and the admittance of women to nontraditional work.[2]

The path to understanding the effect of the First World War on
women wage earners in the United States winds backwards and for-
wards. Studying women wage earners during the war is important

not only for its own sake but also for the attention it draws to significant prewar trends and the foreshadowing of problems and accomplishments yet to come. The war's domestic experience functions as a prism which both reflects and projects a clearer vision of women as workers in early twentieth-century America. Prewar economic organization had a profound influence on the work women would perform from 1917 to 1919. Whether, when, where, and how women earned their livelihoods during the international emergency depended primarily on the organizational revolution then occurring in American business. From the 1870s the nature and location of women's work underwent a major transformation as mass production and mass distribution became facts of daily life in the United States. The increasing bureaucratization of the American economy, specialization of work, and the gender differentiation of labor set limits on the kinds of work women would perform during the war. Essentially, women's wartime employment followed patterns that had been laid down in the generation or two before the European nations took up arms in 1914.

The international conflict not only accelerated previously established labor patterns, but it also created an unprecedented number of employment opportunities for women. Instead of workers begging for jobs as frequently occurred in the labor market, jobs went begging for workers during the war. Particularly as the draft depleted the number of men available for the civilian labor force, women became a precious resource. Acting on the understanding that their historically restricted position in the labor force was breaking down, women eagerly switched workplaces in search of better wages and labor conditions. Although most women remained within the sphere of female employment, the work patterns of white and black women changed markedly during the war. As a result of the new wartime conditions, some women did manage to cross the otherwise rigid gender line into male jobs.

The wartime mobilization imparted a new dignity to women's work for activities which under ordinary circumstances had been taken for granted. From government and industry, women received exceptional recognition for their contribution to the nation's economic welfare. Women took the era's patriotic propaganda seriously. Although they treated their own labor as a resource to be sold to the highest bidder, they refused to allow employers to treat them as mere instruments of production. As individuals and as a group women engaged in job actions to improve their economic status in the course and aftermath of the war. For many months during the war women's demands circumscribed managerial authority. Women's efforts to enhance their welfare told their bosses that women were people first and common laborers, machine tenders, or clerks second.

PREWAR EMPLOYMENT PATTERNS

Between 1870 and 1910 the contours of women's employment changed dramatically. In 1870 most women worked in the fields of agriculture or domestic and personal service. By 1910, as the American economy matured, more and more women earned their livelihoods in factories, offices, stores, and telephone exchanges. In either decade women wage earners constituted a distinct minority among women. In 1870 only 14.8 percent and in 1910 only 24 percent of all females over sixteen years of age worked for wages. The great majority of women wage earners were young single girls whose families depended on their earnings. After marriage most women withdrew from the labor force and only reentered the world of paid employment when their husbands' earnings were diminished or terminated by layoffs, work accidents, or illness, or in the event of desertion.[3]

The birth of the modern corporation marked the beginning of important changes in the location and nature of women's paid labor. The reorganization of capital into corporations facilitated the development of larger-scale manufacture and distribution of goods and created a host of associated commercial enterprises. By the time the United States officially entered the European conflict in April 1917, trusts, interlocking directorates, and multiplant firms had transformed the financial and organizational structure of business. This process virtually eliminated competition in many vital industries and made financial giants of businessmen like John D. Rockefeller, Andrew Carnegie, Gustavus F. Swift, and Gail Borden. As the corporation developed into the nation's dominant institution, determining where and how people would work, what they would purchase, and where they would live, it came to affect every facet of women's employment.[4]

The manufacturing sector expanded and reorganized toward the turn of the century with the development of the metallurgy, engineering, electrical, and chemical industries. At the same time, food processing and canning grew rapidly, as did the manufacture of paper and cardboard boxes. Large factories, designed to make goods for the mass market, replaced older, smaller units of production. Metal-working plants, which manufactured a diverse range of goods from locomotives to needles and pins, grew enormously after 1900. Every morning as many as 6,000 to 10,000 workers filed through the gates of huge new plants, taking their places in one of the rows of machines or benches which stretched as far as the eye could see.[5]

The changes in manufacturing directly affected the nature of work processes and the sex composition of the field. The new corporate control over the production process, from the mining of raw materials to the selling of finished products, and the new pressures to manufacture goods in unprecedented quantities, led to an increasing specialization of work which gradually diluted the skilled trades by separating operations into their component parts and assigning single tasks to men and women with no prior training or familiarity with machine operations. The dilution of craft labor placed a premium on swiftness and endurance, as opposed to the old system which placed a premium on versatility, judgment, and expertise. The traditional division of the manufacturing labor force into skilled craftsmen and their unskilled helpers shifted to a complex hierarchy of machine tenders, craftsmen, and their supervisors.[6]

Women both gained and lost ground in the field of manufacturing as a result of the expansion of heavy industry and the changing nature of work. As skilled work was diluted or new production processes introduced, the position of women within industry was upgraded from that of laborer to the more preferable work of fabricating goods as machine tender. The reorganization of industry which adversely affected the status of skilled craftsmen markedly improved the position and earnings of female operatives. In the two decades before World War I, the number of women in the chemical industry increased sixfold as new formulas and processes were discovered and new products marketed. The invention and manufacture of incandescent lamps, electric fans, irons, and heaters created thousands of jobs for women in small parts production in the new electrical industry. The growing practice of placing newly manufactured articles in individual boxes led to hiring an average of 6,800 new women employees in paperbox production in each decade between 1870 and 1910. Until 1910 the number of women in the older trade of printing and publishing grew at a rapid rate, as the work of the all-round printer became subdivided into a number of separate operations. The expansion of food processing between 1870 and 1910 boosted the number of women in that industry by 20 percent.[7]

Table 1. **Women Laborers and Operatives Employed in Selected Industries, 1870-1910**

Year	Chemical	Electrical	Paper	Printing	Food	Metal
1870	403	—	6,242	4,397	2,460	5,217
1880	862	—	14,126	9,322	4,503	7,668
1890	2,140	—	22,444	24,640	10,169	15,232
1900	3,427	—	27,261	32,938	19,713	21,335
1910	15,198	12,093	33,419	47,640	48,099	56,208

Source: U.S. Department of Labor, Women's Bureau, *Women's Occupations through Seven Decades*, Bulletin no. 218, pp. 123, 133, 120, 121, 95, and 130.

Despite the increases in individual industries, women in the mechanical and manufacturing fields as a percentage of all gainfully employed women diminished from 26.9 percent in 1900 to 22.5 percent in 1910 as heavy industry, which mainly employed males, vastly increased its importance within the sector of factory production. In addition, a rigid gender segregation continued to characterize manufacturing work regardless of the structural changes reshaping the nature of work. Women concentrated in low-paying, unskilled and semiskilled jobs in textile mills, apparel centers, food-processing plants, tobacco factories, and commercial laundries. Men dominated mining, construction, transportation, and heavy industrial production. Even when women and men worked in the same field, they performed different tasks. In canneries, men cooked and preserved the fruit, shipped the goods, and managed sales and other aspects of plant operations. Women cannery workers washed bottles, scrubbed floors, sorted food, bottled, labeled, and filled jars. In the needle trades the women sewed garments which men cut and pressed. In the metal trades women produced small cores, armatures, and coils, tasks which required speed rather than skill. Intensifying the gender differences in employment, craftsmen barred women from apprenticeship programs for more sophisticated, better-paying positions in the metal-working industries. With wages scaled to skill, women often earned only half as much as men. At the same time, unskilled men who had not yet acquired a dexterity and familiarity with their new work might be paid twice the wage of experienced and able women.[8]

Such arrangements meant that the American labor force had two separate work and wage tracks—one for men and another for women. The assignment of women to some jobs and men to others followed the dilution of skilled labor and the introduction of new technologies in industry as regularly as night follows day. The American work force was so rigidly segregated by gender that even wartime dislocations could barely modify this feature.

As industrial production increased in size and complexity, the market for support services expanded and banking, telephone communications systems, insurance firms, advertising companies, and mail-order houses all grew more rapidly. Business consolidation and expansion after 1900 increasingly demanded larger secretarial staffs. At the same time a technological revolution in office equipment and procedures occurred. The widening use of the typewriter, as well as addressograph, calculating, card punching and sorting, and duplicating machines dramatically transformed the speed and methods for performing office work. With the spread of public school education, especially high school training, a growing supply of persons, particularly women, became available and eligible for office employment. These developments resulted in the gradual replacement of the all-round clerk by specialists such as executive secretaries, stenographers, typists, receptionists, bookkeepers, and office-machine operators.[9]

The shift toward specialization was accompanied by a feminization of the clerical field. What had formerly been almost exclusively men's work became increasingly shared by women. In 1870 women comprised only 2.6 percent of all clerical workers in the United States, but their presence in this white-collar employment grew to 37.7 percent by 1910. The number of women employed in offices skyrocketed, as did the total number of clerical workers in the labor force. The rate of women's participation in office work grew even faster than the total number of clerks. In 1910, more than 575,000 women had positions as office workers, while the total number of persons so employed had grown to over 1,500,000. Businessmen welcomed young women into this work because they offered the readiest supply of educated labor and were accustomed to receiving lower wages.[10]

Table 2. The Ascendancy of Women Office Workers, 1870-1910*

Year	Total Number of Office Workers	Number of Women Office Workers	Women as Percentage of All Office Workers
1870	68,819	1,823	2.6
1880	139,819	6,610	4.7
1890	380,141	73,603	19.4
1900	614,509	179,345	29.2
1910	1,525,757	575,792	37.7

Source: U.S. Department of Labor, Women's Bureau, *Women's Occupations through Seven Decades*, Bulletin no. 218, pp. 75, 78, Table IIB: 227.

*Includes stenographers, typists, and secretaries; shipping and receiving clerks; clerical and kindred workers (not elsewhere classified), office machine operators, bookkeepers, accountants, and cashiers.

The change in gender composition of the country's clerical work force was reinforced by a rigid sex-role differentiation in offices around the turn of the century. In most American offices men predominantly served as general clerks, accountants, shipping clerks, weighers, and messengers, while women accounted for a majority of bookkeepers, cashiers, stenographers, machine operators, and filing clerks. Mechanization and specialization resulted in a tri-level stratification of the office labor force: men trained to deal with matters involving judgment, experience, and responsibility; semi-skilled female machine operatives; and unskilled women assigned routine tasks.[11]

Although women's status in clerical work was decidedly inferior to men's, the office as a workplace was especially attractive to women. As compared to domestic service, sales, or factory labor, office jobs gave women higher status, steadier work, and more remuneration. Unlike teaching or nursing, which required extended professional training, clerical positions required skills which could be acquired in a relatively short time. In the hierarchy of women's options, the office occupations assumed a middle position between physically taxing blue-collar work and prestigious professional positions.

Two other fields of white-collar employment to grow spectacularly between 1870 and 1910 also had the effect of widening women's employment opportunities. In the latter part of the nineteenth century the department store began to acquire significant segments of the retail sales market in metropolitan areas. This new institution could facilitate the distribution of novel manufactures and traditional domestic items by taking advantage of economies of scale. These new large stores could thus undersell many kinds of specialty shops, while offering customers the convenience of one-stop shopping in addition to low prices. Resembling the size of new manufacturing firms, department stores employed several thousand workers to buy, stock, display, and sell their diverse consumer goods. As was the case with women in the clerical field, the number of women employed in sales rose rapidly over the course of four decades. By 1910 women represented more than one-fourth of the nearly 1,500,000 workers in this field.[12]

The growth and structural change in telephone communications mirrored developments in the manufacturing, clerical, and sales fields. In the short span of thirty years the telephone industry consolidated its financial operations, standardized its equipment and methods, and centralized its administration. As it grew rapidly from crude local systems to a nationwide service, the handling of telephone calls shifted from a male to a female occupation. The number of female operators jumped 475 percent between 1900 and 1910. From slightly more than 15,000 women in 1900, the number of female telephone operators leapt to 88,000 a decade later. By 1917, the feminization of this work was so complete that women had come to account for almost 99 percent of the nation's more than 140,000 switchboard operators.[13]

Table 3. Women in Sales Occupations, 1870-1910*

Year	Total Number of Sales Personnel	Number of Women in Sales	Women as Percentage of All Workers in Sales Occupations
1870	245,627	9,027	3.7
1880	409,742	31,738	7.7
1890	666,707	98,820	14.8
1900	1,052,642	216,810	20.6
1910	1,474,414	372,271	25.2

Source: U.S. Department of Labor, Women's Bureau, *Women's Occupations through Seven Decades*, Bulletin no. 218, pp. 84, 86, and 228.

*Includes saleswomen, clerks in stores, store buyers and department heads, canvassers and solicitors, traveling sales personnel and agents.

While new jobs attracted women into communications, sales, clerical work, and manufacturing, the relative importance of domestic and personal service as wage work for women diminished. In 1870, 60.7 percent of the women and girls who were engaged in nonagricultural pursuits were employed as service workers in private and public housekeeping. With each successive census, this figure dropped, so that by 1910, only 25.5 percent of working women outside agriculture were members of the servant class. In addition to the new opportunities in manufacturing, the simplication of housekeeping resulting from the popularity of apartment living among the middle class, the invention of domestic appliances, and the commercialization of laundry work and food preparation all contributed to the decline in the percentage of female servants.[14]

Table 4.   Women Employed as Service Workers, 1870-1910*

Year	Total Number of Women Non-agricultural Workers	Number of Women Service Workers	Women Service Workers as Percentage of Women Nonagricultural Workers
1870	1,439,285	873,738	60.7
1880	2,052,582	970,273	47.3
1890	3,235,424	1,302,728	40.3
1900	4,341,599	1,430,692	33.0
1910	6,268,271	1,595,572	25.5

Source: Joseph A. Hill, *Women in Gainful Occupations 1870 to 1920*, U.S. Bureau of the Census, Census Monograph no. 9: 36.

*Includes servants, waitresses, charwomen, cleaners, porters, housekeepers, and stewardesses, based on 1900 classification.

When the conflict in Europe broke out in 1914, women's paid work in the United States was already clearly in transition. The American labor force remained sex-segregated. Domestic and personal service still engaged the largest number of women workers, and the long-standing patterns of female employment in clothing and textile manufacturing overshadowed the use of women machine operatives in new industrial jobs. At the same time, as the American economy diversified and the nature of work became more specialized and subdivided, women were increasingly moving away from home-related work into new and expanding industries and businesses and were finding frequent employment in corporate offices, department stores, and urban telephone exchanges. This trend in women's paid employment had been well established when the United States officially entered the First World War in April 1917. American participation in the struggle abroad reverberated through the domestic economy as material and human resources were mobilized for war. As the country's embroilment in hostilities grew overseas, the movement of women workers into new economic sectors greatly accelerated at home, as did a tendency for women to replace men in some traditional job categories as well.

WARTIME EMPLOYMENT:
PORTRAITS IN WHITE AND BLACK

The international conflict hastened employment changes along
the line with previously established female occupational trends
rather than triggering any major innovations. Between 1910 and
1920, a sharp increase occurred in the number of female office
clerks, semiskilled operatives in manufacturing; stenographers and
typists, bookkeepers, cashiers and accountants, saleswomen and
clerks in stores, school teachers, telephone operators, laborers in
manufacturing, trained nurses, and waitresses. During the same
decade, the number of women earning their livelihood as charwomen and cleaners, tailoresses, laundresses, dressmakers and
seamstresses, as well as servants, significantly decreased.[15]

The changing numbers of women employed in various jobs represented an internal rearrangement of the female wage earners' role
in the American labor force rather than an aggregate change in the
size of the female work force. Unlike the period of World War II,
when the number of women wage earners rose by six million, or
fully 50 percent of their immediate prewar employment level,
homemakers during World War I did not abandon their kitchens
for toolrooms and airplane hangars. The federal censuses of 1910
and 1920 show that the First World War primarily occasioned a
shift within the female labor force, rather than a movement of non-
wage earning women into categories of paid labor. In 1910,
8,075,722 females ten years of age and over were employed,
whereas in 1920, there were 8,549,511, an increase of only 6.3 percent.[16]

The movement of women from one sector of the economy to
another occurred with relative ease because highly routinized skills
in factories, offices, and retail stores could be quickly mastered. A
domestic servant could handle an automatic milling machine after
only three weeks of training, while factory hands could produce
munitions about as easily as they might have previously processed
food on an assembly line. Seamstresses who ordinarily sewed garments at home readily adjusted to the same type of work in a factory
setting. Cashiering in a restaurant amply prepared many women to
be fare collectors on streetcars. Women who clerked in retail sales

Table 5. Increase and Decrease in the Number of Women Employed in the Principal Nonagricultural Occupations, 1910-1920

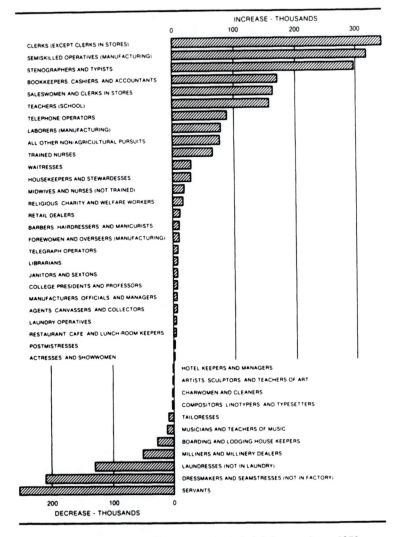

Source: Joseph A. Hill, *Women in Gainful Occupations, 1870 to 1920*, U.S. Bureau of the Census, Census Monograph no. 9: 34.

found that they could easily shift to office clerking, and file clerks could easily adapt to answering telephone calls in a corporate exchange. Farm and urban common laborers could similarly interchange their tasks quite readily.

Women's changing job roles corresponded to the larger economic disruptions caused in the United States by the war. Despite the brevity of American participation in the First World War, a mere nineteen months from April 1917 to the Armistice in November 1918, the war profoundly affected the American economy. The entire industrial machine was wrenched with great violence, forcing extensive readjustments. During the initial phase of the European struggle in 1914, the sudden and vast dislocation of international exchange, trade, and commerce caused a sharp recession in the United States. By the summer of 1915, after the European belligerents had placed substantial war orders with American factories, the United States' economy began to take a turn for the better. The foreign demand for American war materials was accompanied by a full resumption of normal peacetime industrial production. To meet the unprecedented need for quantity production, the country's steel and rubber plants, shipbuilding facilities, and petrochemical industry began to operate at full capacity with overtime production a common occurrence. These wartime conditions required enormous increases in American industrial and agricultural production to meet the needs of customers, allies, and the country's own military machine. The same forces which propelled the demand for increased production understandably placed a special premium on the labor power needed to accomplish this vast task, but the ironies of war simultaneously acted to curtail the availability of America's labor supply. Even before the army and navy enlisted millions of America's young men with work experience and skills, the war had forced a sudden halt in the flow of European immigration to the United States (this immigration was averaging more than a million persons annually before 1914). While the economy's normal labor supply tightened, industry could not even look eastward—as it had been accustomed to do—for cheap replenishments.[17]

As a result of these developments, the prewar overabundance of labor was transformed into a wartime labor shortage, particularly

Figure 1. Vertical milling machine workers. In airplane factories women performed the semiskilled work of operating milling machines as well as the skilled labor of assembling airplane motors. *Signal Corps. No. 111-SC-9225, National Archives, Washington, D.C.*

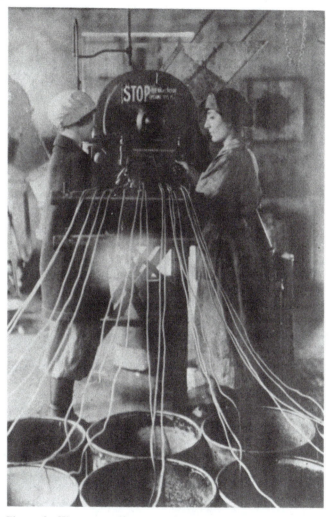

Figure 2. Women tending a cutting press. From explosives to foodstuffs, women participated in the production of wartime necessities. *Signal Corps. No. 11-SC-36040, National Archives, Washington, D.C.*

Figure 3. Drill press operator. Within a matter of a few weeks women learned to handle their new specialized labor. *Women's Bureau No. 86-G-2F-8, National Archives, Washington, D.C.*

Figure 4. Tire finishers. *War Dept. No. 165-WW-589A-1, National Archives, Washington, D.C.*

in fields associated with war production. To replenish the labor supply domestically, employers resorted to hiring workers from two relatively underemployed American population groups. One source of new workers was the pool of blacks in the South. The other labor base was the supply of white women workers whose talents were being underutilized in the wage economy. Newspapers publicized the unusual employment situation with eye-catching notices: "WOMEN WANTED!" For the first time, many job notices now included the word "colored" before the word "wanted." In addition to the tried and true methods of attracting labor, employers now devised ingenious ways to lure new workers. Late in the summer of 1918, when the male labor supply had been depleted by the second armed forces draft, Bridgeport munitions makers literally took to the skies in search of laborers. Companies distributed leaflets from airplanes, urging women to leave their domestic duties for arms production.[18] Before the international emergency, such measures would have been unimaginable.

This extraordinary demand for labor created new employment opportunities for white and black women and set in motion a veritable merry-go-round of job changes. In pursuit of unusual personal challenges or new work experiences as well as higher wages, both single and married women, whether black or white, shifted from one sector of the labor force to another or from one job to another within the same work setting. After the second draft of men into the armed forces, white women substituted for white men in many blue-collar jobs, while black women filled the vacancies left by white women or white boys. For once, women were in a position to weigh the advantages and disadvantages of various jobs instead of walking the unemployment beat every few months or remaining hopelessly imprisoned in routinized, low-paying work.

As a group, female wage earners were acutely aware of the implications of their new wartime opportunities. No matter how modest their employment options, they took full advantage of this occasion to improve their economic status. Women sought information about job openings from the United States Employment Service, combed newspaper advertisements for job leads, exchanged employment information with friends and family, and sought advice from ministers about available positions in either older or newer industries. Their various strategies showed a firm grasp of the labor market situation during this crisis.[19]

In the fields of manufacturing, the meteoric rise in the production of war materials drew thousands of white women from their time-honored employment in domestic service, textile mills, and clothing shops into iron and steel, metal, chemical, lumber, glass, and leather factories. Women produced bombs, grenades, firearms, and ammunition in the iron and steel industry. In other metal industries they supplied the armed forces with wrist watches, clocks, identification tags, eating utensils, and optical goods. From wood they made special furniture and other goods for ships, airplanes, and building construction. Their work in the chemical industry included the production of explosives and fireworks, druggists' preparations, and patent medicines. Leather firms increased their hiring of women for the tanning, curing, and finishing of raw leather hides. Women produced glass for military buildings as well as for optical and scientific instruments and for medicine bottles. To outfit the fighting men, they manufactured cartridge belts, bandoleers, pistol holsters, canteen covers, suspenders, tents, and barrack bags. According to one detailed government survey of wartime production, women comprised 20 percent or more of all workers manufacturing electrical machinery, airplanes (including seaplanes), optical goods, motion picture and photographic equipment, musical instruments, leather and rubber goods, dental supplies, and food, as well as paper, paper goods, and printed materials.[20]

Within these industries white women worked at an impressive array of new jobs. They operated drills, bolt-threading, nut-tapping, milling, and car-bearing machines, as well as turret lathes, angle-cook grinders, hammers, and electric and oxyacetylene and welding tools. In steel works, rolling mills, and machine shops women controlled cranes, riding high above the shop floors, lowering and lifting heavy metal parts to and from their male co-workers. In railroad machine shops they became air brake cleaners, repairers, and testers. A few women were trained for layout work, which involved the careful reading of blueprints and required accuracy in the use of drawing and measuring instruments. To inspect manufactured goods women learned to use various gauges, micrometers, and vermier calipers. In some places women successfully ground and polished metal parts.[21]

In the field of transportation hundreds of white women gave up their jobs as waitresses, clerks, telephone operators, domestic servants, and machine tenders to replace men as streetcar conductors or ticket and station agents. A few women broke down the gender barrier and joined the ranks of longshoremen and stevedores, draymen, and teamsters.[22]

A similar reshuffling of jobs occurred among clerical workers. Attracted by exceptionally good wages and benefits, thousands of stenographers, typists, comptometer operators, and accountants utilized their skills in railroad offices in preference to other businesses and industries. A small number of saleswomen, telegraph and telephone operators, seamstresses, milliners, and factory operatives seized the opportunity to learn routine office work. In search of adventure, thousands of young stenographers and typists from small towns flocked to the nation's capital in response to the government's call for experienced clerical personnel.[23]

Although the number of job vacancies in the fields of manufacturing, transportation, and office work numbered in the tens of thousands, the employment openings were not available equally to all women. Since racial segregation presented as stark a reality as gender segregation, black women's occupational status followed a very different course during the war from that of white women. By and large, black women remained concentrated in traditional forms of female employment to a far greater extent than white women. In 1910, the fields employing the largest number of women of both races were agricultural labor and domestic and personal service. Over 53 percent of all working women earned their livelihood as laborers on the land or in the home, but the significance of this work was even greater for black than white women. In 1910, 95 percent (1,904,404) of the 2,013,981 black women wage earners were engaged solely in these two fields. In manufacturing and mechanical industries black women comprised only 1.2 percent (16,835) of the 1,366,959 female employees. The majority of this group could be found in tobacco and cigarmaking firms as common laborers and machine tenders.[24]

Restrictions on black women's job opportunities extended to other fields as well. In retail houses they served only as custodial staff. Even when they had been trained for better positions as typists or stenographers, employers often refused to hire them. Black telephone operators, secretaries, and receptionists were principally confined to black-owned businesses in black neighborhoods. Given the different work experiences of white and black women, the war understandably affected each group in a distinctive way. As white women entered war industries, black women filled the vacancies left in domestic, industrial, and clerical employment. The wartime opportunities held cardinal importance for black women because as a group they assumed even more responsibility for supporting themselves and their families than did white women.[25]

A combination of economic calculation and necessity reinforced the concentration of black women wage earners in the field of domestic and personal service during the war. In a seesaw manner, the number of black female domestics in northern cities went up as the number of white female servants went down. Taking the decade between 1910 and 1920 as a whole, the percentage of black women in the total number of female servants in the North increased 7 percent, from 11.5 in 1910 to 18.5 in 1920. The actual number of black female domestic servants in this period increased 17.4 percent from 92,318 to 108,342.[26] Although black domestics disliked their long work hours, inferior social status, and the constant personal supervision to which they were subjected, private housekeeping possessed a special appeal to them during the national crisis. Wages paid for household employment increased during the wartime labor shortage, as native and foreign-born white women exchanged their brooms and mops for industrial machines. Black women cleverly maximized their earnings during the war by alternating between jobs as domestics and factory hands. Manufacturers bitterly complained about the high rate of absenteeism among black female wage earners. Whenever they could not make ends meet, they played hooky from their factory jobs and cleaned houses for more money. Domestic service was not always a matter of choice. In some cities institutional racism forced black women to stick to their traditional trade. In Pittsburgh, where prosperity depended on the output of blast furnaces, iron foundries, and steel mills, few industrial opportunities existed for women and those few were reserved for white women. Blatant discrimination in Chicago barred black women from many factory jobs which were open to them in other economically diversified cities.[27]

At the same time, black women's employment showed a marked transition from domestic and other home-related pursuits to industrial labor. As jobs in factories became available, black women sought industrial work for the regular hours and free evenings which left time for recreation with friends and family. One former black servant emphatically declared, "I'll never work in nobody's kitchen but my own any more. No, indeed! That's the one thing that makes me stick to this job [in a paperbox factory]. You . . . have some time to call your own, but when you're working in anybody's kitchen, well, you're out of luck. You almost have to eat on the run; you never get any time off, and you have to work the night, usually."[28] For such reasons, black women left domestic service when they could.

In the field of manufacturing, the tobacco and food-processing industries attracted the largest number of black women during the war. A government study of 21,547 black women conducted immediately after the Armistice found approximately 8400 at work on the manual processes of stemming, stripping, typing, and twisting of tobacco, while another 3300 labored in the stockyards, trimming, sorting, grading, and stamping different portions of the carcasses, separating and cleaning the viscera, and preparing meats for curing and canning.[29]

In addition to their expanded representation in the tobacco and food-processing industries, black women gained entrance to the leather, metal, paper-products, clothing, and textile industries. Although the substitution of black for white women in these industries was heralded by social reformers as inaugurating "a new day for the colored woman worker," statistical data on black women's industrial experience clearly show the wartime changes to have been more modest in proportion.[30] The actual number of black women who entered the world of factory labor was small. According to a study of 150 plants employing almost 12,000 black women, 840 worked in textile mills, 806 in metal plants, 710 in clothing factories,

117 in the paper-products industry, and only 27 in leather shops.[31] The remainder concentrated in industries which had formerly employed black women. These figures nevertheless indicate a breakthrough for those workers who otherwise had had notably few employment choices.

In terms of advancement and wages, black women discovered the best wartime opportunities in the garment trades, government arsenals, and the railroad industry. Seamstresses who ordinarily sewed garments in the cramped quarters of their homes now eagerly applied for factory jobs. In Philadelphia black women successfully cornered 14 percent, or 842, of the 5822 available job openings in 126 garment shops during the war. They assembled, sorted, cut, designed, embroidered, finished, pressed, and trimmed garments. Since the clothing industry had a high proportion of trade unionists, some black women shared in the wage improvements obtained under union contracts.[32] In government arsenals black female workers made and inspected garments, protected by a contract which called for a starting wage of two dollars and fifty cents for an eight-hour day with the guarantee of regular increases and bonuses. These government employees enjoyed a weekly wage of fifteen to twenty dollars, which was often twice the wage of most black women in the industry.[33]

The decent working conditions, steady employment, and high wages offered by railroads drew black female common laborers away from hotels, laundries, restaurants, and private homes. In railroad offices, shops, roundhouses, and yards black women mopped floors, washed woodwork and windows, and polished metal parts, tasks to which they were long accustomed in circumstances of domestic service. A few women wiped engines, while a small number operated electric lift trucks at freight transfer stations and docks, moving lumber and large heaps of scrap iron. Black women also took responsibility for the first time for collecting and distributing linens in Pullman cars. In railroad yards they moved forgings and castings by hand and wheelbarrow. Railroad work constituted a high point in the graph of black women workers' wages during the war. Earning even more than arsenal workers, black female railroad employees took home twenty or more dollars a week, more than two times the wage of common laborers in other industries.[34]

Black office workers also achieved some advancement during the war. About five thousand black women obtained coveted jobs with the United States government as typists, stenographers, bookkeepers, and filing clerks, and five hundred black women received training as billing and addressograph operators or packing or shipping clerks.[35]

The new types of employment opened to black women signified a kind of improvement that differed from the terms of reference applicable in the case of expanded opportunities for white women. Often the entrance of blacks into a new work arena occurred only after white women had rejected jobs in that particular field. Black women substituted for white boys at the most dangerous work in glass factories, carrying to hot ovens the glass products blown by skilled craftsmen. Other black women replaced white men at the highly objectionable and dangerous work of dyeing furs. In mattress factories, some black women took men's places preparing bedding for shipment, which meant constant bending and lifting of 160-pound bundles of mattresses. In most factories they were given the oldest and hardest machines to operate. As if to signify their lowly position, employers restricted them to the darkest and worst-ventilated sections of factories and gave them the smallest and dirtiest of the available rest rooms. Where piecework provided them with a chance to increase their wages, employers forced them to accept a lower weekly rate than the one given to white women. Managers usually found "reasons" to pay black women workers substantially less than their white counterparts.[36]

Segregation further marred black women's wartime opportunities. The insidious color line was drawn in offices, forcing women with distinctly negroid complexion and features to work and take breaks in separate quarters from white women. Tobacco companies continued to exclude black women from the preferred job of manufacturing cigars and cigarettes by machine, while food-processing concerns similarly barred black females from the canning and wrapping of meat and meat by-products. Only the most light-skinned black applicants were permitted to work in government offices, forcing darker-skinned stenographers and bookkeepers to earn their livelihood in factories. Department stores hired black women as stock girls, elevator operators, store maids, and cafeteria waitresses, but continued to prohibit them from waiting on customers as sales clerks. For positions in which black women performed their duties in full view of customers, store managers preferred to select women who might pass for white, reserving for darker members of the race the stockroom labor and other less visible tasks.[37]

In objective terms, black women's wartime opportunities were definitely more narrow and meager than those of white women, but job options implied varying subjective realities as well. What constituted an opportunity depended primarily on a black woman's assessment of her former work experiences and her present choices. A fine example of the meaning of job alternatives was offered by a former black domestic servant who during the war secured a job as a common laborer in a railroad yard.

All the colored women like this work and want to keep it. We are making more money at this than any work we can get, and we do not have to work as hard as at housework which requires us to be on duty from six o'clock in the morning until nine or ten at night, with might little time off and at very poor wages. . . . What the colored women need is an opportunity to make money. As it is, they have to take what employment they can get, live in old tumbled down houses or resort to street walking, and I think a woman ought to think more of her blood than to do that. What occupation is open to us where we can make really good wages? We are not employed as clerks, we cannot all be school teachers, and so we cannot see any use in working our parents to death to get educated. Of course we should like easier work than this if it were opened to us, but this pays well and is no harder than other work open to us. With three dollars a day, we can buy bonds . . . , we can dress decently, and not be tempted to find our living on the streets. . . .[38]

The railroad worker spoke not only for her black sisters but also for many white female wage earners. A change of pace, place, position or payment could provide relief from the ordinarily limited range of employment choices that were open to black and white women alike. The cleaning of railroad cars at decent wages was favored over sweeping offices and hotels at subsistence wages.

Figure 5. Cannery operatives. Ordinarily barred from industrial work, black women gained entry in limited numbers to food-processing, tobacco, leather, metal, and paper-products factories. *War Dept. No. 165-WW-587-5, National Archives, Washington, D.C.*

Figure 6. Racial segregation in the garment industry. In terms of advancement and wages, black women discovered the best wartime opportunities in garment shops, government arsenals, and railroad yards. Their opportunities were usually limited by racial segregation. *Women's Bureau No. 86-G-2A-5, National Archives, Washington, D.C.*

Figure 7. Black women at work in a brick yard. Often the entrance of blacks into a new work arena occurred only after white women had rejected jobs in that particular field. In most workplaces black women performed the hardest, dirtiest, least desirable tasks. *Women's Bureau No. 86-G-65-3, National Archives, Washington, D.C.*

Working year-round as a switchboard operator for the Bell System clearly offered a woman more security than a job dipping chocolates in a candy factory only a few months a year. Dangerous work in glass factories ranked higher than washing strangers' clothing in private households. Conducting streetcars allowed women more freedom than performing highly routinized factory labor under constant supervision. The technical expertise for these newly opened jobs was quite similar to work previously performed by women, but the social context and monetary rewards of the new employment differed substantially. Many women greeted even modest improvements in their work situations with genuine enthusiasm.

Young women between the ages of eighteen and twenty-one who had experienced the confining and restrictive atmosphere of clerking in a department store or the monotony of running single-function machines in factory settings were thrilled to drive motor trucks for the hauling of freight from platforms to warehouses. The war opened opportunities barely fathomable to such women before the European crisis reverberated through the American domestic economy. Now dressed in crocheted tams, sweaters, and bloomers, they expressed great pleasure in work they likened to "air ship flying." Teenagers who wanted to escape from overcrowded homes and sheltered family life eagerly became block house operators for the nation's steam railroads. When off-duty, these women used their rail passes to travel aboard trains to experience the excitement of speed and the freedom to roam. A Pennsylvania woman who tired of her first career as a physical education teacher had the opportunity to learn the art of mechanical drawing during the war. A recent high school graduate who was deemed sweet and demure would likely have become a secretary had it not been for the war, which inadvertently opened a job to her in an electrical repair shop. There she helped a "troubleshooting gang of men" splice cables, locate electrical disturbances, and repair all manner of electrical breakdowns. For women like the newly hired haulers, block house operators, mechanical drawers, and electrical repairers, the wartime economy did indeed offer unusual challenges and choices.[39]

On the whole, the wartime rotation of jobs rewarded women with better wages than they had been accustomed to receiving. The increased need for labor and the sharp decline in immigration benefited unskilled workers. In 1915 the real wages of unskilled workers rose 5 percent over the figure for 1914, while in 1916 and 1917 each registered a further 6 percent improvement. Unskilled labor made its greatest advance during the last year of the war, when the draft further depleted industry's supply of unskilled workers. Real wages in 1918 jumped over 12 percent, constituting a 19 percent rise over the 1914 level.[40] This rise is corroborated by a National Industrial Conference Board comparison of women's weekly earnings in seven industries from September 1914 to March 1919. In the metal, cotton, wool, silk, and paper industries women's weekly wages outstripped the cost of living. Only in the rubber and the boot and shoe industries did women's pay packets fail to keep pace with prices for groceries and housing.[41] Even when the jobs available to women were dirty and physically taxing, many women shared the sentiment of a black woman who took a job as a streetcar-track cleaner that the "almighty dollar" made the work worth the physical effort.[42]

WOMEN AND THE WARTIME LABOR REVOLT

Money alone did not influence women's perception of their value as workers during the war. Other economic, social, and political conditions unique to the war gave women confidence in their power to improve their economic status. At times during the war, groups of women expressed simultaneously their frustration over job limitations and their heightened self-confidence as workers by organizing or participating in various strikes and other job actions. Women's wartime militancy was part of an endemic labor restlessness among both organized and unorganized workers throughout the United States. This widespread labor "revolt" can best be understood as a response to the wartime pressures for personal sacrifice, patriotism, and productivity.

From the government's point of view the successful prosecution of the war depended on the development of a committed army of civilian workers as well as the enlistment and training of millions of men for the various branches of military and naval service. The industrial system had to be organized into a nationwide munitions plant and the labor force drilled into an effective human war machine. To realize its goals, the Wilson administration assumed greater control over the production and distribution of food, munitions, fuel, clothing, and propaganda. As never before, the American government turned its attention to price-fixing, stimulating and standardizing production, and determining economic and social priorities.[43]

Civilian life was dramatically altered as the federal government launched a nationwide campaign to "sell the war" at home while it "sold peace" abroad. Publicity and advertising experts employed by the government issued millions of pamphlets in diverse languages, spreading zealous, patriotic propaganda throughout the country. Everyone was urged to prepare wheatless and meatless meals, conserve precious fuel resources, and buy Liberty bonds and war-savings stamps. By conserving food, increasing the rate of personal earnings, and decreasing the production of consumables, the nation could better muster its resources to meet immediate military needs.[44]

Day in and day out, government and industry beseiged workers with pleas to "smash the Hun." In every conceivable way wage earners of both sexes and all nationalities and races were told repeatedly how absolutely essential they were to winning the war. Three- and four-minute patriotic speeches were delivered in production plants, movie theaters, public halls, and churches. Every morning as workers assumed their posts, ready for the moment when the power would be turned on, they heard continuous appeals to work, work, work. Frequently attached to their machines were small, mass-produced United States flags, symbolizing the government-employer-worker coalition whose very unity would defeat the enemy. Workers might find their pay envelopes stuffed with letters from government or army officials exhorting them to demonstrate their patriotism by exceeding production quotas. Movies regularly importuned workers in eight hundred munitions plants in fifteen cities to take pride in their country and in their trade. Two million posters repeated the message, "NOT JUST HATS OFF TO THE FLAG, BUT SLEEVES UP FOR IT." As Liberty bonds were issued, factories competed for the highest subscription tally. Army officers in their newly acquired uniforms made impassioned pleas to workers for monetary support for the war effort. Ardent and ambitious foremen pressured their workers to buy bonds, even calling in fellow employees and other supervisors to influence recalcitrants.[45]

As part of the mobilization, women received special commendation for their role in wartime activities. Suddenly, new respect and public recognition were accorded women's responsibilities in the workplace and in the home. In diverse ways women were told that the fighting men's accomplishments abroad depended on the organized support and effective labor of women on the home front. Daily newspapers reported women's activities and on Sundays fullpage accounts with photographs sung women's praises for patriotic dedication. Stories lauded women who entered munitions factories, climbed aboard streetcars as conductors, cleaned railroad yards with picks and shovels, sewed army shirts in their homes, handled hundreds of emergency telephone calls, and tended the voluminous paperwork in government offices.[46]

The spotlight was also turned on women's domestic responsibilities. Careful use of food materials, always the mark of a good housewife, was linked during the war to the nation's commitment to international peace. Wartime propaganda preached thrift as a matter of more than mere personal concern, stressing that a nation of thrifty families spared scarce resources for the prosecution of a war which would make the world safe for democracy and appreciative of the American economic system. Even in the realm of life conservation, through organizations like the Red Cross, women found their responsibility and influence widening from a personal concern for their children to the moral protection of other women's sons and daughters who were meeting the hazards of the war in distant places across the seas.[47]

Large colorful posters issued by the federal government immortalized women's contributions to the war effort as workers, volunteers, and homemakers. One poster entitled "Will you have a part in Victory?" depicted a young white woman draped in an American flag sowing seeds for her vegetable garden. An equally famous scene showed a secretary seated at her desk gazing upon a shadowy image of a soldier poised for military action. Looming in the distance was an outline of the Capitol. The poster boldly stated in red letters, "Stenographers! Washington needs you!" In an advertisement for military recruitment a woman attired in a seaman's uniform proudly proclaimed, "GEE!! I WISH I WERE A MAN. I'D JOIN THE NAVY." No matter what their station in life, women were repeatedly applauded during the war for their contributions to the national effort.[48]

By definition, the nationalist sentiment stressed the unity of the populace, the oneness of workers and employers, and the combined efforts of men and women. Propaganda necessarily masked the separateness of people's experiences in terms of their socio-economic status, ethnicity, and gender, although the realities of daily life were defined by such differences.

While workers produced and economized more than usual, some businessmen exploited human and material resources during the war. The greater the stress on patriotism, the more sensitive were wage earners to the disparity between their own and their employers' actions and earnings. As individual sacrifices mounted unequally, women and men voiced their outrage, frustration, and moral indignation at these inequities. They looked to the federal government to correct injustices because they firmly believed that the state had a fundamental obligation to protect its citizens from exploitation.

From Seattle, Washington, one woman complained to the secretary of labor, William B. Wilson, about a construction company which refused to sell scrap wood to its employees and later destroyed it for no good reason. She implored the secretary not to "ask the common laborer to waste not, and then let the employer use such tactics. It only created dissatisfaction and unrest."[49] An elderly woman from Savannah, Georgia, expressed contempt for southern manufacturers who sold their products for twice the prewar prices but refused to raise their employees' wages. The combined effects of low wages and rising prices had forced the writer's family to withdraw one teenager from high school and send her to work. "[L]et me beg you to recognize this as a grievance of the working women. [T]hey are forced to pay the same prices for their rents, their groceries and all that men have to pay and yet only mak[e]

Figure 8. Patriotism in the factory. These female punch press operatives were reminded each day by the flags on their machines that the government counted on their productivity. *Women's Bureau No. 86-G-2J-6, National Archives, Washington, D.C.*

Figure 9. Women and patriotism. World War I posters appealed to women's sense of patriotism and depicted the importance of women to the American war effort. *National Archives, Washington, D.C.*

about half the salary. . . ."[50] Her family clearly suffered because women often earned as little as children for their labor but paid as dearly as men for their necessities. By late 1918, all women could agree with the sentiments expressed by a female clerk to the secretary of navy, "What could be done in regard to oppression a couple of years ago, cannot be done now without serious consequences to all concerned. We only want to be treated as human beings, not as . . . oppressed humanity."[51]

Besides looking to the federal government to protect their interests, women also fended for themselves. Contrary to the stereotypic image of women as passive, docile, timid wage earners who rarely asserted their rights, they were very active in their own behalf during the war, both as individuals and in groups, in private and in public. To provide for their own welfare, women constantly searched for better work, a traditional method of self-help which intensified during the period of labor scarcity. Women might accept several different jobs from various employers in the course of a day and return to the employer who offered the best conditions. Such behavior both reflected and intensified the labor shortage. For employers, labor turnover became a critical problem. The manager of the General Electric Company in Philadelphia had to hire 125 women to replace twenty-five operatives in one week. Telephone companies, which were unwilling or unable to pay the market price for salaries during this high-wage period, suffered a breakdown of normal service because of high labor turnover. Black female factory operatives demonstrated a strong sense of initiative and enterprise by staying away from their factory jobs for several days to work as domestics whenever factory piece rates paid less than a day's domestic service.[52]

Private employers were not alone in suffering this problem. The relatively low salaries, the severe housing shortage, and the lack of recreational facilities made it very difficult for the federal bureaucracy to retain experienced secretaries in Washington, D.C. The first surge of patriotic fervor brought a wave of clerical workers from New York to the capital, but the disparity in salaries between the two cities sent most of them packing again within a month or two. Shop and office talks by employers about their severe labor needs only reinforced women's sense of their economic value.[53]

Apart from labor turnover, women sought to improve their working conditions by striking and bargaining collectively. Such job actions were very common during the war. Workers of all skill levels in diverse sectors of the economy demanded wage increases to meet the rising cost of living, adjustments in the number of working hours, and recognition of their unions. As unemployment declined, no field of work escaped class conflict. In 1917 and 1918 alone, shipbuilders, longshoremen, machinists, packing-house, and sugar-cane workers all struck. So too did potters, textile and garment workers, hatters, cigar makers, lumberers and molders, as well as teamsters, retail clerks, street railway employees, and telephone operators. Women participated in many of the more than six thousand strikes which erupted during the United States' involvement in the war.[54]

The surge of union growth during the war also affected women. Until the war, women wage earners had been only weakly organized into trade unions. Their youth and their concentration in the unorganized fields of agriculture, domestic and personal service, trade, clerical work, and professional occupations placed them outside the labor movement, the strongholds of which were the mining industry and the building trades. During the war, union membership grew rapidly both in male-dominated fields and those employing large numbers of women. The wartime labor shortage enabled unions to move from a defensive to an offensive position, dramatically increasing their membership. From 2,716,900 trade unionists in 1914, the number rose to 3.1 million in 1917, 3.5 million in 1918, 4.2 million in 1919, and finally to 5.1 million in 1920. Wartime organizing drives achieved their greatest success among women in the clothing, textile, and shoe industries, which together accounted for 223,000 of the 397,000 women organized by 1920.[55]

Numbers tell only part of the story of women's wartime labor activity. The labor revolt touched workers who were themselves not inclined to use the power of collective action. For no group was militancy more unusual than for the new white-collar workers: the accountants, bookkeepers, stenographers, typists, and operators of multigraph, stenotype, comptometer, and other office machines. Thousands of women office employees joined their male co-workers in an unprecedented challenge to managerial authority. These

workers contested the terms of their employment with the federal government, the railroads, and giant corporations like General Electric and American Locomotive Works. They shed their shell of complacency and joined the ranks of the National Federation of Federal Employees, the Brotherhood of Railway Clerks, and the Stenographers, Typists, Bookkeepers, and Assistants' Union.[56] Encouraged by the militancy of other workers and drained financially by the high cost of living, these workers developed a new view of themselves as wage earners. In the words of the Schenectady, New York office employees, a new order was in the making. In their petition to the National War Labor Board they admirably summarized this new perspective.

Underpaid at all times in the past, the members of our profession have never organized as other branches of industry have done. This was due to tradition, but the present abnormal times have put so many past usages on the discard, we ask your Honorable Board to consider us as workers, and give us, as such, a standard of living in accord with the present, rather than a class recognition, which, while appealing to a few with aspirations, does not pay prosaic grocery, shoe and rent bills.[57]

The most militant female wage earners came from another white-collar group—telephone operators. During the war and the immediate postwar period, thousands of teenage girls and young women used the power of collective action to cripple telephone communications for weeks at a time, from coast to coast. Thousands of sixteen- and seventeen-year-olds momentarily brought the American Telephone and Telegraph Company, the country's largest corporate monopoly, to its knees.[58]

Such massive strikes should not overshadow the myriad of smaller, shorter work stoppages and job actions in which women participated. Laundresses in Little Rock, Arkansas and Kansas City, Missouri, who believed themselves to have been treated like chattel by their employers before the war, refused to wash, starch, or iron clothes until their wages and working conditions were improved. Fifty women spontaneously walked out of a fireworks plant in Seattle when their boss refused to let them watch the April 1918 Liberty parade. Domestics in Kansas City and Norfolk met in

small groups in their respective cities and agreed to demand a two-dollar a day wage from their housewife-employers. By 1919 household workers had formed local organizations for the purpose of bettering their wages and working conditions in Mobile, Alabama; Fort Worth, Texas; and Tulsa and Lawton, Oklahoma. Female streetcar conductors in Kenosha, Wisconsin joined their fellow carmen in a strike to raise their wages. Women teachers in Seattle demanded that their school board give them the same "war bonus" paid to men. The list of examples could go on and on. In small and large cities, among young girls and middle-aged women, from every sector of the female work force, a spirit of labor revolt radiated.[59]

As might be guessed from the mere mention of job actions among domestic servants and laundresses, black women, as well as white women, participated in the wartime labor rebellions. Contemporary observers of black women wage earners emphasized how new they were to industry, how much they lacked "factory sense" and how vastly ignorant they were about industrial employment. Black women have usually been viewed as "unprepared," "immature" workers who stumbled into factories and offices and did not know how to cope with their wartime dislocations.[60] This characterization is unfair. Although few black women had worked in factories or offices before 1914, they expressed the same sense of self-worth during the war as other more seasoned blue-collar and white-collar workers. In terms which they deemed appropriate, black women asserted some control over their conditions of labor.

Throughout the war black women expressed a distinct sense of racial identification and separateness. Long familiar with the indignities of segregation, they expected better treatment from their employers during the war because of the nationwide government and business campaigns for home-front solidarity. Racial discrimination was unacceptable to them because it contradicted the ideals for which the war was presumably being fought. When black women were abused, they thought of the mistreatment as a dishonor to their nationalist sentiment. After a young Cleveland woman was rejected for a telephone operator's job, she asked a local newspaper advice columnist to explain why. "Does it make any difference," she wondered, "what nationality helps to bring this most awful war to an end? Our girls have brothers, sweethearts, and husbands over there fighting for democracy for all nationalities." "No, it does not make any difference," the columnist asserted. "Everybody's help is going to be needed to bring the war to a successful conclusion, but the help of each . . . must be applied in [its] place."[61] Such an answer was found wanting. Black women expected a fairer share of the wartime jobs.

Black women looked to the day when their inferior status would be just a bad memory. They registered their complaints for abuse on the job by quitting, as an entire group of young black women did their first day of work after a foreman in a sheet-metal plant cursed at them for protesting against undesirable working conditions. They also collectively abandoned their jobs when they discovered wage discrimination based on race. Ordinarily blacks and whites worked in different parts of a factory, conveniently reducing the likelihood of wage comparisons between the two groups. When black and white women labored side by side or in close proximity, discussion of earnings often revealed the extent of black women's second-class citizenship. In protest, black women would walk off their jobs.[62]

A significant minority of black women in industry cleverly made segregation work to their own advantage. Seclusion in a separate unit, room, or building encouraged these women to develop informal work groups of trusted, mutually supportive co-workers. As a group, they insisted on supervisors of their own race, women with whom they felt more comfortable and from whom they received a more just treatment. If they were going to be told what to do, they wanted one of their own people to issue the orders. According to the 1920 Women's Bureau study of black women's wartime employment, twelve of 150 plants had hired black forewomen because their black employees had demanded it of them. One manager of a lampshade factory which employed black women as skilled workers reported to a government investigator that when he had temporarily replaced an absent black forewoman with a white woman, the black workers turned the shop into utter "chaos" by refusing to follow the substitute's instructions. The boss gladly welcomed the black supervisor back to her former post.[63] In this case, the forewoman was particularly important because she drew and drafted the lampshades which workers then sewed. The women's productivity depended directly on their superior's capability.

The efforts of black women to obtain their own supervisors could be found in other industries as well. A manager of a large mail-order house reported that 340 black women stopped work for half a day when he replaced the forewoman of their race with a white person. Elsewhere, an employer discovered much to his satisfaction that absenteeism dropped a full 80 percent when a black woman was hired to oversee 260 women.[64] Perhaps black women responded more positively to members of their own race because black supervisors represented to them a real chance for promotion. Whatever the explanation, black women unquestionably exercised some control over this condition of their employment.

Little is known about trade union organization among black women during the war for there are no nationwide tabulations of their membership in unions. Given the limited number of women who entered organized industries, it can be safely assumed that black female trade union members constituted a small group. The bits and pieces of information which can be assembled on this question indicate that black women either tended to be ignorant or suspicious of unions. A wartime study of 175 black women industrial workers in New York City found that only twenty-one or 12 percent had joined a union. Those few were affiliated with the Amalgamated Clothing Workers, the Fancy Leather Goods Union, and the International Ladies' Garment Workers' Union, which had made substantial inroads into the union organizing of male and female clothing workers. One hundred twenty-four or 71 percent of those women interviewed for the New York study had never even heard of trade unions. Employed in the lowest-paid industries making candy, toys, and paper boxes, these women had no more familiarity with collective bargaining than their white female and male co-workers.[65]

When presented with the opportunity to join a union, black women sometimes joined and at other times remained unaffiliated. Although there is no definitive data to sort out the reasons and circumstances which determined whether black women would accept union membership, their responses may have varied according to the permanence of their employment. Perceiving themselves as only temporarily employed as munitions workers, not one of the five hundred black women who worked in the Frankford Arsenal in Philadelphia during the war would join the National Federation of Federal Employees. In contrast, all of the black railroad workers in Philadelphia organized into the Railroad Coach and Car Cleaners' Local No. 16702. In the first instance, black women knew that the arsenal would dramatically curtail its production of munitions after the war, raising the likelihood of their dismissal. In the second instance, the women could assume that railroads would continue to need the services of large numbers of maintenance personnel. Their trade union affiliation was part of an effort to retain their common labor jobs.

The more hospitable the environment for unionism, the more likely a black woman was to sign a membership card. As a center of trade union activity among government workers, Washington, D.C. offered a receptive setting for the union affiliation of black women. A notable example was the organization in September 1918 of the Charwomen's Branch of Washington Local 2 of the National Federation of Federal Employees, which enrolled women office cleaners. This branch was strengthened by another independent branch of black women members of Local 2; these women worked as machine operatives in the Bureau of Printing and Engraving, which for the first time had begun to hire black women for such work. These two branches of black women joined with white females employed by the bureau in an effort to win a new classification system for federal workers, to raise the wage level for unskilled women, to obtain a retirement program, and collectively resist the introduction of efficiency schemes in government agencies. These organizations of black federal employees demonstrated the potential organizing force of black women.[67]

Trade unionism among black and white women wage earners constituted only one part of a many-faceted female labor revolt in the United States during the war. These restive women workers forcefully made their special needs known to their employers, the government, and the public at large. The wartime emergency gave women workers some leverage in doing so, as their services had suddenly become valuable, even though the basic problems they faced predated the war and would long outlast it. In terms drawn from their own experience, these women forced their employers and government agencies to pay special attention to what women had to say about their wages, hours of work, and other conditions which affected their labor.

CONCLUSION

The war came at a time when many fundamental changes in American economic life had begun to gather inexorable momentum. Corporate capitalism was reorganizing the country's financial arrangements, utilizing new technologies, introducing new jobs, and designing new labor policies. Within this developing web of new economic infrastructure, the changing contours of women's paid employment were increasingly affecting the opportunities and workplace autonomy of millions of women. The war then propelled women's work patterns along the paths already evolving before the European conflict had begun. Job shifts occasioned by wartime economic circumstances intensified during the international crisis, giving American women greater latitude for choosing work than they had ever had. Acutely attuned to the importance of this unprecedented situation, both white and black women wage earners weighed and evaluated their options, choosing those jobs which best matched their daily routines, family obligations, skills, and physical stamina. What appears in aggregate statistical terms as a modest wartime change was for thousands of individual women a time of enormous personal change and adjustment.

Working women took advantage of their new strength. They seized opportunities for changing jobs, petitioned the government for fairer labor policies, struck at their workplaces for better pay and conditions, joined trade unions, and challenged the authority of their bosses in a myriad of ways to say no to exploitation. When male co-workers, foremen, unions, and even social reformers attempted to block the aspirations of these women workers, the newly heightened awareness of their own worth made them a substantial collective force with which to be reckoned. Many women took literally the wartime propaganda which corresponded to their own experience and hopes, that the rhetoric of democracy and human dignity should have meaning in women's work.

2   The technical and the human: managing women workers

> The greatest business today is the human problem of labor and the wise handling of men. . . . On the one hand, lie the possibilities of steady production, cooperation, contentment and good will; on the other, the possibilities of strife, of organized social revolt and even the wrecking of the present organization of industry. Syndicalism and socialism . . . are more than empty shadows. We must look to the future as well as the past.
>
> Ernest Fox Nichols, President of
> Dartmouth College, 1916[1]

In urban and rural America women enlisted in the home-front effort to win the world war. As wage earners women answered the call to work in various nontraditional jobs. Dressed neatly in the police uniform of jacket and skirt, women directed the rush-hour flow of car, trolley, truck, and wagon traffic. Garbed in the traditional male attire of coveralls, teenage girls worked in teams of two to deliver huge blocks of ice to urban homes and restaurants. On the doorsteps of residences women greeted occupants with their daily mail. In barber shops females could be seen shaving men's beards and cutting their hair. In the industrial world women could be found operating cranes, tending railroad gates, conducting streetcars, toting shells, and painting huge steel tanks. Throughout the countryside girls and women replaced men in the harvesting of crops. America at war had come to depend on the employment of women at home as a national necessity.[2]

The efficient utilization of women wage earners in American industry drew the attention of employers and government officials as women frenetically changed jobs, entered nontraditional work, and stood up for their rights as employees. For decades efficiency in industry had been a consuming interest of employers, but the war gave the problem a new sense of immediacy. Businessmen wanted to know what kinds of work women could handle, which training programs would best prepare females for unfamiliar tasks, and which conditions of labor would best meet women's personal needs.

In response to the wartime labor shortage, corporations experimented with training programs for women. At the same time, the federal government created agencies to establish safe and sanitary working conditions for women, to oversee the introduction of women into male-dominated work, and to monitor male-female relations on the shop floor. From the standpoint of the history of wartime labor management, two of the most important programs for women were undertakings of newly created government agencies—the Women's Branch of the Ordnance Department of the United States Army and the Women's Service Section of the United States Railroad Administration. The policies of these bodies represented an amalgam of two previously independent approaches to labor management, scientific management and corporate welfare work. By focusing attention on the worker as well as on the design of work, these new government agencies reflected and reinforced the growing interest in a more inclusive approach to personnel management.

The movement for scientific management of business and the general set of practices known as industrial welfare work had developed simultaneously in the late nineteenth century. Scientific management concentrated on technical changes in the actual performance of work, while welfare measures focused on the cultural, educational, recreational, medical, and financial aspects of workers' lives. Scientific management made its greatest inroads before the war in the metal-working and telephone industries, whereas welfare work flourished chiefly in department stores, textile factories, mines, and steel mills. The war helped to forge a union between the scientific management of work and the cultivation of human relations.

The female reformers chosen to run the Ordnance Department and Railroad Administration's agencies for women workers attached special meaning to the efficient management of female wage earners. In their mind's eye they held a vision of an efficient industrial system emancipating women from exploitative, dead-end employment. The women reformers coupled these feminist sentiments with a socially conservative theory of labor relations that emphasized individual efficiency and "proper" work habits. Their solution to the economic degradation of women relied in part on the molding of women into model workers and the careful matching of the "right" worker with the "right" job. The reformers undertook their wartime responsibilities with the twofold purpose of promoting new opportunities and benefits for women in industry while encouraging women wage earners to achieve high productivity levels, but lasting and large-scale employment improvements for female workers fell far short of the social reformers' ideal.

The ethic of efficiency resulted in few of the benefits for women workers that the reformers had envisioned. For all their efforts the reformers could not insure women wage earners equal pay to men's for the same work, employment security, or long-term job opportunities. Employers were mostly interested in hiring women workers to solve the wartime labor shortage or to be used as a threat against male workers who might collectively organize to improve their working conditions. Since employers' motives for hiring women differed substantially from the reformers' goals, businessmen implemented only those labor policies which served their own interests. The reformers' enforcement powers and their policy roles in the government were limited. Under such circumstances the reformers' ideal could not be translated into a lasting reality.

TAYLORISM AND INDUSTRIAL WELFARISM

Frederick Winslow Taylor and the system of labor control which bears his name are justifiably at the heart of any historical discussion of modern labor management. In the early twentieth century, when the ethic of efficiency had virtually become an American mania, Taylor and his disciples promoted it as a technique of industrial management.[3] Taylorism, known also as scientific management, was an attempt to use the methods of engineering for the adaptation of labor to the needs of capital. Taylor's goal was to make every factory operate with the precision and exactitude of an efficient machine. Every feature of factory operation fell under Taylor's scrutiny. He analyzed the entire factory setting in terms applicable to a machine's productivity rating, arguing that wasted movements, parts, and materials represented avoidable costs which lowered potential profits. Of all the facets of factory life, workers' pace and productivity preoccupied Taylor. In place of the customary tradition of craftsmen establishing what they considered a proper day's work, Taylor aimed to establish a "scientific" basis for workers' performance. With stopwatch in hand, he tried to determine how long a physically fit worker should take to do each job in a shop. He then turned this information into a formula for what he considered a fair day's work for a fair piece rate. In tandem with such time-and-motion studies, Taylor advocated standardization, systematization, planning and routing of work in manufacturing processes. He also urged the use of careful selection, instruction, and supervision to weed out all but the most productive employees, and encouraged the use of material incentives in the form of sliding wage payments to maintain the prescribed rates of productivity.[4] Taylor boasted that this system increased workers' efficiency and earnings, developed their manual ability, and elevated their standard of living. For employers, scientific management offered hopes of higher profits through increased output, lower costs, and greater labor-management harmony. Despite such claims and hopes, the economic and social effects of Taylor's management reforms—on workers and employers alike—have been matters of profound controversy.[5]

Before World War I scientific management was vigorously discussed in management circles, but few employers adopted the Taylor system in its entirety. Since the principles of scientific management drew heavily from those practiced in mechanical engineering, Taylor's ideas found the greatest receptivity in American machine shops in the early twentieth century, although a few textile and clothing firms also experimented with scientific management. In the approximately twenty-nine firms which adopted Taylor's ideas between 1901 and 1917, changes were instituted in the classification and standardization of materials, in tool and storeroom procedures, in the adjustment and replacement of machinery, as well as in industrial architecture and internal plant design. The American Telephone and Telegraph Company applied the principles of scientific management to the design and operation of its many urban telephone exchanges.[6] In contrast to the technical and structural innovations of scientific management, Taylorism showed no comparable sensitivity to the human dimension of production. Taylor was more concerned with work design than with workers' personal adjustment to his system. He believed that an incentive pay system, a careful selection and training of workers for job assignments, and a well-organized flow of production would discourage labor disputes. Only when craftsmen militantly contested the introduction of time-and-motion studies and incentive pay plans did Taylor's followers begin to pay closer attention to the knotty problem of labor-management relations.[7] The more systematic evaluation of human relations in the workplace developed when the fields of industrial psychology and sociology won a wide enough following in American industry.[8]

In contrast to the school of scientific management, which focused on the planning, execution, and control of production, welfare work proponents sought direct reforms in wage earners' living and working conditions. Interest in these facets of workers' lives arose in the late nineteenth century in response to the influx into American industry of millions of immigrants from eastern and southern Europe and the increasing unrest among all workers as expressed in absentee rates, turnover, and work stoppages. The surge of interest in welfare capitalism surfaced after the acrimonious and often bloody labor disputes of the decade of the 1870s and the year 1886. In the two years following the violent Haymarket Affair of 1886, approximately twenty-four firms initiated welfare programs. Between 1905 and 1915, a decade of widespread labor-management strife, at least forty additional U.S. firms introduced extensive welfare measures.[9]

With roots in the philanthropic and paternalistic traditions of labor management and humanitarian reform, welfare work emphasized the provision of cultural, educational, recreational, financial, and medical services for workers. It sought to change native and foreign-born workers' social attitudes, work habits, and life styles. Unlike scientific management, welfare work did not have a rigorous set of guiding principles. Its underlying tenet was the belief that employers' active concern for the health and welfare of their workers would improve employees' loyalty and morale, promote congenial management-labor relations, and discourage the growth of trade unionism. Welfare work included all provisions for the health and comfort of employees which were not otherwise required by law—specifically, first-aid facilities, free ice water, rest rooms, rest periods during work hours, vacations with pay, pay for legal holidays, insurance and retirement pensions, as well as profit-sharing, bonus, and premium plans.[10] The textile and machinery manufacturers, Bell System telephone companies, large department stores, and, to a lesser extent, the iron and steel industries, offered comprehensive welfare programs, while hundreds of other plants adopted particular measures of welfare reform. Nearly all the companies with well-developed welfare programs before the war were large concerns, and many of these firms were already employing hundreds of women wage earners.[11]

In the world of scientific management, the time-and-motion study expert was central to the implementation of changes in production processes, whereas the key person in welfare work was the social secretary who served as the bridge between capital and labor. As the stopwatch expert studied the physical operations involved in work, the welfare secretary examined working and living conditions in order to suggest and institute changes. In contrast to the pioneers of scientific management, much less is known about the welfare workers. The limited available evidence suggests that most industrial social secretaries were women with training in nursing and teaching or experience in religious, philanthropic or social settlement work. Employers looked for persons possessing "good health, good sense, good taste, good manners, good character," as well as sympathy and tact. Firms that engaged in social welfare work between 1880 and 1920 sought persons with middle-class characteristics rather than graduates of a particular professional program.[12]

The actual work of the social welfare secretary varied from firm to firm. In the 1880s at the H. J. Heinz food factories in Pittsburgh,

"Mother Dunn" variously supervised the hiring and firing of women employees, investigated absenteeism, and offered a sympathetic ear to those in need of counsel. At the William Filene & Sons Department Store of Boston, welfare work began in the 1890s when a woman took charge of evaluating working conditions, handling grievances, and helping to operate various clubs, services, and activities for workers. At the textile mills owned by Joseph Bancroft & Sons in Wilmington, Delaware, Elizabeth F. Briscoe assumed responsibility from 1902 until 1919 for maintaining a proper moral atmosphere, overseeing benefit programs, and handling complaints at the mills and company boarding houses.[13] As suggested by their duties, the three welfare secretaries were part of larger company reform programs to improve wage earners' working conditions and influence their social lives. Dressing rooms, washrooms, and lockers, as well as sewing and cooking classes, recreation facilities, and social clubs, were normally provided at firms employing special welfare administrators.

Welfare work varied so widely that it is difficult to assess its effects on labor management. At some firms the introduction of a welfare secretary offended workers' sense of dignity and self-respect. Employees were especially uncomfortable with the interference of management in their family and home situations. When Lena Harvey Tracy, a former deaconess, was hired by the National Cash Register Company to develop welfare programs, hundreds of women employees greeted her with a mixture of "wonder, doubt, and expectancy." Jean Hoskins, the welfare secretary at a Maine manufacturing company, was also greeted by employees with "hard suspicious glances," and workers at Joseph Bancroft & Sons dubbed Elizabeth Briscoe the "lady detective."[14] Workers' decided lack of enthusiasm for welfare work and the vague and uncertain cost benefits of welfare measures contributed to a growing dissatisfaction with this approach to labor management on the part of some employers. By World War I many businessmen had begun to look elsewhere for innovations to counteract labor force instability because welfare reforms were not appreciably resolving the problems for which they had originally been introduced. The appeal of the ideal of industrial welfare was greater than its visible successes. However, as welfare work lost favor among some employers, it gained popularity with others. For those managers who had not yet introduced welfare measures, the war acted as a sudden spur for its widespread adoption.[15]

Between 1910 and 1920 welfare work gradually gave way to a new interest in personnel administration. Increasingly, the cost of labor unrest encouraged businessmen to concentrate more on the careful recruitment and selection of workers. Personnel administration most often took the form of a labor or employment department with responsibility for the recruitment, selection, instruction and discharge of workers. In varying combinations, some employment managers also handled training programs, discipline, and grievance procedures, as well as research and welfare provisions. While the scope and functions of employment departments varied considerably, they shared a common intent, which was to remove control over certain employment duties from the hands of foremen and invest these tasks in a new managerial elite who would presumably be more amenable to company direction and would work with greater rigor and precision. This development suggests the degree to which management was becoming interested in placing the "right" worker in the "right" job as a strategy for curbing labor turnover. Outside the corporation, the necessity for adjusting workers to their jobs gave rise to a complex of academic disciplines aimed at developing new ways to select, train, and motivate workers. The fields of industrial psychology and industrial physiology originated in this prewar labor problem.[16]

WARTIME LABOR MANAGEMENT

This new concern for managing the worker intensified during the war and took many different yet complementary forms. The wartime labor scarcity fostered discussion of potential labor resources and prompted experimentation with methods for utilizing women, older men, physically disabled workers, and black agricultural and domestic labor in the manufacture of war materials. In the private sector alone, some 200 firms installed employment departments, while more than 400 experimented with welfare measures, such as medical facilities, lunchrooms, rest rooms, savings plans, libraries, and social clubs, to attract and retain their employees.[17] New techniques for evaluating workers were also popularized during the war. Psychological testing was used on a larger scale than ever before. The federal government provided the major impetus for the extension of this method when the army hired Walter Dill Scott, the pioneer industrial psychologist who had developed intelligence tests for industrial workers, to screen more than three million conscripts. Civilian agencies of the federal government also helped to legitimate the new profession of personnel management. In 1918 the War Industries Board sponsored programs for training employment managers. By 1919, more than a dozen colleges offered courses in the new specialty. In addition, the war's disruption of the labor market led to the creation in January 1918 of the United States Employment Service and to the inauguration of training programs for unskilled workers sponsored by the Federal Vocational Board.[18]

As women's presence increased dramatically in the munitions plants, manufacturers sought information about precise methods for training and adjusting women to industry. In 1918 the Industrial Welfare Committee of the Cleveland Chamber of Commerce and the National Industrial Conference Board, which represented employers' associations throughout the country, undertook detailed studies of manufacturing training programs.[19] Employers wanted to know what work women could perform successfully and what special facilities were needed for their health and safety. Significant questions in the studies concerned the comparative productivity of women and men as well as the reaction of men to women's introduction into their fields. The findings from these and similar investigations were publicized regularly in such trade journals as *Iron Age, Iron Trade Review, Electric Review, Industrial Management,* and *Machinery.*[20]

Two wartime training programs received widespread publicity for their effectiveness in both training techniques and labor relations. The instructions offered by the Recording & Computing Machines Company of Dayton, Ohio and the Lincoln Motor Company of Detroit, Michigan were chosen as model programs by the Council of National Defense, through its section on Industrial Training for the War Emergency. The federal government issued separate pamphlets describing these programs for distribution to metal-working establishments throughout the United States.

Significantly, the Ohio wartime training program for women was designed by Charles U. Carpenter, who had headed the first modern personnel department in American industry at the National Cash Register Company of Dayton, Ohio in 1901.[21] As works manager of the Recording & Computing Machines Company, Carpenter recommended five principles to guide the employment of women: a separate training department, continued supervision by a job boss on the shop floor, special attention to inefficient workers, a "fair" system of pay with bonuses, and a system of supervision to prevent operatives from overworking. For the 5,000 women in its wartime work force of 8,600, the Recording & Computing Machines Company carefully designed a mechanical training department in a well-lit room away from the factory.

One of the company's expert mechanics, a man known for his "gentlemanly" manner, headed the training school and supervised a staff of carefully chosen female teachers who had already proven themselves to be excellent production workers. The women instructors acted as role models to boost the morale and confidence of "frightened" and "nervous" newcomers who were first entering machine shops from previous employment in stores, restaurants, and schools. In each stage of the training, women were programmed for as efficient a performance as possible. Before the instruction began, the trainees were separated into two groups: the more physically able worked on heavy machines while the rest were assigned to lighter equipment. During the lessons, care was taken to correct women's mistakes "in the most kindly manner" possible. After ten days' training at a low day rate of pay, the trainees were transferred to regular shops where they were supervised by skilled machinists called job bosses and were paid according to a piece-work rate.[22]

The company program stressed moderation and group effort. In order to insure a relatively uniform rate of production from each employee, every job boss was paid a bonus which depended on the output of the entire group of women under his supervision. In frequent meetings, company officials cautioned the male machinists, foremen, and supervisors against driving individual women at an exhausting pace to compensate for slower workers.[23]

For the social welfare of its workers, the company provided a hospital and several restaurants and company bands. In its published report the firm congratulated itself for paying "especial attention to the health and spirit of our employe[e]s and . . . look[ing] out for their interest as a matter of justice pure and simple. These plans have resulted in a very large increase in output, a well satisfied body of employe[e]s, and an organization that will respond to any urgent request that may be made upon it."[24]

The Lincoln Motor Company training program resembled procedures followed by the Dayton firm. A skilled machinist with "an engaging personality, patience, and enthusiasm" instructed American-born women over twenty-one years of age in assembly, machine, or inspection work. During the training period women worked with other partially trained female operatives to develop confidence in their mechanical ability. Like the women at the Recording Company, the women at Lincoln shifted from an hour wage to piecework upon completion of their course.[25]

A system of strict surveillance distinguished the Lincoln Motor Company's program from that of the Recording & Computing Machines Company. In a booklet entitled "Announcement Regarding Women Workers in Lincoln Motor Company" written by Henry M. Leland, president of the firm, employees were emphatically instructed to be on their best behavior at all times. According to company policy only women with "good character" were even admitted for training. Once on the job, women and men were not allowed to mingle with one another. They were assigned different rest periods, opposite entrances to company restaurants, and alternate quitting times. Foremen and subforemen were held personally responsible for the conduct of those in their departments. Immediate dismissal awaited any craftsman, no matter how valuable, who violated the conduct code. Women were expressly forbidden to flirt or even talk with male employees, inspectors, clerks, or foremen.[26]

In order to "bind women together by ties of good fellowship and to create loyalty and interest in the plant," Lincoln Motors created a social club to hold monthly dinners for the women. As of December 1918, the firm's welfare department was considering a women's orchestra, a singing club, and bowling and basketball teams as means for further extending the company's involvement in the women's lives. Lincoln Motors clearly intended its "threshold" school, as it was called, to initiate the women into a world associated with the company both on and off the job.[27]

As these programs and plans suggest, the war accelerated the merging of the technical and social dimensions of labor management. In both the private and public sectors, special efforts were made to train women, curb their turnover, and promote good work relations between men and women. Responding to the impact of war, the policies and personnel of the Women's Branch of the Army Ordnance Department, the Women's Section of the United States Railroad Administration, and private industry provided a transition between the independent, prewar development of scientific management and welfare work and the emergence in the postwar period of systematic personnel administration.

TWO MODEL AGENCIES FOR ORDNANCE PLANTS AND RAILROADS

The creation of a special women's branch in the Army Ordnance Department was a direct result of the unprecedented wartime demand for enormous quantities of metal products. The army required cannons, rifles, cartridges, shells, fuses and detonators, shrapnel, high explosives, and other forms of ammunition and military equipment. The need for such materials coupled with the trend toward the standardization of work, the use of single-purpose machines, and the rise of labor shortages increased the number of women in the metal trades. According to a Women's Bureau survey of the war years, women accounted for barely 3 percent of the total work force in iron and steel in 1914 and little more in 1916. Seven months after the first military draft, in February 1918, the percentage leaped to 6.1, and four months after the second draft, in October 1918, it reached 9.5.[28]

Because of the increased number of women in the metal-working industries, the first government agency to declare a policy on the employment of women was the production division of the Bureau of Ordnance of the United States Army. The Ordnance Department was responsible for procuring a vast assortment of military equipment, operating all of the government arsenals, and ordering materials from private manufacturers, as well as inspecting, storing and transporting 75,000 to 100,000 different items.[29] Gauged by the volume of its business from April 1917 to December 1918, which ranged between $3.5 billion and $4 billion, the Ordnance Department became the greatest single industrial organization in the United States.[30] To facilitate the utilization of women in wartime manufacturing, the Ordnance Department established a Women's Branch in its Industrial Service Section in January 1918.[31]

The Ordnance Department's interest in the recruitment and adjustment of women workers derived from its larger concern for the relationships of people at work. Since 1909, when Frederick Winslow Taylor and his associates tried to install several technical and managerial innovations at the Watertown Manufacturing Arsenal, the Ordnance Department had pioneered in the movement for scientific management. Much to the army's dismay, efforts to change production and work relations did not wholly succeed. In 1911 the Watertown molders, who resented the Taylorite usurpation of control over their labor, began a campaign to outlaw time study and incentive pay policies. By 1915 they had convinced Congress to ban these practices in government arsenals. As a result of this bitter conflict between management and labor, the chief of ordnance and the arsenals' commanding officers considered ways to modify the Taylor system and make it more palatable to workers. After 1915 the department was increasingly forced to obtain the consent of craftsmen for changes in their working conditions, wages, and tasks.[32]

During the war the Ordnance Department expanded and strengthened its ties with advocates of management reform. By 1918, one-third of the active members of the Taylor Society had become reserve officers in the production division in ordnance.[33] These men brought to government service the philosophy of industrial management that had germinated in the prewar years. In the Ordnance Department they found an organization both favorably disposed toward this philosophy and experienced in implementing it.

As one of its first wartime labor measures, the Ordnance Department on November 15, 1917 issued General Order No. 13, drafted by Morris L. Cooke, a leading member of the Taylor group, and Mary van Kleeck, a noted expert in the problems of women wage earners. In the interest of uninterrupted wartime production the directive argued for optimal efficiency in the manufacture of war products. The order specifically recommended the restriction of the workday to eight hours, the need for a fair wage scale, the right of negotiation between employers and employees, the need for limitations on the physical work performed by women, the enforcement of existing state legal standards for women's employment, the payment to women of wages equal to men's for the same work, and the prohibition of child labor. The pronouncement demonstrated the growing compatibility between efficient production and good working conditions, and it formed the basis for similar policies issued by other government bodies during the war. The army's creation of the Women's Branch within the Ordnance Department's Industrial Service Section was part of a more comprehensive effort to stabilize the work force in the munitions industry. To curb labor turnover and cope with the shortage of labor, the Ordnance Department also established a housing branch to construct dwellings in war-boom communities and an employment service to install special departments in factories for the purpose of recruiting, selecting, and training workers. Together with these branches, the women's agency was mandated to facilitate labor productivity and promote congenial labor relations.[34]

The Women's Service Section (WSS) of the United States Railroad Administration shared the Ordnance Department's interests in both improving the lot of women workers and in fostering steady, high levels of wartime production. Both agencies were concerned with working conditions and wages as well as with the introduction of women into new work, the preservation and enforcement of regulatory laws, and the careful selection and training of women. The two federal agencies, however, differed markedly in their emphasis. While the Ordnance Branch stressed the importance of changes in the design of work, the Women's Service Section emphasized the primacy of changing the worker as a person. The Ordnance Branch focused on the technical concerns of production involved in the operation of machines, whereas WSS accentuated efforts to shape workers' social attitudes, work habits, and life styles. The WSS tried to mold women into model workers, while entrusting to management the provision of a physically and morally wholesome work environment. On balance, the Ordnance Branch followed the Taylorite tradition and the Women's Service Section pursued an industrial welfare approach.

The difference in emphasis was due in part to the particular reasons for the creation of the Women's Service Section. The WSS was created as part of a larger organizational change in the railroad industry during the war. The absolute necessity of maintaining uninterrupted operation of the railroads, the weak financial condition of the industry, and the widespread militancy of railroad employees forced the federal government to assume control of the rails on December 28, 1917. In order to stabilize the work force, the Railroad Administration promptly adopted some policies which were expressly favorable to labor. The official recognition of workers' concerns by the government ended a particularly bitter chapter in the long history of strained relations between railroad unions and owners.

The entire period of federal operation of the railroads, which lasted until March 1920, was generally characterized by harmonious relations between the Railroad Administration and its employees. The new management-labor cooperation was strengthened by the selection of W. S. Carter, President of the Brotherhood of Firemen and Enginemen, as Director of Labor for the Railroad Administration. Carter chose either active union members or people sympathetic to the labor movement for positions in his department. In addition to sanctioning rapid unionization, federal control brought extensive changes in working conditions, including the enforcement of an eight-hour day with time-and-a-half payment for overtime work; elaborate provisions for promotion, seniority, and grievances; elimination of piecework; standardization of pay scales; and recognition of equal rights for women and black workers.[35]

To deal specifically with labor difficulties relating to the employment of women, the Division of Labor of the Railroad Administration created the Women's Service Section on August 29, 1918, under the direction of Pauline Goldmark. According to the Railroad Administration's General Order No. 27, Article 5, the WSS was instructed to establish safe and suitable working conditions for women, to enforce state labor laws regarding conditions of female employment, and to guarantee equal pay for women performing the same class of labor as men. The WSS could investigate all other matters pertaining to the employment of women, but it had no powers of implementation and could only make appropriate recommendations for areas outside its immediate authority.[36]

PROFILES OF FEMALE SOCIAL REFORMERS

The spirit in which the Women's Branch of the Ordnance Division and the Women's Service Section of the Railroad Administration entered upon their work reflected a particular moral and social orientation. The women chosen to work for each agency brought to their work an outlook and expertise which complemented the government's concern for efficiency and scientific management. The women staff members belonged to a generation of independent middle-class and working-class social reformers who devoutly believed that social problems could be solved through a combination of timely diagnosis, moral exhortation, and legislation. In contrast to a former generation of reformers, these women spurned a theory of economics based on laissez-faire and a concept of law that, above all else, sanctioned private property. Instead, they asserted that individuals could control their environment. Their commitment to reform grew from an awareness of social problems created by the rapid and expansive growth of the American economy.

The female reformers accepted the reality of the new factory system with its specialized, mechanized labor. They understood that the backbone of the American economy had shifted from self-employed farmers, craftsmen, and shopkeepers to large, impersonal corporations. They accepted women wage earners as a permanent part of the industrial labor force, but they bemoaned the fact that millions of women were slaves to the industrial system of labor. Their understanding derived from their first-hand investigations of women's employment at home, in factories, stores, and telephone exchanges. Study after study had convinced them that women workers were exploited, cheap labor driven to work at inhuman speeds under wretched conditions. Their investigations of women's work had brought them face to face with the physically abusive, mind-numbing drudgery of industrial production. Since they had

Figure 10. Mary van Kleeck, industrial sociologist. Early in her long career as a social researcher, van Kleeck showed an abiding interest in management-labor relations. *Women's Bureau No. 86-G-9F-44, National Archives, Washington, D.C. Permission of Bachrach, Inc.*

Figure 11. Mary Anderson, trade unionist and social reformer. In the first six years after Anderson left her native Sweden, she worked at ten different jobs in three fields of work in three states. She is best known as the first head of the Women's Bureau of the Department of Labor. *Signal Corps. No. 111-SC-9216, National Archives, Washington, D.C.*

Figure 12. Pauline Goldmark, social reformer. Like her sister Josephine, Goldmark distinguished herself as a crusader for better working conditions for women wage earners. *From Survey 35 (November 27, 1915): 214.*

either observed or worked under the pulse and pressures of mechanized labor, they fully appreciated the detrimental effects of industrial monotony and industrial fatigue. Their personal encounters with women wage earners had made them sympathetic to the plight of Italian cannery workers, Polish stockyards employees, Jewish and Italian seamstresses, native-American bookbinders and shoemakers, black laundresses, and thousands of English-speaking saleswomen.[37]

The women reformers recognized the need for some form of enjoyment or fulfillment in paid labor. They believed that night work, seasonal employment, wages far below the cost of living, and unsanitary and unsafe working conditions destroyed the fabric of family life and made women into pawns of the industrial system. As a social reform measure to unite women wage earners with each other and with their male co-workers, they endorsed the extension of trade unionism to all sectors of the economy. Accommodated to the growing presence of huge factories, offices, and telephone exchanges, they dedicated themselves to abolishing what they considered to be the most destructive aspects of mechanized labor. By publishing investigations of women's work, testifying before government agencies, and pleading their cases before law courts, they hoped to reduce seasonal employment, abolish night work, set wages in relation to the actual cost of living, and develop vocational training programs for women. To their way of thinking, the corporate capitalist system needed more efficient and careful management, which would result in benefits to women workers as well as men and in increased company profitability.[38]

The chief of ordnance appropriately chose Mary van Kleeck and Mary Anderson as principal advisors on ordnance matters pertaining to female workers. Van Kleeck came to Washington with fourteen years' experience as a social scientist. After her graduation from Smith College in 1904, she worked as an investigator of employment and housing conditions for the Alliance Employment Bureau, a New York City philanthropic agency for the placement of women and girls in factories and offices. Later, when she joined the staff of the newly established Russell Sage Foundation, she compiled detailed information about women wage earners for the development of employment standards. From September 1914 to

June 1917, van Kleeck lectured on industrial disorders at the New York School of Social Philanthropy. By 1917 she had become well known for three books on the problems of female factory operatives and industrial homeworkers.[39]

Like many of her peers, van Kleeck placed special emphasis on the cooperation among social scientists, government officials, and industrialists. In her scheme of social change, the expert played a central role in investigating conditions and suggesting solutions for problems. She sincerely believed that by studying the opposing interests of employers and workers, the government, representing the whole people, could learn to mediate conflicts by enacting appropriate laws for workers and by forcing industry to minister to the "national good."[40] In a statement about the philosophy of the Russell Sage Foundation, van Kleeck seemed to voice the essential components of her own personal perspective on the amelioration and adjustment of social conflicts.

The Foundation is concerned with the labor movement from the viewpoint neither of employers nor of workers, but as representing the public interest. The public interest may sometimes square with the interest of workers, and sometimes with the interest of employers. Sometimes it may be in conflict with the immediate interests of both. Conflicts are inevitable, but the important thing is that employers, workers, and the public should understand the facts and know the tendencies involved in action. The Foundation has tried to describe the facts, and . . . its investigators have sought not to influence conclusions, but to help to establish the habit of making facts, rather than prejudice or self-interest, the basis for conclusions.[41]

Not surprisingly, van Kleeck fervently believed in the war's potential for initiating a new order in industry and society. As the head of the Women's Branch in the Army Ordnance Department, she inspected arsenals and consulted with government officials and ordnance contractors about the best methods for maintaining industrial standards while accelerating production. She undertook her wartime work with the staunch conviction that social scientists could engineer a new society by slightly modifying the basic structure and prerogatives of corporate capitalism in the workers' favor.

The woman who assisted van Kleeck came from a very different ethnic and class background. In 1889, at the age of sixteen, Mary Anderson left an impoverished farm in Sweden to seek a more secure way of life in the United States. Like many self-supporting female immigrants, she undertook various kinds of labor, spending her first six years in America employed at ten different jobs in three fields of work in three states. In 1895, when she changed from household labor to factory work and made contact with the labor movement, she began to distinguish herself from other women workers. At the age of twenty-two, she joined Stitchers' Local 9 of the International Boot and Shoe Workers' Union while working as an operative in a Chicago shoe factory. Later, she served as a union delegate to the Chicago Federation of Labor and as an executive board member of her international union.[42] She became one of a small but significant minority of working-class women who remained single and actively devoted to the labor movement.

Like van Kleeck, Anderson brought to her wartime work a commitment to management-labor responsibility and accountability. Cooperation, adjustment, and accommodation were the essential features of her perspective. She believed that wage earners and middle-class reformers could work together to ameliorate industrial conditions.[43] As a social welfare progressive and seasoned trade unionist, she fully expected the government to launch a comprehensive program of social and economic regulation which would substantially benefit women workers. Eight months after her government appointment, Anderson expressed her attitude and hope to a friend, declaring in a letter, how ''I sincerely believe that this time, with [our] liberal government . . . we can do more for the labor movement on the inside of the government than on the outside.''[44]

By the summer of 1918, when Pauline Goldmark became the head of the Railroad Administration's Women's Service Section, she was also a well-known veteran of social reform. As one of seven daughters of a former member of the Austrian Parliament who had taken a leading part in the Revolution of 1848, she was imbued with her family's liberal social conscience. As the sister-in-law of Felix Adler, founder of the Society for Ethical Culture, and of Louis Brandeis, a Boston lawyer and justice of the United States Supreme

Court, she had important connections in American cultural and political circles. After her graduation from Bryn Mawr College in 1896, she devoted herself to industrial investigations and social work. For two years she worked as an assistant director of the Bureau of Social Research at the Russell Sage Foundation under the supervision of Mary van Kleeck.[45] By the early twentieth century, Goldmark had also gained valuable reform experience as assistant secretary of the National Consumers' League.

The league actively promoted a new public role for middle- and upper-class women. League members frowned upon patrician benevolence and a conception of womanhood which sanctioned idleness and detachment from social problems. In order to publicize the importance of protective legislation, the organization engaged college-trained experts to gather facts about the conditions under which wage earners labored. In its consumer program, the league united economic activity with moral and personal considerations, and it campaigned to encourage women to purchase only those goods made under decent working conditions. Every business transaction was regarded as part of a larger social process.[46] As one of the league's hired staff, Goldmark brought to her wartime work a sense of middle-class social responsibility, a watchdog mentality toward management, a belief in state regulation of industry, and a commitment to individual accountability.

Three of the four staff members who worked in the Women's Service Section under Goldmark during the war came from backgrounds similar to Mary van Kleeck's. Florence Clark, Helen Ross, and Edith Hall mastered the techniques of social research in the course of their respective studies at the University of Chicago, Bryn Mawr College, and the New School of Philanthropy. Clark had studied political economy, social psychology, and civic government and had taken courses from Edith Abbott and Sophonisba Breckinridge, two outstanding pioneers in social investigation and reform. Ross had worked with Susan Kingsbury, an industrial researcher, on inspections of department stores, railroad shops, and sweatshop piecework in the home. Hall came to the government with recommendations from Goldmark herself and with extensive experience in researching municipal and child labor problems. Each woman had had some contact with the railroad industry prior to her employment by the Women's Service Section.[47]

The fourth WSS staff member, Rose Yates, who was a railroad worker and dedicated trade unionist, was unique among the field agent team. Although she had completed teacher education training, she earned her living at different times as a telephone operator, file clerk, and railroad service agent. Like Mary Anderson of the Ordnance Department, she brought to her wartime position a rich work experience and an active trade union membership which qualified her for the government assignment. Her intimate knowledge of railroad operations and affiliation with the Brotherhood of Railway Clerks more than compensated for her lack of formal industrial research training.[48]

All the personnel in the Women's Ordnance Branch and the Women's Service Section agreed that the successful employment of women during the war depended on educating employer and employee about their "proper" industrial roles. The reformers believed that wise management of industry required a combination of personal and social efficiency. The American economy would function smoothly and harmoniously, in the reformers' vision, if workers and managers fulfilled their mutual obligations to one another. Women wage earners owed their employers hard work and diligence in return for realistic production demands, fair wages, and decent working conditions. Since the reformers viewed the substitution of women for men workers as an important, though very difficult, wartime experiment that could advance women's postwar economic status, they wanted women wage earners to succeed in their new wartime jobs in keeping with the reformers' own larger vision of social change. They saw in the efficient operation of industry the emancipation of women workers from routine, dead-end employment. They were so eager for women to get into promising and more lucrative "men's" jobs that they happily promoted women as efficient workers and encouraged them to demonstrate higher productivity. The government employees accepted the idea that women had to perform better than men ordinarily did at the same tasks to prove themselves worthy of good jobs. The reformers saw themselves as promoting the extension of new job opportunities to women while eliminating the most exploitative features of industrial labor.

The themes of efficiency and feminism were inextricably interwoven in the reformers' view of wartime developments. Their ability to shape circumstances to the ends they most desired was an entirely different matter. Formidable obstacles blocked their wartime attempts to set American industry on the course they envisioned.

THE WOMEN'S BRANCH OF THE
ORDNANCE DEPARTMENT

Under van Kleeck and Anderson's supervision, the Women's Branch served the immediate needs of the production division of the army and the long-term interests of industry by helping to establish a fund of knowledge about ways to introduce and train women workers. In particular, the Women's Branch assumed responsibility for three tasks: advising ordnance establishments on matters pertaining to the substitution of women for men, employment methods, and standards for working conditions, hours, and wages; supervising the conditions of work and employment of women in munitions plants; and handling requests from employers for exemptions from state laws regarding women wage earners. Mary van Kleeck aptly summarized the general aim of her work as "setting free the best energies of the workers" by "finding out . . . the obstacles to satisfactory production."[49] In short, the Women's Branch focused attention on both the "human" and technical sides of industrial organization and management.

To carry out her assignment, van Kleeck hired a special staff of three for her Washington, D.C. office to study employment management, health problems, and training techniques. Anderson was assigned responsibility for inspecting munitions plants and interpreting the government's labor policy to both men and women wage earners. By the end of 1918, the Women's Branch had opened eleven district offices to serve ordnance plants. The Washington headquarters served as a clearinghouse for reports of the district agents and for information about industrial policies, labor supply, and plant management.[50]

The Women's Branch facilitated the wartime dilution of skilled labor, by which the variety of work ordinarily performed by a machinist or other highly trained worker would now be separated into several component operations. One or another particular task would then be assigned to women with little or no prior training in machine work. Each woman investigator served as a laboratory model for the dilution of labor and job analysis. Whatever work she herself could perform, by actual trial, she sanctioned for other women. Whatever conditions facilitated her production, she recommended as policy to promote the work of others.

The ordnance personnel promoted the principle of assigning the "right" worker for the "right" work with the least disruption to production. Like scientific management experts, the Women's Branch personnel were concerned about the number of rest periods, the degree of nervous strain, the amount of strength, and the frequency and duration of motions necessary to perform a job. In effect, the agency provided manufacturers with government-paid production consultants and analysts. When a munitions firm, for example, requested permission from the Ordnance Department to employ women as welders, a Women's Branch investigator visited the plant, learned how to weld, and then determined what modifications in training and working conditions were necessary for the successful utilization of women. As a result of the investigator's positive experience, women were trained as welders and introduced into metal factories.[51]

The Ordnance Department's efforts on behalf of the Bethlehem Steel Company illustrate the government's role in standardizing and rationalizing production and facilitating the employment of women. Bethlehem found the services of the Ordnance Department very much to its liking because the corporation had long-term interests in the use of scientific management and the employment of women wage earners to maintain corporate control over its thousands of male employees. Significantly, Bethlehem's concerted efforts to change the design of production processes and increase the number of its women employees coincided with the steel industry's first major union-organization drive in a decade. The training of women was one way that Bethlehem reacted to the new conditions in the steel industry created by the war. As a result of the wartime labor shortages, the federal government's guarantee of the right of workers to organize into trade unions, and its vigorous public proclamations about the importance of labor to the war effort, steelworkers began to join labor unions. Both the government's official sanction of trade unions and workers' new solidari-

ty dismayed steel manufacturers.[22] Women specialists and all-
round machinists may well have been seen by steel company executives as a reserve labor supply to replace men deemed to be trouble-
makers.

In June 1918, when Bethlehem had fallen significantly behind in
its scheduled production of war materials because of a severe labor
shortage that left hundreds of machines idle, the company requested permission from the government to place women on three eight-
hour shifts, an arrangement which would violate the Pennsylvania
law prohibiting women's night work. The demand for artillery was
so great that the Ordnance Department sent consultants to the
company's steel plants. The inspectors determined that the low
output at Bethlehem was due to a combination of inefficient production methods, a thirteen-hour workday, a complicated bonus
system, a shortage of proper housing facilities, and conscious
restriction of output by machinists, as well as a genuine labor
shortage.[53]

The Ordnance Department performed several valuable services
for Bethlehem in an attempt to improve productivity. United States
production officers took charge of installing a new system of organization for Bethlehem's twenty-five thousand employees. A
special planning department in each shop with progress charts
designed by Henry L. Gantt, a scientific management expert, carefully monitored production. The government team simplified Bethlehem's operation by reducing the variety of guns produced at the
plants and striking a better balance between the number of shops
responsible for forging and finishing.[54]

After these changes had been completed, a woman inspector
from the Ordnance Department assessed the particular conditions
of women's employment. By the summer of 1918, Bethlehem had
already made considerable strides in preparing for the hiring and
training of approximately one thousand women. It had installed an
employment department for women and a well-equipped training
school which was graduating one hundred women per month into
the production shops. The new workers learned to operate drill
presses, gun-boring lathes, turret lathes, planers, shapers, and
milling machines. Instead of training women to perform only one

operation as had become typical during the war, Bethlehem now intended to make women all-round machinists capable of a wide range of tasks, including blueprint reading and the use of precision-measuring instruments.[55]

Bethlehem's arrangements for women wage earners favorably impressed the woman investigator, who suggested additional ways to improve conditions for women's employment. On the stipulation that Bethlehem expand its industrial welfare measures, the inspector approved the company's request for three shifts of women workers. She urged Bethlehem to provide better transportation to take women to and from work, adequate facilities for their health, comfort, and safety, and matrons to supervise women's behavior in both the plant rest rooms and shops. She further emphasized the importance of the personnel manager in reducing labor turnover by bettering the physical and social conditions of employment and reducing losses in working time.[56]

The female ordnance officer also played the role of a government emissary to the male workers. In order to decrease the men's hostility to the employment of women at Bethlehem, the officer discussed production problems with the men and encouraged them to work as efficiently and as hard as possible during the day so that fewer women would be needed at night. According to her report, the men agreed to apply themselves to their jobs only if substantial improvements were made in their wages and hours. Her response was to recommend that Bethlehem give the men material incentives to apply themselves.[57]

Like many employers, Bethlehem evaluated the government's several recommendations. Under intense pressure from its employees and the government, the company declared an eight-hour day—an astounding change in view of the industry's long adherence to a twelve-hour workday. Without any reluctance Bethlehem added facilities for women's health, comfort, and safety in order to obtain government approval for employing women in shifts around the clock. The company considered such welfare measures temporary deterrents to labor turnover and unionization.[58]

The success of the female ordnance agent at Bethlehem was mirrored in the growing interest by employers in the new expertise in personnel management. The Women's Branch of the Ordnance Department specifically promoted the new profession. Because of the enormous labor force fluctuations during the war, traditional methods of hiring and firing workers seemed grossly inadequate. Manufacturers increasingly relied upon employment managers who were trained in designing employment departments, detailing job specifications, developing training schools, and controlling working conditions. The employment manager was popularly known as the "labor-cost accountant." By the middle of 1918, van Kleeck had assigned to every one of the government-operated manufacturing arsenals a female personnel manager whose function it was to ease women into their new work through training programs and to safeguard against declines in production by insuring that women could actually perform their jobs.[59]

When the Ordnance Department offered its first course in July 1918 to train women for war work in labor relations, women enthusiastically welcomed the experiment. Circulars were sent all over the United States announcing that the management training course was open to women who wanted to work in munitions plants. According to one woman who evaluated the applications, the school commanded a lot of public attention. Women from every part of the country and from every occupation and class applied for the training courses: "fine, able women, with experience in other fields, who wanted to 'do something' to help win the war; wealthy women who had had no training in any trade or profession but sentimentally and largeheartedly offered their housewifely and motherly backgrounds to the 'working girls'; school teachers and others, tired of the routine of their jobs and looking for change and excitement."[60] Out of the thousands of applications fifty women were chosen.

Because of the large number of munitions plants in Cleveland, the city's Case School of Applied Science was chosen to host the program. In contrast to men with extensive shop experience who enrolled in management courses sponsored by the government at the University of Rochester and Harvard University, many of the fifty women chosen for training in Cleveland were college graduates without any previous contact with industrial production. The women's two-month course consisted of daytime factory work and evening classes in employment office practice, labor economics, and industrial management. This training was designed to familiarize the women with the operation of only one machine and with the different kinds of employee problems they would later confront in their role as personnel managers. Cleveland manufacturers welcomed the students into their shops, thus making it possible for the women to obtain some practical experience. The Cleveland steel, hardware, and metal makers fully appreciated the experiment in the new applied science of "human" management, since their own experience had already attested to the profitability of paying close attention to the matter of shop management in introducing women into their operations. In some instances the very same employers who had installed extensive welfare programs years before the war now pioneered in the development of personnel management.[61]

The positive reception accorded by management to certain of the Women's Branch efforts did not extend to all of its endeavors. While employers shared an interest in the dilution and management of labor, arsenal commanders and private manufacturers did not respond favorably to the Women's Branch attempts to inspect working conditions and insure women wages equal to men's for the same work. Years later Mary Anderson recalled, above all else, the distrust expressed toward the Women's Branch.

[O]n the whole I do not think that we accomplished as much as we should have, chiefly because there was a great deal of antagonism to us in the division. Dean Schneider was an excellent chief, but the men he had to depend on did not like us to be in on the ground floor. Many of the men appointed had been employment managers in stores or connected with industry. . . . They were put in uniforms and felt that they had to run the show. As usual, they did not want women to interfere in any way.

[Furthermore,] women had not, before that time, taken any part in the work of the War Department. We were a new phenomenon and they were distrustful of us. I think they thought of me particularly as what they probably called a "red-eyed labor leader" who would be destructive rather helpful.[62]

Ironically, as Anderson points out, the women shared the men's concern for productivity and efficiency. Anderson not only wanted to better working conditions for women, she also wanted to obtain the highest levels of production possible. Although she firmly believed that the fulfillment of wartime production demands could best be accomplished by improving the conditions and wages of labor, her immediate superiors evidently did not appreciate such methods of boosting productivity.

Anderson's expectations for her work in the Women's Branch were considerably dampened when she discovered the immense difficulty of her assignment. The inspection of factory conditions demanded that the investigator be both aggressive and combative. Anderson was too unaccustomed to such work to outmaneuver recalcitrant employers or military personnel. In her autobiography she suggests that other women investigators experienced similar problems. Two incidents in particular discouraged her so much that she planned to "pack up and go back to Chicago."[63]

I remember going to Bridgeport with a group of several men and one other woman to inspect some factories and see that production was facilitated by proper working conditions. The group never got into a factory. We waited for the head of our expedition to tell us when we could go into a factory to see what the conditions were. Day after day he put us off saying the management was "about" ready to let us in. After nearly a week of waiting we left in disgust.

Another time, Mary van Kleeck and I stopped in Pittsburgh for one day to see conditions in some of the many ordnance plants there. We were met by an officer from the Ordnance Department the minute we got to the hotel, were taken to the office, taken to lunch, taken through one plant in the afternoon, taken to dinner that night. We were so closely chaperoned that until we took the train that night we could not so much as say "hello" to one another. Naturally, we did not find out much about the conditions of women's employment.[64]

When they did get inside plants for inspection, the investigators often reported that women were not paid the same as men in munitions plants.[65] Much munitions work was in the hands of subcontractors, who had no direct contractual relation with the government and over whom the government's power was accordingly limited. Due to subcontracting, wages for men and women metal workers fluctuated from shop to shop. Those employers with highly profitable contracts could afford to pay the higher wages demanded by workers during the war, but those employers with contracts for fixed sums often found it difficult to keep pace with wage demands.[66] Under such circumstances the Women's Branch could do little to enforce policies for fair wages.

During a visit to the Rock Island Arsenal, a female ordnance investigator complained to the commanding officer that the maximum rate for skilled female labor was $3.20 per day, whereas the starting minimum day rate for male labor was $3.68. Similarly, women who inspected the production of metal parts at the arsenal received one payment for their work while men with machinists' ratings received another. The machinists objected both to the employment of women and to the wages paid to the women, which tended to lower the pay scale in the trade as a whole.[67] As an alternative to the industry's myriad classifications and piece rates, the machinists fought for a system of classification of wages with a minimum wage scale for each skill level, but the union was not able to obtain a new wage system.[68] Since work was frequently redefined by the dilution of labor during the war, women were frequently paid according to the whims of private employers and arsenal commanders.

The Women's Branch, despite its uneven accomplishments, represented a middle ground between the older concerns for welfare measures and scientific management and the newer interest in personnel administration. The ordnance personnel combined the functions of welfare secretaries, job analysts, and factory inspectors. In the area of working conditions, the women reformers urged the acceptance of a well-paced workday both for workers' welfare and production maximization. For the same reason, the Women's Branch tried to encourage enforcement and prevent the repeal of various states' legislation regulating the conditions of women's employment. Anderson and van Kleeck also stressed the importance of measures to improve the physical environment of the factory, particularly sanitary and safety provisions. The branch encouraged new employment procedures as a way of promoting women's success and curbing labor turnover. By appointing employment managers to enforce federal standards and to interview, screen, and place women in positions in industry appropriate to their experience and ability, the ordnance division directly promoted the new profession. The army ordnance operation thus demonstrated to many employers that the control of workers involved the subdivision of labor processes, material incentives to attract workers during periods of labor scarcity, and a more rigorous approach to labor management.

THE WOMEN'S SERVICE SECTION OF THE RAILROAD ADMINISTRATION

The Women's Service Section of the Railroad Administration performed two very important functions. Officially it acted as a regulatory agency for all matters affecting the industrial welfare of women railroad employees. Unofficially it served as a women's rights advocate. To encourage a just treatment of women, Pauline Goldmark and her staff carefully monitored employment records for wage discrepancies, listened to individuals' grievances, taught women how to submit formal complaints, ordered the installation of dressing and sanitary facilities for workers' comfort, and generally looked after women's well-being in terms established by the Railroad Administration. In the area of labor welfare protection, the WSS carefully assessed women's working conditions. Employers were informed of the need for rest and lunch breaks, adequate rest rooms, local matrons, rules for proper dress and conduct, the inspection of housing facilities, the applicability of state labor laws, and the prohibition of night work for women under the age of twenty-one.[69] The field agents sought to intervene in cases of improper dismissal, assignment to physically strenuous work, personal abuse by male employees and supervisors, denial of women's rights to union membership, misinformation about seniority privileges, and discrimination based on race as well as sex.

In general, the WSS performed very well in its role as special labor regulatory agency for women. With the encouragement of the Labor Division of the Railroad Administration to which the WSS reported, the field agents exercised their full power. One unexpected by-product of the agency's efforts, however, was the hostility of many railroad officials. Railroad managers and foremen frequently objected to the work of the Women's Service Section, since its agents interfered with management's decisions and its treatment of workers. Railroad officials further resented the WSS because it signalled the growing power of organized labor in the railroad industry. A few examples clearly illustrate the kinds of abuses addressed by the WSS and the agency's positive efforts on behalf of women workers.

When women clerical and shop workers lodged a complaint against their local superintendent for unfair dismissals at the Harrisburg Division of the Pennsylvania Railroad, Florence Clark used verbal threats and a measure of bodily force to secure information about the women's work records. In a letter to Goldmark she described in detail her strategy for getting the facts of the case. After officials initially refused to give her any information,

I said [to the local supervisor that] I wanted to have all the material and intended to have it. . . . I put myself in the doorway and told him that he could not get out. . . . Before we left he tried to take the material . . . out of my hand. I told him I intended to hang on to it. . . .

To the next higher official she said

that if he refused to give all the material I asked for he would have to write . . . a statement as to his reason and I would return at once with it to Washington. He then let me have the material and I sat next to him while I copied it, so he could see that I did not tamper with it.

It was much more evidence than I had hoped I could get. There was no scene about it all and the whole performance was very quietly done. It sounds pretty undignified but it was not.[70]

Her assertiveness helped to settle the case in the women workers' favor.

When railroad officials tried to punish women as a group for the mistakes of one person, the WSS interceded on women's behalf. Pauline Goldmark protested a May 1919 order of the Delaware, Lackawanna and Western Railroad prohibiting the employment of any women highway gatekeepers after a fatal accident in Buffalo,

New York. The ruling was issued because one woman neglected to protect a truck driver from an oncoming train. Goldmark dealt directly with the DL&W Railroad federal manager and secured his promise that women would not be removed from their jobs as gate-keepers unless they were definitely incapable of performing the work. "It would . . . have been extremely unfair," she said, "to the 22 women in the service of this railroad to remove them without cause."[71]

In some instances the WSS field agents were able to aid women who had been mistreated by their local supervisors. An especially unusual case was that of Mrs. Jennie Hadley, an elevator operator in the Pittsburgh office of the Pennsylvania Railroad. In February 1919 Hadley was accused by four men in her office—the station-master, the chief clerk, a clerk, and a messenger—of being pregnant. Although Hadley reported that she was not about to become a mother, the men told her that "the only way" she could certify the truth of her statement was to submit to a medical examination by a railroad doctor. During the course of her medical evaluation, Hadley was examined by three physicians on three separate occasions. The first two physicians refused to take a stand on the matter and referred her to a third doctor who listened for fetal sounds and concluded that Hadley was not pregnant. As a result of this experience, Hadley complained that she had become "sick, nervous, and humiliated." At her request the WSS agent secured a written apology from the general superintendent of the Pennsylvania Railroad in Pittsburgh, certifying that Hadley had been subjected to gross mistreatment.[72]

Although the WSS deserves praise for the vigor with which its staff endeavored to minimize sex discrimination, its policies were not exclusively informed by a commitment to equal rights for women. The feminist orientation of the WSS was coupled with a socially conservative theory of labor relations which emphasized the primacy of individual efficiency and "proper" work habits. The WSS concern for good behavior and moral conduct was by no means unique. Since the development of the Lowell textile mills in the mid-nineteenth century, women workers in industrial America had been subjected to a rigorous system of supervision. For re-formers like the WSS agents, efforts to shape employees' work habits and life styles held a special meaning. The ethics of efficiency and social control for occupational mobility were a feminist reformer's cause. Many Progressive social reformers believed that the best chance for the advancement of underpaid, unskilled, and mostly unorganized women workers lay in the initiative and efficiency of individual women. While trade union organization and protective legislation were considered important, individual accomplishment was accorded the highest value.

Because the WSS personnel believed that the international crisis severely hampered the possibilities for any radical alterations in the usual procedures for hiring, training, or advancing workers, the field agents encouraged women wage earners to perform well so that individual accomplishment would bring them some measure of advancement and job security in the railroad industry.[73] The women reformers understood that the rapid introduction of female labor into railroad work, and especially the increased employment of women in traditionally male occupations during the war, was accomplished by reducing job training to its bare essentials and by dividing work into specialized tasks which demanded only a limited knowledge or skill. In a letter of instruction to one of her field agents, Pauline Goldmark reasoned that

[m]en in the railroad service have a great advantage over the women in their greater familiarity with the various forms of work. For this reason it is all the more necessary that women should be given the best instruction. I think there is a temptation both on your part and mine (which is fully justified by the facts) to conduct this inquiry in such a way to prove the need of *radical change in methods of employment*. But we must hold ourselves strictly to the present point of approach, namely, the *training of women . . .* to a *higher standard of work*. [T]he other line of approach [must be] a subordinate one. . . .[74]

Training women to "a higher standard of work" depended on an evaluation of the workers' habits and character. The WSS staff perceived wage earners as "types" in a manner which sharply reflected the agents' own cultural bias. Women wage earners were categorized as either of the "poor white," "poor negro," "inferior," "loose," or "superior type." The WSS classified women based on their appearance, intelligence, spirit, and deportment. Women workers were referred to as "material" to be trained or replaced as the situation might demand. Those who dressed shabbily or did not use "proper" language received an "inferior" rating. "Superior" workers fitted the middle-class model of correct behavior defined by neatness, cleanliness, and good manners. The reformers identified and sympathized with the plight of women railway workers, yet regarded them with varying degrees of condescension.[75]

The WSS reports on women wage earners reflect the growing interest in the worker as a person. The emphasis on character as a determinant of work efficiency lacked any "scientific" basis, such as was then being attempted, for example, in the army's evaluation of conscripts' mental and physical fitness. To advance the cause of efficiency, women railroaders were exhorted to be punctual, trustworthy, accurate, tactful, cooperative, able, and pleasing.[76] In addition, the WSS promoted the strict control of workers, the use of women supervisors for female employees, and regular investigations of women's performance. The women's agency feared that the hasty selection or poor supervision of women would have negative consequences for working women once the wartime labor shortage was over. Since the misconduct of one woman in whatever way could be used by management as an excuse to discredit all women, the WSS wanted to insure that women had a fighting chance to succeed in their new jobs. By regulating the work environment they hoped to aid women.

As outlined by Goldmark and her colleagues, the supervisors' duties primarily concerned worker adjustment and efficiency. The ideal supervisor encouraged her work force to be disciplined, polite, and efficient. Since the supervisor had her workers' best interests at heart, she was expected to help her "better" employees bid for higher-paying jobs. According to field agent Edith Hall, a female supervisor at the Baltimore and Ohio General Office in Baltimore approached the ideal. She had chosen, trained, or retrained all her employees to fit model worker behavior. She demanded that the women be neat and well-groomed. Her personal control extended to regulating workers' every movement, even to insisting that women request permission whenever they wanted to leave the office for any reason. From Hall's point of view, her one shortcoming was a reluctance to secure better positions for her employees by waging an aggressive effort against discrimination. Thus, Hall reported regretfully that while the supervisor recognized "that the women are tacitly barred from the revision desks by prejudice, she seems to accept the limitation, and [does] not urge them to break through and put the matter to rest by bidding in." Hall praised the Baltimore supervisor for her good work, even while admonishing her to push her workers up the employment ladder.[77]

Despite the enthusiasm for such supervision shown by the Railroad Administration, women workers themselves sometimes resented the degree of control exercised by their superiors. Female supervisors were well aware of this reaction. At a conference held by the Women's Service Section in October 1919, some supervisors even suggested that their title be changed to something less offensive, such as "head of women's service."[78]

The WSS also assumed responsibility for investigating male-female relations, especially in situations where women worked alongside men. Detailed reports were written on individuals suspected of moral misconduct. Reprimand, transfer, or dismissal was recommended for workers found guilty by local personnel of inappropriate behavior. The WSS reports concentrated on the quality of labor management provided by the roads. A case in point concerned workers engaged by the Baltimore and Ohio in its Wheeling, West Virginia railway crossings. Field agent Rose Yates reported in January 1919 that

Wheeling has been one of the places that the employment of women . . . has created a great deal of ill feeling both among the general public and among the men employees. . . . The general public resented the type of women being hired at the crossings and the fact that [white] women . . . in the Benwood Shops were working with gangs of colored men. . . . It is said . . . in the town that women of openly bad reputation were put on as crossing tenders and that the man supervisor winked at the actions of these women. They were unsuitably dressed, flirtatious, and careless about their duties. Finally . . . the man supervisor was removed and a woman was put in his place. She proceeded to remove the women and hire in a different type. . . . When one sees how the situation at Wheeling has been clarified it gives some hope for the future of women on railroads.[79]

The agents considered the absence of strict supervision a sign of disorder and a threat to women's reputations and chances for improved occupational mobility. Even though in its reports the WSS chastised men involved in the "improprieties," the field agents put the burden for moral rectitude on the women workers.

Individual achievement assumed critical importance during demobilization, when Goldmark explicitly instructed her staff to promote efficiency as a way of mitigating the wholesale dismissal of women.

[T]he most emphasis should be put on the importance of increased efficiency on the part of all employees. . . . The wartime emergency is over which caused a diminution of efficiency on account of the introduction of so many employees without previous experience, but . . . now with the return of labor to the railroads each employee should be on her mettle to give the best possible service and that only in this way can the women be secure in the[ir] positions.[80]

Neither individual excellence nor the exhortations of the WSS, however, determined the shape of the postwar labor situation on the railroads. Good moral conduct and efficiency proved to be insufficient weapons against the larger forces of supply and demand and the traditions of different work for men and women; these were the factors which dictated whether women would be hired or fired.

Ironically, the WSS emphasis on individual achievement conflicted with the agency's attempts to protect women from unsuitable kinds of employment. The WSS occasionally ruled that certain work was inappropriate for women. For example, because of the demand for heavy labor and the need for women to work with men in gangs at long distances from any house or station, the use of women as section laborers was considered harmful to women's physical and moral well-being. Objection was also taken to the employment of women as truckers in depots on account of the excessive physical exertion required. Despite the protests against dismissal by women who had been employed in such positions, the WSS placed protection above job opportunity when the situation demanded a choice. "How difficult it is," Goldmark admitted to one of her agents, "to stand for the rights of women and also for their protection."[81]

CONCLUSION

The labor policies of the Ordnance Department and the Railroad Administration reflected the growing role of the federal government in management-labor relations and factory operations. The wartime disruption of the labor market served to accelerate and spread an interest in both technical processes and welfare measures as avenues to increased efficiency. In this regard, the female reformers in the Women's Branch and the Women's Service Section publicized the need for a more systematic approach to labor problems. The staffs of both agencies acted as analysts of work design, inspectors of working conditions, welfare workers, and labor advocates. To varying degrees, each expressed concern about the adaptation of work to women's strength and training and the enforcement of standards of wages and hours to protect women from physical and economic exploitation. The realization of these efforts was substantially circumscribed by the wartime commitment to production at any cost.

The subdivision of technical processes and the paternalistic and moralistic approach of management to labor resulted in an adjustive, manipulative theory of labor relations. Aware of the wartime experiments in government arsenals, machine shops, and railroad operations, employers benefited from the efforts to manage female labor and attempted to develop and refine techniques for managing employees of both sexes. The 1920s saw the continued interest in the "human relations approach" to production problems. While the design of work itself continued to receive special attention, managerial practice in the postwar decade was built on the assumption that workers would respond positively to personnel programs designed to consider their feelings, attitudes, and interests. Professionals like Mary van Kleeck and Pauline Goldmark secured a place in postwar managerial circles for their work in this area.[82] As a frequent contributor to the *Bulletin of the Taylor Society*, van Kleeck utilized her prewar and wartime experience to promote personnel management. For the twenty years after the termination of the Women's Service Section in 1920, Pauline Goldmark served as an advisor for problems related to women's employment for the American Telephone and Telegraph Company. Reformers of the van Kleeck and Goldmark type joined industrial sociologists, psychologists, and personnel managers in the postwar period to assist employers in the development of programs to promote workers' appreciation, loyalty, and efficiency. With the war's end there began a new era of labor management. The wartime experience, by offering a period of gestation and an opportunity for experimentation in the personnel management of women wage earners by women reformers, had provided the impetus for the new era.

3 The limits of opportunity: working for the railroads

Supreme devotion to country, an invincible determination to perform the imperative duties of the hour while the life of the nation is imperilled by war, must obliterate old enemies and make friends and comrades of us all. There must be cooperation, not antagonism; confidence, not suspicion; mutual helpfulness, not grudging performance; just consideration, not arbitrary disregard of each other's rights and feelings; a fine discipline based on mutual respect and sympathy; and an earnest desire to serve the great public faithfully and efficiently.

Railroad Administration Order No. 8[1]

Had women been asked during the First World War which industry offered them the most favorable wages and working conditions, they surely would have chosen railroad work. During the period of federal control of the railroads, the government directly introduced some fundamental improvements in the industry's working conditions nationwide. All wage earners were granted an eight-hour day, decent wages, a well-designed grievance procedure, and a seniority system for regulating promotions and layoffs. In railroad offices, yards, and machine shops throughout the United States, women could expect to be treated with fairness. The war emergency provided the stimulus for a national policy of equal pay for equal work under which women could gain entrance into unconventional employment, enjoy occupational advancement within the ranks of railroad labor, and gain trade union protection as well. These benefits attracted tens of thousands of women to the industry.

Because wartime policies governing railroad labor were relatively favorable to women, railroad employment provides an illuminating case study of the enduring problems women faced under the best of conditions. Although the Railroad Administration preached comradeship among workers and between workers and bosses, the reality of work relations contrasted sharply with this ideal. Women faced a variety of problems in the "enlightened" railroad industry, but most complaints were related to specific categories of women's railroad work. The object of the women's grievances changed with the work situation and focused at various times on male supervisors, government investigators, and co-workers in offices, yards, or machine shops.

Gender segregation rigidly defined the nature of women's office employment. Sexual harassment was a fact of life in railroad clerical work, reinforcing women's subordinate position. Male bosses and male co-workers challenged women's right to higher-paying, skilled clerical jobs. In railroad yards, regulations to protect women ironically forced many women from their well-paying common labor jobs, and racism and sexism on the part of carmen denied black and white women union protection. In railroad shops, the dilution of labor which accompanied women's introduction into metal work angered skilled craftsmen, and they developed a number of different strategies to get rid of women. Gender segregation, sexual harassment, regulatory policies, white racism, sexism, and craftsmen's control of skilled jobs interacted in complex ways to circumscribe women's wartime opportunities dramatically. In turn, demobilization presented female clerical, yard, and shop workers with a host of new problems. The postwar labor reduction hit all women hard. Management and male co-workers lined up against them. Local officials denied women the right to use their seniority standing to bid for available jobs, while unions often fought to preserve existing jobs for men.

In the face of such obstacles, women did the best they could to protect their integrity and their jobs. Only infrequently did they protest collectively against their supervisors' or male co-workers' abuse. As individuals, some women filed complaints with their unions or with the Railroad Administration's Women's Service Section, an agency established specifically to monitor the conditions of women's work during the period of federal control. Most women tried to weather the adversity they faced by doing the best job possible under trying circumstances. They struggled at all costs to avoid being dismissed from railroad work.

WARTIME CHANGES IN THE ROADS

The story of women railroaders is part of an intricate web of changes that occurred in the railroad industry as a result of the First World War. In terms of financial status, technical operation, and labor relations, the United States steam railways were fundamentally unprepared to handle the special burdens of the war. Since 1910, the politics of railroad rate regulation under the Interstate Commerce Commission had favored the interests of shippers against those of the railroads. As the profits of the railroad industry decreased, the roads were understandably hard pressed to raise funds for extensive improvements in equipment and service— improvements which became critically important if wartime demands for the movement of troops and materials were to be met. Wartime inflation only heightened the railroads' managerial dilemma. By the fall of 1915, the future disposition of fourteen important railroads and a host of lesser companies was uncertain. By then the number of railroad receiverships had reached an all-time high. The lack of uniform design in locomotives, track gauge, and railroad cars, as well as car supply shortages and freight congestion, had long retarded the development of an efficient nationwide rail system. Operational difficulties were now further compounded by the attraction of workers to the shipbuilding and munitions industries, where wages soared above employees' earnings in the railroad industry. Those workers who remained with the roads threatened to halt the flow of goods and personnel in order to win substantial wage increases. Faced with the immediate threat of a massive tie-up of train service by the railroad brotherhoods and with the financial breakdown of the rail system, the federal government took control of the industry in December 1917 and launched an intensive campaign to forge the existing network of railroads into a standardized, transcontinental system.[2]

Federal control brought fundamental changes in labor policies. The necessity for a truce between labor and management forced the government to extend special benefits to all railroad employees.

During the twenty-six months that the Railroad Administration governed the industry, from December 1917 to March 1920, every aspect of working conditions and wage payments was examined in detail and at length. The capstone of the modifications in working conditions was the formal recognition of the workers' right to bargain collectively. Before the war, union contracts mostly covered train personnel and shop employees. The National Brotherhoods of Engineers, Conductors, Firemen, and Trainmen, known as the railroad "Big Four," represented the highly skilled on almost all Class I roads. As of December 1917, 80 percent of all eligible train service workers in the four categories bargained collectively, but since the Big Four represented only 20 percent of the entire railway labor force, the extent of unionization remained limited. Second in union strength were the skilled shop craftsmen who had negotiated contracts with 70 percent of the Class I roads. Outside the ranks of organized labor stood the mass of railway employees—the carmen, telegraphers, clerks, station tenders, freight house workers, and maintenance-of-way employees.[3] This situation changed markedly with federal control. Relieved of opposition by private management and encouraged by the favorable climate for trade unions, the railway labor organizations expanded rapidly in the period of federal control, especially among previously unorganized, unskilled, and semiskilled workers.

In numbers alone the rise of organized labor was impressive. The Brotherhood of Carmen grew from 50,000 to 200,000 between 1917 and 1920, while the Brotherhood of Railway Clerks jumped from 6,800 to 186,000 in the same period. Simultaneously, the telegraphers' organization attracted 34,000 new members, bringing its strength to 80,000. Similarly successful, the organization of maintenance-of-way employees multiplied tenfold, from 30,000 in 1917 to 300,000 in 1920. As of March 1920—when federal control ended—organized labor had enrolled 90 percent of train service workers and 80 percent of all other railway employees.[4]

Substantial changes in working conditions and pay followed the recognition of collective bargaining. The scrutiny of wages began with the creation of a four-man commission headed by Secretary of Interior Franklin K. Lane. In its report of April 1918 the Lane Commission found the standard of railroad wages well below the cost of living and the existing pay rates in other war industries. In order to close the substantial gap between the existing railroad pay scales and those of other war industries and to protect those hit hardest by wartime inflation, the commission recommended large increases in wages for the lower-paid railroad workers and much smaller increases for those with higher starting wages. Using the December 1915 base, the commission recommended that employees earning fifty dollars per month be raised 43 percent to seventy-one dollars and fifty cents, while those commanding two hundred fifty dollars a month received no increment. Four weeks after the commission issued its findings, Railroad Administration General Order No. 27 officially mandated adoption of the commission's recommended new wage schedule.[5]

By awarding substantial increases to members low on the wage scale, the commission's award clearly upset established wage differentials in the railroad industry. Ill feeling toward the Railroad Administration erupted immediately among employees who benefited least from the settlement. Workers' dissatisfaction forced the director general of the Railroad Administration to reopen the issue by creating a Board of Railroad Wages and Working Conditions for the specific purpose of advising him on further changes in wages. As a result of the board's efforts, new supplements, addenda, and reinterpretations of the settlement extended the wage reassessments to shopcraft, maintenance-of-way, clerical, and telegraph employees.[6]

In addition to pay scales, nationwide control over working conditions also concerned the railroad unions. The unions used their leverage to win high rates for overtime, a more detailed job classification system, the elimination of piecework, and the adoption of the seniority principle. For all working hours in excess of eight and all hours on Sundays and holidays, the federal managers were obliged to pay time and one-half. A classification system defined in detail the work of each class and grade of employee. Within machine shops hourly wages replaced piecework rates. The principle of seniority, which had previously been recognized only among those in train service, became the basis of promotion for all workers as long as their ability and merit were deemed sufficient for the job by their immediate bosses.[7]

All these changes substantially strengthened the control of railroad employees over their conditions of work. Before federal control some carriers had recognized unions, others had not. Wages had varied from one road to another and from one part of the country to another. Some workers could rely on their seniority for job security, while the arbitrary decisions of foremen controlled the duration of employment of others. Although most of the measures undertaken by the Railroad Administration had been put into effect on one or another railroad before federal control, it was not until the government took over the entire railroad system that a uniform and universal policy defined railroad operations. By standardizing rates of pay and working conditions, the federal labor administration abolished local differences. Under federal control a car cleaner in a small town in Pennsylvania now received the same pay as a car cleaner who worked in a metropolis such as Boston. A telegrapher in Springfield, Illinois earned no less than his counterpart in Seattle. The new uniformity in wage rates and job classifications eliminated many arbitrary distinctions and extended its principle of equal treatment for equal work into categories which flatly defied conventional norms of the era. In one federal administrative stroke, the principle of uniformity was extended in practice to all workers—whether white or black, whether male or female.[8] The necessity of the railroads to the successful prosecution of the war and the importance of organized labor resulted in the far-reaching standardization of working conditions for nearly two million wage earners. These changes had a profound effect on the lives of one hundred thousand women.

WOMEN RAILROAD WORKERS

Women sought railroad jobs for their excellent wages, job opportunities, and employee security policies. Most of the female clerks who began work in railroad offices during the war came directly from non-railroad clerical jobs. They were joined by women whose employment experience derived from factory or service work. The female common laborers employed by the roads were similarly well-seasoned and hard-working wage earners. These women shifted their employment from laundries, hotels, restaurants, and private households. The newly employed female was the exception. The economic exigencies of the war accounted for the entry into the job market of some previously non-employed women. Widows, deserted wives, wives whose husbands were in military service, and other women were forced to seek paid work for the first time because of the increased cost of living caused by the war,[9] but these women were in the minority.

The number of women drawn to railroad work climbed dramatically during the course of the war. Quarterly statistics were gathered by the Railroad Administration on the number of women employees in various railroad occupational classifications. The data for twenty-one job classifications from January 1918 through October 1920 provide a numerical picture of the war's effect on women's railroad work. Women's employment increased 47.2 percent in this thirty-four month period, from 61,162 to 90,052. The number of women employees rose continually until October 1918, when a total of 101,785 women were engaged in railroad work. This figure represents a gain of approximately 224 percent over the 1917 employment level of 31,400 women. Significantly, the employment peak for women coincides very closely with the war's end.[10]

Women railroad workers benefited substantially from the high wartime wages paid by the Railroad Administration. Most women in office employment earned between $87.50 and $105 a month for a 48-hour work week. Station cleaners received between $70 and $80 a month for a 48-hour week, while car cleaners brought home $93.60 per month for their more taxing 60-hour week. As compared with other women's railroad wages, only laundresses and seamstresses employed by the roads were conspicuously underpaid, earning as little as $60 per month for a 48-hour week. With the exception of the laundresses and sewers, women railroad workers received either decent or exceptionally high wages as compared with their usual remuneration for similar work outside the railroad service.[11]

INSIDE THE RAILROAD OFFICES

Most women railway workers performed clerical or semiclerical tasks. Of the 101,785 women employed by the railroads on October 1, 1918, 72 percent (73,620) worked in one capacity or another in railway offices. Women's clerical work ranged from the routine and mechanical to the highly skilled and technical. As might be expected, women were unequally distributed among the various categories of clerical work. In the generation preceding the war, clerical employment increased in tandem with the consolidation and expansion of commerce and manufacturing. The technological revolution in office equipment and the spread of public school education contributed not only to women's growing role in the clerical sector, but also to an increasing specialization and gender segregation among office personnel. Railroad offices followed this pattern. In a 1919 inquiry of eleven large offices in different parts of the United States, the Women's Service Section of the Railroad Administration found that women comprised 78 percent of the workers in the car accountants' offices, where typewriting, comptometer operating, and card punching for Hollerith tabulating machines predominated, whereas they held only 32 percent of the jobs in the offices of the auditors of disbursements, where a broad knowledge of railroad operations was needed.[12]

The prevailing patterns of gender segregation and work specialization meant that most women newly employed in railroad offices lacked familiarity with all-around clerical training. In terms of skills, women were most accomplished as machine operators. Accordingly, the railroad industry set no fixed educational standards for office workers. Of 676 women clerks who offered information about their educational backgrounds to Women's Service Section investigators, almost 50 percent had only an elementary education, 47 percent had high school experience, and 3 percent had some college training.[13]

In their search for office workers, railroad officials tested female and male applicants for general intelligence and "quickness." Some companies administered a psychological examination to evaluate the applicants' knowledge of everyday facts and their ability to follow instructions accurately. A typical exam question devised by a railroad office in St. Paul, Minnesota asked, "If you believe that Edison discovered America, cross out what you have [just] written, but if it was someone else, put in a number to complete this sentence: A horse has _____ feet." For prospective clerks there were arithmetic tests. Typists and stenographers had to prove their accuracy and speed. Interviewers made informal notes about the candidates' personalities. On the basis of physical appearance and mannerisms, applicants could be rejected out of

Figure 13. Clerical workers. Women clerical workers comprised the single largest group of female employees hired by the steam railroads. Their work ranged from the routine and mechanical to the highly skilled and technical. *Signal Corps. No. 111-SC-2482, National Archives, Washington, D.C.*

Figure 14. Training of railroad dispatchers. During the war women underwent training alongside men to become railroad dispatchers. Telegraphy had usually been reserved for men, but the war created opportunities for some women in this field. *War Dept. No. 165-WW-595E-12, National Archives, Washington, D.C.*

hand.[14] Once hired, women were assigned particular railroad jobs in which they were expected to stay for the duration of their employment, whereas newly hired men were more often groomed for careers as railroad clerks and could generally look forward to the possibility of promotion.

The tendency to channel women into particular jobs was reinforced by the attitudes toward women widely held by railroad superintendents, assistant superintendents, master mechanics, and chief clerks. The otherwise unspoken attitudes of railroad officials toward women were brought into the open during the war as a result of the public attention accorded to women's railroad work. The evaluation of one chief clerk typifies the prevailing male view that women deserved only dead-end jobs at low wages. The clerk, who was in charge of a car accountant's office, stated matter-of-factly to a Women's Service Section inspector that he personally saw "no special difference" between men's and women's work. His explanation of this remark, however, indicates a rather condescending view of women as workers.

I prefer young women to young men and I am going to continue to employ them. We have employed women since the '80's. For our class of work they are steadier than boys. They are not so damned anxious to get out and rustle around. Women are more content with the detailed monotonous work because they are filling in between school and marriage. They never think of themselves as General Managers of a railroad and are content to work along. Boys want to move on too quickly to do our work well.[15]

Dismayed, Florence Clark reported to her WSS superior, Pauline Goldmark, that this clerk "has so narrowed each person's opportunities that there is not much to learn and not far to advance. Ease in breaking people in and getting the work [done] today seem to be his [only] standards." Most of the women office workers spent their time "hanging little pieces of paper on pegs day after day."[16] It never crossed the chief clerk's mind that women's limited employment opportunities and their boss's low expectations served to reinforce their reported lack of initiative.

Different versions of the same attitude could be observed in several parts of the country. In the Baltimore and Ohio Railroad general offices in Baltimore, women received little encouragement from their bosses. No supervisor discussed employment options or ways that women could improve their job standing. On an inspection in the fall of 1918, Rose Yates, a WSS inspector, noted that the women "have been tolerated and that's all." A year later Yates' colleague, Edith Hall, reported that the outward attitude, of the male officials towards women at the B&O office of the auditor of disbursements in Baltimore was courteous and pleasant enough, but when caught off guard, the men observed that women were "successful at certain work . . . with distinct limitations." The WSS field agent reported that women who used their seniority standing to bid for a "position worth a man's while to want" would have "trouble" getting it. Understandably, no such bid had yet been made. During inspections conducted nearly a year apart, Helen Ross and Florence Clark noted that women employed by the Santa Fe Railroad in Topeka, Kansas were discouraged from applying for better jobs. Most women were assigned specialized, routine jobs with no opportunity for advancement, initiative, or creativity. The adjectives "routine," "dead-end," and "monotonous" punctuate the WSS inspection reports for twenty-three states and the District of Columbia, covering the work experiences of 13,000 women railway employees.[17]

The prevailing notion that women were docile, undistinguished workers found expression in the supervisors' treatment of women, in the words of one woman clerk, as "either jokes or pets."[18] Abusive personal treatment of women by male supervisors and foremen ranged from verbal discourtesy and incivility to physical assaults. In the Cincinnati auditor's office of the Southern Railroad, women clerks complained that four men tried to handle them all the time, by lifting up their skirts, pinching their breasts, and touching their necks. To add insult to injury, the office supervisor reportedly misused his authority in a brazen fashion by lavishing wage increases on those women who submitted without complaint to his molestations, while refusing raises to those who protested. In the yardmaster's office of the Great Northern Railroad in Cut

Bank, Montana, the man in charge thought nothing of thrusting his hand down the back of one of his female clerks in the presence of his wife and a government inspector. The assistant chief clerk of the revision office of the Chesapeake & Ohio Lines in Richmond, Virginia violated the standards of propriety so many times that higher management finally terminated his employment.[19]

Women developed various ways to cope with the limitations of their jobs and the persistence of sexual harassment at work. Their responses ranged from collective protest to resentful acquiescence. Women who operated office machines eight or more hours every day, six days a week, exerted informal control over the pace of their work. Subject to "speed-ups" to keep pace with the enormous volume of paperwork generated by the wartime crisis, the women variously loafed on the job or feigned illness to avoid nervous exhaustion from their workload. They used their rest rooms as a refuge from the pressure of their daily routine and as a place to socialize briefly in relative privacy. When reprimanded for taking prolonged or too many rest room breaks, women openly defied their bosses and congregated privately with still greater urgency, to figure out "who squealed on them."[20]

Although most women were offended by sexual harassment, they rarely initiated official complaints. Fear of losing their well-paying jobs served to discourage the filing of formal grievances. According to some reports in the WSS files, women acknowledged having silently suffered the sexual advances of their bosses because these men threatened to spread ugly rumors about their character or make their work lives miserable in other ways. Railroad authorities were known to accuse women of flirting with their bosses or wearing provocative clothing on the job. Women feared not only being harassed sexually, but having their own complaints of such abuse turned against them. They could not rely on railroad officials to conduct trustworthy investigations of harassment. As a WSS agent observed of one instance, "It was another case of Adam pointing to Eve as the cause of trouble."[21] Women were equally hesitant to tell their stories to the male representatives of the local protective committees of the Brotherhood of Railway Clerks, for fear that these men might also belittle them. Often, then, women swallowed their pride and allowed their bosses to abuse them. They reasoned that high-paying railroad jobs under less than optimal conditions were more desirable than lower-paying office jobs which offered no guarantee that their superiors would behave any better. Most cases of sexual harassment reported in the Railroad Administration records were uncovered by Women's Service Section field agents who were openly disdainful of such blatant sexist behavior.[22]

Such instances of benign neglect and intentional mistreatment suggest the operation of an ironclad law of custom which kept women in a subordinate position. Other wartime experiences of women railroaders qualify that conclusion. The seniority principle and the wartime labor shortage did give women an unprecedented opportunity to bid for better jobs, which they used to their own advantage. As women entered nontraditional office jobs in the railroad industry, male superiors and co-workers challenged the women's right to enter this "male" domain. More subtle challenges to the women's new social mobility predominated, however, so that railroad offices during the First World War became an important testing ground for women workers' claims to equal treatment with men for equal work.

Unfortunately, there are no precise figures available on promotions of women during the war, but WSS reports contain many examples of talented and experienced women who gained access to responsible, often supervisory, positions during the period of federal control. For one woman, twelve years of service in revising local and interline waybills placed her in especially good stead when she applied for the job of reviser in an overcharge claim bureau, a position second only to the head clerk. The shortage of revisers in another office made it necessary to instruct both men and women in this work. As a result of such special training, one woman was promoted to a supervisory position over four male assistants charged with revising local waybills. For the first time women could also be found as heads of correction account units and tracing bureaus. Executive jobs which required less technical railroad knowledge, but which demanded considerable ability to direct others in routine office work, were now also filled on occasion by women. In one office, two women directed comptometer bureaus, each of which had thirty or more machine operatives.[23]

The coveted position of chief clerk was also sought and won by women. In Miles City, Montana, an experienced clerk was promoted by the master mechanic to head the office staff. During federal control, women who had been performing the work of chief clerk, but who had been misclassified and mispaid, demanded an adjustment of their rank and wage scale. One of these women, Ella Barnett, of the return ticket department of the New York Central Railroad in Grand Central Station, had carried out the duties of chief clerk in her office for years, yet was listed and paid as an assistant chief clerk. Publicly supported by all the women in her office, she formally requested in January 1919 to be reclassified and properly rated. She had worked for the roads since the age of fourteen, and having advanced by slow degrees through every grade of work from ticket sorter—or "peg hanger"—to chief clerk, she was now especially delighted to receive her promotion. As she told WSS inspector Helen Ross following her victory, she felt vindicated on behalf of all women who were struggling for equal recognition and equal rights. [24]

The promotions held special significance for women. Advancement liberated workers who had long ago reached the top of the job ladder within the "female" domain of office work. Especially in cases where women were the sole supporters of their families, opportunities for advancement ranked high on their list of employment concerns. In St. Louis, Adrianna Freiss, the wife of an invalid, had been told before the war that she had advanced as far as a woman could go in her office. During thirteen years of continuous railroad employment for the Wabash Company, she had worked her way only from comptometer operator to head comptometer operator. The war suddenly provided her an opportunity to exercise her seniority right and break out of her traditional line of employment. She became a station remittance clerk, a position which required accounting skills, supervisory responsibilities over several clerks, and correspondence duties as well. Her goal had been realized. As even her boss acknowledged, Freiss had entered railroad work with the same eagerness for advancement as many a man, so she was delighted finally to have the chance to learn new work and to earn much more money. [25]

Not every woman who deserved to be promoted received her just due. The outcome of bids for promotion depended, among other factors, on the responses of local railroad officials and male clerks. Part of the procedure governing promotion involved the evaluation of an applicant's ability and merit by local railroad officials. Subjective factors could, of course, play a major role in such assessments. In 1918, after working thirteen years for the B&O Railroad, assistant chief clerk Mabel T. Gessner applied for a promotion to chief clerk. Although acknowledged to be "an unusually capable young woman," she was denied promotion by her superintendent, who simply preferred that she continue as second in command. Gessner had very much wanted the more responsible job and its higher pay, but she would not appeal her boss's decision because she feared jeopardizing her present position. As the sole support of an invalid mother, she would not gamble with her earnings. Although the case seemed unjust to a WSS investigator, Gessner steadfastly refused to pursue the matter.[26]

In bidding for skilled jobs and gaining access to them, women also triggered confrontations with their male co-workers. In contrast to the ordinarily strained relations between male supervisors and female subordinates, co-worker relations were generally congenial. This was especially true because the differentiation of office work along male-female lines did not ordinarily put women and men in direct competition. With no fears for their own job security, male clerks could relax in the presence of women and enjoy the particular ambience of an integrated work setting. In a more rivalrous situation, the atmosphere became charged with ill feeling and suspicion. As discussed above, in January 1919 Ella Barnett of the New York Central Railroad requested a change of job classification and pay from assistant to chief clerk to bring her title and salary in line with the work she had been performing for some time. Her right to the position was challenged by men of greater seniority, who argued that the change of pay and title meant that a new position was being created and should by right be opened for bid to the senior employees. Even after the job was opened to other applicants, Barnett was selected as the best qualified person. This decision was further challenged by local members of the Brotherhood of Railway Clerks, who supported the candidacy of a member who had requested a thirty-day trial period in which to prove that he could handle the work. According to Barnett, the challenge to her position was rooted in male jealousy and a desire on the part of the union to have one of its own members in charge of the office. Ironically, most of the women in the office were themselves members of the union, but they backed Barnett and were "very sore over the action of the Brotherhood." In March 1920, the case was resolved by the Division of Labor of the Railroad Administration in Washington, D.C. in a ruling which accorded Barnett the head clerkship as a matter of simple justice.[27]

Preferential treatment to help women quickly acquire the necessary expertise to assume jobs ordinarily reserved for men could also poison male-female relations. In the Chicago office of the loss and damage department of the Chicago, Burlington, and Quincy Railroad, women were given excellent advanced training in work that required knowledge, judgment, and responsibility. During the war, the shortage of skilled male claims adjusters prompted the federal auditor to devise an innovative and accelerated training program for women. Considered a "railroad trade," the highly skilled investigators' work demanded a comprehensive understanding of freight construction and transport. In groups of five or six, a total of thirty-eight women received a month's training in all aspects of claims work. They attended lectures about their new duties, travelled to various railroad yards, acquainted themselves with types of freight cars, inspected stations, and followed in detail the procedures involved in shipping freight. The women even visited railroad shops in Aurora to witness the actual construction of freight cars. The trainees also observed packing and shipping procedures in furniture factories, bottling works, and mail-order houses. Under the supervision of experienced investigators, the women spent a second month preparing actual claims of a simple nature. In this aspect of their preparation, some women received more training than regular male investigators, who usually were expected to learn the work on the job in the process of tackling complicated claims.[28]

Of the thirty-eight trained women, all between the ages of twenty-five and thirty-five, only eighteen were still employed as investigators at the time of the WSS field agent's report in September 1919. More than half of these women typified a common female pattern: some had left the training program because they felt unqualified, others had married and quit their employment altogether. Those who stayed proudly voiced satisfaction with the work and hoped to advance in the department. Agent Helen Ross noted that these women had "never thought railroad work could be so interesting." With earnings of $120 to $150 a month, these freight claims adjusters ranked among the highest-paid female railroad employees.[29]

The newly trained women found themselves in an unusual position for two reasons. Not only were they relatively well paid in recognition of their skill, training, and responsibility, but they came to be accused by male employees of having been favored on account of their gender. The men who did similar work complained of discrimination. Although the usual discriminatory situation entailed the underpayment of poorly trained women, in this instance male railroad insurance investigators argued that the women were earning more money and had received more training than they. The men submitted a formal protest in Washington with the Railroad Administration's Division of Labor, but the women claims investigators were allowed to retain their positions. It was surely more than a coincidence, however, that local officials discontinued the hiring of women as soon as male trainees became available during the postwar demobilization. The Chicago male claims agents could look forward once again to an exclusive hold over their trade.[30]

In some local offices, the hostility of male clerks toward women was rooted in prewar situations. Because women had on occasion been employed at lower wages and willingly used as strikebreakers and scabs, their increased employment under federal control made some men apprehensive. Ugly, vivid memories of past labor-management confrontations colored the men's feelings toward the women. They feared that women would again underbid them and prove resistant to union membership. With disdain and anger they recalled that female strikebreakers had gratefully received promotions before the war for their loyalty to management. Under such strained circumstances the men believed that their status would be severely and perhaps irrevocably weakened upon the eventual return of the roads to private control. While the Railroad Administration's wage orders and its policy of union recognition temporarily decreased the likelihood of these possibilities, local railroad officials fanned male fears by using special agents to discourage union organizing among women. Where formal bars against women's union membership existed, women could easily be influenced by their superiors' informal comments against unions. There was often a fine line between "friendly advice" and the threat of reprisal.[31]

Despite the jitters of some male trade unionists, female clerks demonstrated a noticeable awareness of themselves as workers, not least through their union activities. In the Brotherhood of Railway Clerks, where female membership had been negligible in 1910, women accounted for approximately 35,000 members in 1920. This figure included about 50 percent of all female railway clerks and represented almost 19 percent of the 186,000 railway clerks with union membership. Some women became officers of their locals, while several achieved distinction as members of the union's system boards.[32]

As members of organizations with clearly defined grievance procedures, women unionists handled the violations of their personal and occupational rights with greater facility than women who did not join the ranks of organized labor. Young women new to railroad service more readily accepted union membership and used the union and governmental channels available for adjudicating their complaints more often than women clerks who had been employed by the railroads for some time. These women remembered the bitter antiunion sentiment that characterized private ownership of the roads. While the Railroad Administration provided ample machinery for dealing with grievances, women who were not union members showed reluctance to fight their cases through proper channels. Instead, they complained privately to the WSS field agents about the many abuses they suffered. At the same time, they pleaded with the field agents not to take any action that would make their complaints visible and possibly provoke vindictive treatment from their male superiors.[33]

In contrast, union members more securely pursued their grievances to some resolution. The Brotherhood of Railway Clerks gave women emotional support and provided legal expertise in dealing with the government's bureaucratic procedures. The local assisted women employees in obtaining redress for discriminatory treatment on the part of railroad authorities in a number of cases that came to the attention of the Women's Service Section. On occasion, the grand president of the Brotherhood, J.J. Forrester, intervened on women's behalf. Such persistent union endeavors educated women about their rights as workers. Mayme Hayes, for example, could testify to the union's beneficial influence in encouraging women to stand up for their rights. She was one of the few women to submit an official grievance against a chief clerk for indecent conduct. As a local union activist and organizer, Hayes felt confident that her accusations would be taken seriously by the union. Her confidence was rewarded when Forrester backed her complaint and demanded that the accused man be duly reprimanded for his abusive behavior.[34]

Railroad office employment, then, offered women a mixture of preferable and undesirable working conditions. The standardization of wage rates guaranteed women unusually handsome remuneration for their work. The wartime labor shortage and the seniority rule improved women's chances for occupational mobility. At the same time, gender segregation and the specialization of work restricted women to certain jobs. Women had to work under the supervision of bosses who controlled the fate of many employees. Under such circumstances, women could become easy prey for sexual exploitation by their male superiors. Those women who in turn proved fortunate enough to break out of the female job ghetto were likely to be confronted by angry challenges from male co-workers. Women could not escape the dual reality of their office jobs. Opportunity and discrimination alternately defined and redefined their employment.

IN THE YARDS AND ROUNDHOUSES

Problems facing female common laborers employed in the railroad industry during the war differed in kind and degree from the difficulties facing railroad clerical workers. Ironically, objections from the Women's Service Section—rather than from male workers or supervisors—curtailed wartime employment opportunities for women workers in railroad yards. Racial and sex discrimination in the labor movement additionally frustrated women's efforts to obtain protection of their right to work as common laborers.

In October 1918, the second largest group of women railway workers was the 5,600 women (5 percent of the total) who toiled in offices, shops, roundhouses, and yards as cleaners and sweepers. A small number of women wiped engines while others operated electric lift trucks at freight transfer stations or worked on docks, moving lumber in lots of one to two hundred pounds or lifting large heaps of scrap iron. Previously employed as unskilled labor in hotels, laundries, restaurants, and private homes, these women eagerly sought railroad work for its better working conditions, steadier employment, and higher wages. For the same class of labor they had previously performed, the women now earned between seventy and ninety dollars a month, about twice their former incomes.[35]

Black women who had worked before the war as coach cleaners gained employment during the war on scrap docks, in freight transfer stations, and in supply departments. As employees of the Missouri Pacific Railroad in Kansas City, for example, black women would sort and put away supplies dumped in the yards. They would pick up twenty-five pound forgings and castings and move them in their arms or in wheelbarrows to supply bins. In storerooms and yards they swept and tidied the premises. Such common labor sometimes involved moving 250-pound couplers and heavy oil barrels.[36]

Whether yard work required excessive physical exertion is difficult to assess. Foremen often chose large-boned, sturdy-looking women to perform this labor. According to WSS field reports, several women acknowledged that they did not perform all the heavy tasks expected of them, but rather, that some male workers would regularly lend a helping hand.[37] Still, according to supervisors, the women's efforts basically measured up to the tasks. The Women's Service Section thought otherwise. It finally decided that the common labor in the railroad yards demanded more physical strength than women could easily manage. In September 1919, the director general of the Railroad Administration ordered the roads to discontinue the employment of women as section hands and truckers. One railroad alone transferred or dismissed 223 laborers and 193 truckers as a result of this order.[38]

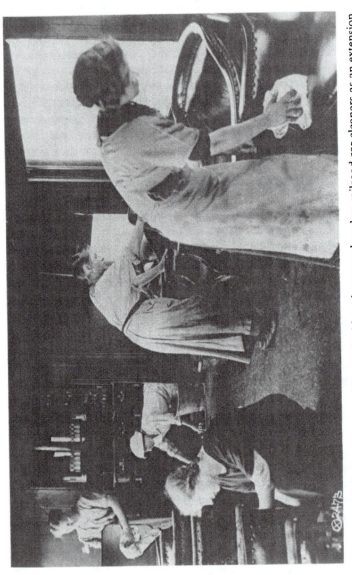

Figure 15. Women car cleaners. Women had long been employed as railroad car cleaners as an extension of traditional female domestic work. *Signal Corps. No. 111-SC-2473, National Archives, Washington, D.C.*

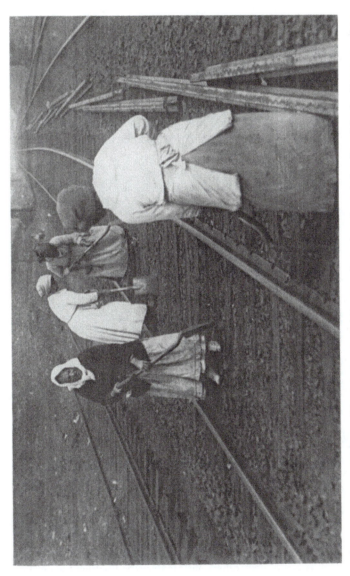

Figure 16. Track Walkers. Women common laborers cleaned and tended railroad beds. Foremen often chose large-boned, sturdy-looking women to perform this work. *Women's Bureau No. 86-G-6T-4, National Archives, Washington, D.C.*

Figure 17. Woman oiling a railroad engine. A small number of women gained admittance during the war to nontraditional jobs in railroad yards. Some wiped engines, while others operated electric lift trucks at freight transfer stations or worked on docks, moving lumber or lifting heaps of scrap iron. *Women's Bureau No. 86-G-6T-2, National Archives, Washington, D.C.*

Figure 18. Railroad yard common labor. Woman at work on a scrap heap in one of the Baltimore & Ohio Railroad yards. *Women's Bureau No. 86-G-6T-6, National Archives, Washington, D.C.*

Figure 19. Women railroad workers and engine no. 940. Women pose before
locomotive, symbolizing their new roles in wartime railroad service. *Women's
Bureau 86-G-6T-1, National Archives, Washington, D.C.*

Despite the physical demands of the manual labor, the black and white women who received the relatively high pay this work commanded and who enjoyed the other benefits of railroad employment, such as seniority rights and overtime wages, resisted the protective regulation which would deny them these particular jobs. The anxiety to retain their jobs was especially pronounced among all black women, not only those subject to transfer or dismissal. Black women's work habits, particularly their regularity and their meticulous character, impressed WSS field agents. Described by their superiors as dependable, the women tried their best to keep their common labor jobs. One scrap dock worker who had been brought from Atlanta with her husband and children to work in the Cleveland shops of the New York Central Railroad eagerly explained to a field agent her motives for working so hard. She said that her husband worked as an ashpit man in the roundhouse. With their four children they lived in a three-room boxcar provided by the railroad in a boxcar community of twenty other similarly employed black families. Speaking as a concerned parent, she said, ''I am working with my husband so we can get along. You know the children have to be dressed better than most people who live in box cars.''[39] The second salary provided the margin of respectability.

Despite vigorous protests by the affected women to the Railroad Administration and to their unions, the women were nonetheless dismissed from heavy labor jobs which the new federal regulations deemed unsuitable for females. The companies often did not have alternate work for these women, so enforcement of the federal regulation effectively meant dismissal. When seventy-two female truckers employed by the Minnesota Transfer Company were dismissed, the women searched elsewhere for jobs with the aid of the state employment service. It appears that five women found temporary jobs and only twelve found permanent positions in other industries. According to a supervisor, others returned to their homes in the country. Some of the women received adequate support from husbands and discontinued working. Those who found new employment received an average of forty-eight dollars per month, which compared quite unfavorably with the seventy to ninety dollars paid them for railroad work. Despite the well-meaning intention to protect the women physically, the new federal regulations in practice discriminated against them financially.[40]

During the women's tenure as common laborers in the railroad industry, their satisfaction over wages and benefits seems to have been sufficient compensation even for the special work rules, pressures, and penalties that were applied to them *as women*. Railroad personnel strictly supervised women's behavior and put almost the entire burden for moral rectitude on women. A case in point concerned the yard workers employed by the Santa Fe Railroad in Topeka, Kansas. One WSS field agent wrote approvingly in October 1918 that

Men and women work together in the warehouse, but all seemed orderly and businesslike about their work. A foreman keeps strict supervision over them. When the women were first employed, the General Foreman talked to all the men telling them that the women were to be regarded as equals and that no intimacy was to be tolerated. Several of the first women were dismissed because their conduct was not proper, and this had a wholesome effect on the rest of the women as well as on the men. So many women have applied for the work that a vacancy is filled easily. Both the men and the women recognize therefore that their employment depends on good behavior. No woman is allowed to go into a box car except to take her load if so required. If she is found there for any [other] purpose she is dismissed.[41]

Unlike clerical workers, the women newly hired in common labor jobs did not complain about the daily social controls and double standard of morality imposed upon them by their supervisors. These women wanted above all to keep their jobs. Aware of their precarious tenure, which resulted directly from the wartime labor shortage, they were accordingly quite careful to avoid jeopardizing their positions by some inadvertent infringement of a work rule. Decently paid, steady jobs of an unskilled nature were, after all, very hard to find. Most women, therefore, tolerated the constant supervision without overt complaint.

Opportunities for women in railroad yards were defined not only in terms of their presumed physical strength or social behavior but also by racial considerations. Car cleaning, for example, was divided not only between male and female tasks, but also along color lines. In the Long Island yards of the Long Island Railroad, black women were barred from cleaning dining cars and were restricted to work in coaches. Even in their time off the women cleaners were assigned to segregated, although identical, quarters in a new locker room facility.[42]

Racial and sex discrimination merged in the carmen's attempts to organize car cleaners. The Brotherhood of Railway Carmen attempted to increase its economic strength by claiming jurisdiction over cleaning crews in many railroad yards during the war. The brotherhood failed to offer, let alone provide, equal representation to two principal categories of car cleaners. Interested only in white males, the carmen withheld membership from black men and women on the one hand and white women on the other. In the St. Paul, Minnesota district, the carmen specifically proposed in the spring of 1919 to organize three separate groups—white men, white women, and blacks of both sexes. According to a WSS field agent's report on the situation, neither the women nor the black men were to be given the same degree of protection as the white male car cleaners. This proposal was offered at a time when demobilization was making more white men available for work, and it constituted a way of pushing white and black women as well as black men out of their jobs and replacing them with white men. The express purpose of organized labor may be seen in the statement of the American Federation of Labor to the WSS field agent assigned to the case of the Minnesota car cleaners. Even though the AF of L had no explicit information on the situation in Minnesota, it indicated how important racial considerations were for organized labor by stating that it was not customary for the white and black car cleaners to belong to the same locals.[43]

In comparison, then, the problems which female common laborers faced were different from those experienced by women office workers. Women in clerical jobs had to deal with sexual harassment and denial of promotion from male superiors. The more highly skilled female office workers also encountered challenges from male co-workers for their jobs. Obstacles to women in common labor jobs were largely indirect in nature. Newly introduced protective legislation served covertly to terminate women's employment as section hands and truckers, while racism and sexism within the labor movement denied black and white women the same union protection as white men. In one sense, common laborers were in a no-win situation, in which they were either overprotected by middle-class reformers or not protected enough by organized labor. Middle-class reformers employed by the Women's Service Section, eager to guard the women from physically strenuous work, established regulations against the employment of women in certain common labor jobs. A policy of prohibiting the employment of women as yard workers was implemented over the protests of the female laborers. The organized carmen also disregarded the women's wishes. Instead of organizing women on the same terms as white men and closing ranks as workers, the carmen refused to safeguard the rights of black men and women and white women car cleaners. The denial of employment and the denial of union protection had the combined effect of substantially worsening laboring women's prospects for keeping their jobs. Demobilization would strike the final blow.

IN THE SHOP

The substitution of women for skilled male workers brought far more resistance from craftsmen in railroad shops and roundhouses than it had from skilled male clerical workers in railroad offices. Although even at the peak of female railroad employment in October 1918 there were relatively few women in skilled labor categories, these women were nonetheless regarded by their co-workers as intruders. The shopmen not only feared the loss of jobs to women, but they perceived an even greater threat. Because women's introduction into the shops was accompanied by the dilution of skilled labor and the subdivision of labor processes, the shopmen perceived women's employment as a threat to their craft. In many ways the haughty shopmen actively attempted to discourage the hiring and retention of women. They harassed their female co-workers, refused them admittance to the machinists' union, and pressed for the introduction and enforcement of state legislation to prohibit or restrict women's employment.

Most women employed in railroad shops during the war performed the work of helpers. Within the larger occupational designations women throughout the country accounted for thirty-five blacksmiths, six boilermakers, fourteen coppersmiths, sheet-metal workers, and pipe fitters, fourteen electricians, and 370 machinists.

More specifically, women operated bolt-threading, nut-tapping, and car-bearing machines as well as turret lathes, angle-cock grinders, pneumatic hammers, and cranes. Garbed in a uniform known as "womanalls," females worked as air-brake cleaners, repairers, and testers, as well as electric welders, oxyacetylene cutters and welders, and core makers.[44]

The largest single group of women in the shop crafts was the machinist group. The new training programs for machinists presented a threat to the craftsmen's sense of craft because they ran counter to the machinists' traditional practices. The challenge which women represented was particularly evident in the case of female welders. Ordinarily, welding had been one stage in the apprenticeship of a machinist. During the war the process was separated for the first time from this larger training program and women who were unknowledgeable about machine-shop production were taught welding skills. Of twelve women investigated at the Mt. Clare shops of the B&O Railroad in Baltimore, eleven had worked in typical female jobs before the war. One woman had run a power sewing machine, another had worked in a button factory, a third in a cigarette factory, and a fourth in a silk mill. Others had variously earned their living as timekeeper, telephone operator, cashier, spooler and spinner in a cotton mill, home dressmaker, and weaver. Two of these women had worked in a munitions factory before coming to the railroad. Like other women in new wartime railway work, they uniformly enjoyed welding and the income it provided.[45]

The employment of women as core makers in railroad foundries presented molders with a similar challenge to their craft. Even though women had been employed in some foundries as small core makers for as many as fifteen years before the international emergency, their visibility increased during the war as their employment was extended to workshops which had never before hired women. At the same time, in those foundries in which women had produced small cores, they were allowed to manufacture heavier, more intricate ones. Since the production of cores was a distinct stage in the training of apprentices, the molders' union strongly objected to the separation of core making from the entire program of training, a program solely reserved for white males.[46]

The dilution of labor accompanying women's introduction to metal work was the first of two important reasons for the craftsmen's objections to women's employment. Friction also resulted from the different attitudes men and women held toward production standards. In well-organized industries, craftsmen brought to their daily work a carefully defined ethical code which shaped their performance on the job. The code defined an output quota, commonly known as a "stint," above which workers would not labor. To the craftsmen, as David Montgomery has pointed out, a restricted output was synonymous with "dignity, respectability, defiant egalitarianism, and patriarchal male supremacy."[47] Setting this stint was a form of workers' control which craftsmen aggressively guarded from erosion by employers. In unionized settings the code of behavior was carefully formulated in the enactment and enforcement of craft work rules which specified the terms of apprenticeship, defined the work of unskilled helpers, and established the kind and amount of labor for which members were responsible. Such regulations were intended to set a group norm and to discourage individually determined work practices. Worker-established norms also represented a significant form of resistance to managerial encroachments in the workplace. Unions even struck to win acquiescence to their rules from management.[48]

The women who now came to operate lathes and drill presses, wind armatures, shape, grind, mill, solder and weld, polish and buff metal parts, make cores, and serve in other industrial operations did not share the craftsmen's code of work conduct. Many women entered the metal trades during the war with experience in seasonal industries, where they had become accustomed to working at a break-neck pace in order to maximize their incomes during the industry's peak months and save enough money to tide them over the period of unemployment which followed. Accustomed to unrestricted output, they brought to their wartime jobs an individual work ethic rather than a commitment to group regulation. In contrast to the craftsmen, they were used to accepting available work which involved routine chores and intrinsically uninteresting mechanical tasks.[49] They entered machine shops during the war to earn as much money as they could and to learn new trades; the dilution of these trades did not concern them.

The demands for uninterrupted production throughout industry aroused employers' interest in the comparative output of men and women. During the war, manufacturers undertook detailed studies of the differences between men's and women's work performances. In April and May 1918, the National Industrial Conference Board, composed of management representatives from national industrial associations, conducted a survey of the employment of women in manufacturing processes in metal-working plants. The report showed that for sixty-four of the ninety-seven establishments furnishing specific information on this point, women's productivity equalled or surpassed men's. A highly favorable account of women's exceptional efficiency came from an automobile plant which employed women in twenty-three departments. The firm reported one instance in which a woman with only a week's experience on a nut-tapping machine turned out double the amount of work produced by the man working next to her. "After endeavoring to equal her speed for a few days," the report continued, "the man quit and was replaced by a woman who is now very nearly the equal of the first." A gear manufacturing firm where women sandblasted, ground, drilled, and broached metal parts disclosed that women's output averaged 15 to 25 percent more than that of their male co-workers. In a munitions plant making fuses, women drill press and milling machine operatives produced 25 to 50 percent more than men. The National Industrial Conference Board concluded with satisfaction that women did not restrict the work pace by curtailing output as skilled men ordinarily did.[50]

The same was true of women's work performance in railroad shops. In the Pennsylvania Railroad plumbing shop in Pitcairn, the shop foreman reported that five young women who were employed at the triple valve bench to disassemble, clean, and assemble triple valves of various kinds averaged twenty valves a day in contrast to the ten or twelve valves usually processed by men.[51]

The wartime influx of women into machine shop jobs previously performed only by craftsmen threatened to undermine the relatively privileged position of these skilled men. In the name of nationalism, the government called upon skilled workers to teach their crafts to newcomers who might later force down wages and ruin their trade and standard of living. For these men the war created a horrifying vision of the future. A cartoon published in the *Machinists' Monthly Journal* in 1917 aptly expresses the craftsmen's view of the war's effect on labor. In the cartoonist's hands the war is personified as an aggressive knight in armor whose blood-dripping saber testifies to his commitment to do violence to everything around him. Shown in an aggressive posture, the knight is seen marching toward a machine shop, pulling an unwilling black man with one arm, while pushing a reluctant and frail white woman with the other. Underfoot he tramples "safety laws," "hours legislation," and "wage agreements."[52] Any craftsman who thought about wartime changes in those terms would understandably react with outrage to the employment of women. With little understanding of the larger consequence of their own new work for the established skilled male workers, the women were unprepared for the craftsmen's responses.

Shopmen developed a number of strategies to preserve their control over working conditions. To protect themselves from the prospect of permanent competition from unorganized female wage earners, the members of the International Association of Machinists passed a resolution in April 1917 to organize women into their union. The IAM reasoned that women as union members would act in solidarity with male machinists for the protection of the craft as a whole. The IAM constitution permitted women to organize with men or in separate locals as specialists or helpers. Women responded well to the organization drive, which covered not only railroad machine shops, but also many other metal-working establishments throughout the United States. By June 1918, women accounted for nearly 12,500 of the 229,500 IAM members. At the peak of the wartime labor shortage, slightly more than one machinist in eighteen was a female in American metal-working establishments with IAM representation.[53]

Although the IAM policy to organize women was carried out in most workplaces, considerable opposition appeared in several railroad machine shops. Some men figured that it would be better to discourage women from joining the IAM and in this way let them know that their employment could only be expected to last the war's duration. At the B&O's Mt. Clare shops in Baltimore, women gained admittance to the union only infrequently and in the

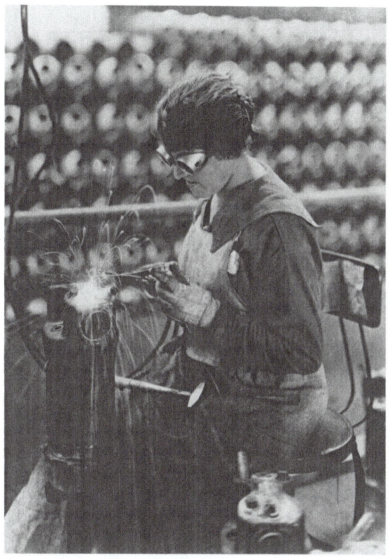

Figure 20. Electric welder. Garbed in a uniform known as "womanalls," females worked in railroad shops as electric welders, oxyacetylene cutters and welders, and core makers. Male craftsmen interpreted the introduction of women into railroad shops as a direct challenge to their job security and control of work standards. *Women's Bureau No. 86-G-7A-24, National Archives, Washington, D.C.*

Figure 21. "Another Military Expediency?" This cartoon, published in the *Machinists' Monthly Journal* in July 1917, aptly expresses the craftsmen's view of the war's effect on labor. White craftsmen who thought about wartime changes in these terms reacted with outrage against the employment of women and blacks.

face of great reluctance on the part of male machinists. In the Pitcairn plumbing shops of the Pennsylvania Railroad, men repeatedly ignored women's requests to join the union. To get the women's
production standards in line with their own, these men persuaded
the women to slow down the pace of their work. As a result, the
number of valves cleaned each day by the women dropped 40 percent. At the same time, without telling the women, the shopmen
petitioned the general foreman "to get rid" of these same newcomers. In the Riverside yards of the B&O in Baltimore, women
employed as valve testers were not only misclassified and mispaid,
they were also given the cold shoulder by local union members. [54]

Women welders in Baltimore received the worst treatment of all.
The male machinists not only opposed women's membership in the
union, but they also refused to help or work alongside the women.
According to the Women's Service Section agents, some women
reported that "the men had tried to drive them off the job with
their torches or with the riveting." In the case of one woman welder
who had been put on boiler work, the men refused to work with
her, had her taken off the job, and protested her employment to the
local secretary of the International Association of Machinists. [55]

Despite the negative experience of women machinists, valve
testers, and welders at various railroad shops, the International
Association of Machinists as a whole was responsible for a significant increase in the number of women enrolled in union ranks,
including a number in the railroad industry. In terms of official
union policy, the experience of the Molders' and Foundry Workers'
Union forms a notable contrast to that of the IAM. The MFWU
directly fought the employment of women by stringently enforcing
its regulation mandating the expulsion of members who taught
women any part of the molder's trade. Another of the strategies
used to deter women from certain work in railroad-related jobs
involved the use of protective legislation on the state level, which
had been enacted for the ostensible purpose of benefiting women in
the labor force. In order to stop employers from hiring women, the
molders' union pressed for the enforcement of the Pennsylvania,
Massachusetts, and New York laws which expressly limited the
weight that women were allowed to lift in the course of their
employment. The laws effectively restricted women's foundry work

in those states to the production of very small cores, an activity in which they had long established themselves.[56]

As early as 1915 the International Molders' and Foundry Workers' Union had lobbied in Ohio for provisions in foundry codes to regulate the employment of women. With the expanded employment of women in foundries in 1918, representatives of the union requested that the Ohio State Federation of Labor use its influence with the Ohio Industrial Commission to expand the state foundry code to prohibit the employment of women in all foundry molding departments. The Federation of Labor decided that even more drastic action was appropriate. In cooperation with the Ohio Consumers' League, it designed a bill to block women's admittance to many occupations, including molding. During the 1919 Ohio legislative session, the General Assembly translated the federation's recommendation into law. Once the governor signed the bill, women were prevented from working as gas or electric meter readers, section hands, express drivers, bellhops, taxi drivers, jitney drivers, baggage or freight handlers, and freight or baggage elevator operators, as well as molders. In one legislative blow, the employment of women in places as diverse as furnaces, mines, quarries, shoeshining parlors, bowling alleys, and trucking firms was also made illegal in Ohio.[57]

The molders were not alone in the use of protective legislation to limit the employment of women. The practice appeared in railroad-related work as part of a national pattern affecting diverse industries. Attempts to invoke female "protective" laws for the preservation of male dominance in certain work categories occurred as well in the field of coal mining. In May 1918, when anthracite coal companies in western Pennsylvania attempted to replace men and boys with forty-two foreign-born girls and women in one of the above-ground coal-producing operations, miners at the Lehigh Coal and Navigation Company staunchly objected. Despite a pronounced labor shortage, they refused to admit women into their ranks. They appealed to the Pennsylvania Department of Mines to enforce an old law which restricted the employment of females in the coal-mining industry to clerical work. The miners won their dispute with the company, and women remained barred from this nontraditional employment.[58]

Despite the different strategies of the machinists and molders for combatting the introduction of women into their crafts, the two groups agreed unequivocally that women simply did not belong in their occupations. Women, of course, disagreed. If male and female railroad shop workers had expressed their perspectives in verse, they might well have described their respective sentiments in terms used by employees of the Jones and Lamson Machine Tool Company of Springfield, Vermont. By late 1918, two hundred women, dressed in special uniforms, worked alongside men at the Jones and Lamson Company and the neighboring Fellows Gears Shaper Company and Bryant Chucking Grinder Company. In one of the lighter exchanges of the war the men composed a verse of good-natured ridicule, to which the women offered an appropriate rejoinder.

The Reason Why

The shop girls had a meeting
They came from far and near
Some came from Bryant's J and L
And some from Fellows Gear.

But before inside the hall
They were allowed to look
They had to take their bloomers off,
And hang 'em on a hook.

Then into the hall they went at once
With courage ever higher
But hardly were they seated
When someone shouted "Fire."

Then out they ran all in a bunch,
They had no time to look,
And each one grabbed a bloomer
At random from the hook.

They got their bloomers all mixed up,
And they were mighty sore,
To think they couldn't have the one
They had always had before.

And that's the reason that you see
As you go 'round the streets,
Each one will stop and take a look
At every girl she meets.

And hence the reason that the girls
Who are not so very stout,
Have to take 'em in a bit,
And the fat ones, let 'em out.

The women replied in kind:

She Hands Him a Lemon

My man, you're really out of date
And now before it is too late,
I'll try to set you right;
We never mixed our bloomers, clown,
They fit just like a Paris gown,
They're neither loose nor tight.
The simple, tender, clinging vine,
That once around the oak did twine,
Is something of the past;
We stand erect now by your side,
And surmount obstacles with pride,
We're equal, free, at last.

We're independent now you see,
Your bald head don't appeal to me,
I love my overalls;
And I would rather polish steel,
Than get you up a tasty meal,
Or go with you to balls.
Now, only premiums good and big,
Will tempt us maids to change our rig,
And put our aprons on;
And cook up all the dainty things,
That so delighted men and kings
In days now past and gone.

Now in your talk of shouting "fire,"
You really did arouse my ire,
I tell you, sir, with pride,

That you would be the one to run
While we would stay and see the fun,
And lend a hand beside.
To sit by your machine and chew
And dream of lovely Irish stew,
Won't work today you'll find.
Now, we're the ones who set the pace,
You'll have to bustle in the race
Or you'll get left behind.

We're truly glad we got the chance
To work like men and wear men's pants,
And proved that we made good.
My suit a badge of honor is.
Now, will you kindly mind your "biz"
Just as you know you should.[59]

On one level, the verse could be interpreted as mutually harmless banter between men and women who worked together under unusual circumstances. On another level, the poems reveal how very differently each group perceived the entrance of women into a traditionally male field. The men depicted their co-workers as hysterical, foolish females masquerading as men, while the women's reply asserted that their new work had affected them more profoundly than the superficial change of garb might seem to suggest. As a consequence of their machine shop experience, they had been transformed from weak, dependent women into "free," "equal," and self-reliant individuals. Even if few women personally experienced such a dramatic metamorphosis, the mere expression of this general change undoubtedly threatened the men's self-image.

The shopmen's bitter reaction against the women's employment in railroad shops and roundhouses reveals the complex way in which craft protection and discrimination against women combined during the war. The machinists and molders reacted with hostility against women, both because women's employment brought with it a dilution of skilled labor and a subdivision of production processes, and also because the new wartime workers happened to be women instead of men. The male machinists and molders resisted the structural changes in their craft by resisting the employment of women workers. In such a situation, the men's acceptance of women workers would have implied an acceptance of the accompanying changes in their craft. The machinists and molders could conceivably have fought management's dilution of their skills and could also have admitted women to railroad machine shops by opening their apprenticeship programs to women. The men's unwillingness to pursue such a strategy suggests the degree to which they perceived their crafts in exclusively male terms. They firmly believed in a gender-segregated labor force. Working alongside women was simply unacceptable to the proud, manly craftsmen.

DEMOBILIZATION

After the signing of the Armistice in November 1918, women employed in railway offices, yards, and shops faced the critical problem of job retention. The end of battlefield confrontations abroad ushered in a labor force contraction at home. Women lost their jobs after the Armistice when servicemen formerly employed by the railroads were reinstated and the Railroad Administration inaugurated a drastic austerity program. Both actions decreased the ranks of women in railroad jobs because women workers generally had less seniority than male workers. There were other factors as well which put women at a great disadvantage during demobilization. Local railroad officials and male workers conspired to oust women from their jobs. The decision to retain, furlough, or fire employees touched off local confrontations between women and their supervisors on the one hand and between women and their local unions or male co-workers on the other.

Postwar layoffs were supposed to be governed by the seniority principle which made a worker's length of service as important as fitness and ability. Theoretically, the adoption of the seniority principle by the Railroad Administration offered women a new standard of justice, but in reality justice depended on the good will and integrity of local managers. The shift from separate company policies to a single railroad labor policy during the war had removed much of the authority over job classifications, pay rates, and discipline from the hands of local managerial personnel, but during demobilization, as the return of the railroads to private management drew closer, local male supervisors came to exercise increasing control over layoffs and discharges. Chief clerks, foremen, and master mechanics often paid more attention to efficiency, gender, and marital status than to seniority, the result being a drastic reduction in the size of the female work force.

According to the Women's Service Section investigations of demobilization, the Pennsylvania Railroad was the worst offender of women's seniority rights in the railroad industry. Other railroads were also known for the mockery that they made of women's rights, but their reputation for unsavory conduct never equalled that of the Pennsylvania Railroad. As part of a strategy to break the union spirit among employees and bring about a "passive group . . . too afraid" to exercise its job rights, Pennsylvania Railroad officials consciously disregarded the Railroad Administration's orders pertaining to layoffs. As a result, the clerks, car cleaners, storeroom attendants, yard employees, and shop workers—in Jersey City, New Jersey and Olean, New York, as well as in Washington, D.C., and in Oil City, Harrisburg, and Altoona, Pennsylvania—were subject to the whims of their local bosses, to whom the company delegated broad authority.[60]

Railroad officials laid off or dismissed women from their jobs on the basis of efficiency. According to the master mechanic in the Harrisburg shops of the Pennsylvania Railroad, his way of handling the process of demobilization was to "weed out dead wood first, and then govern by seniority."[61] The man's written statement to affected women captured the essence of many railroad officials' feelings about female labor just after the war.

[I]t is necessary to re-establish, in a broad sense, the efficiency of our service. In the stress of affairs during the war period the temporary employment of women . . . became an absolute necessity. . . . [T]he results obtained have not, as a rule, been happy; nevertheless we appreciate what the women have done for us in the past months. . . . [M]en must be re-instated for the good of all and women should lend a willing obedience to that fact.[62]

Pennsylvania Railroad officials interpreted the charge of inefficiency in any way that suited them. Two women in the Altoona yards were dismissed because of "the language they used."

Another was fired because she supposedly "got drunk repeatedly." A third woman—who had been actively sought out to work for the railroads during the war, when workers were scarce—was dismissed after the war despite her seniority ranking when a local official recalled a prewar maximum age limit for new employees. Often the foremen offered no explanation other than "inefficiency" for dismissing women. When pressed to give a more specific evaluation for firing a woman clerk, the head of one office said that to comply he "would have to cast a slur upon the girl's character."[63] Similar innuendos were used by other local officials as well.

Supervisors frequently violated women's seniority rights by refusing to post rosters required by the Railroad Administration which detailed each worker's standing according to length of service. Those supervisors who did post seniority rosters often refused to include women's names on the pretext that the women had originally been hired only for the duration of the wartime emergency and hence had not earned any job security.[64]

Marital status was also used as an excuse for dismissing women. Officially, the Railroad Administration orders did not recognize the state of marriage as a legitimate basis for reducing its work force. Local officials nonetheless acted on the basis of their own sense of morality, which no doubt was widely shared in the community. Thus, in Topeka, Kansas, married women office workers employed by the Santa Fe Railroad were dismissed, in the words of a WSS report, by "pious members" of the management who zealously argued that they were "protecting the sanctity of the home."[65]

Some master mechanics attempted to get rid of women shop workers without illegally dismissing them. In the Jersey Erecting Shop of the Erie Railroad, the master mechanic tried to make women resign by creating an uncomfortable work atmosphere. A visiting field agent noted the hostility among the shopmen and the "ugly spirit" of the male apprentices. In the same shop the assistant master mechanic reportedly threatened to fire a woman who intended to report his misclassification of her as a common laborer, when she was actually performing the work of a machinist's helper.[66]

The chief clerk in the voucher department of the Wabash Railroad general office in St. Louis expressed his own allegiance to male employment prerogatives by indicating that as long as men walked the unemployment lines, he had no intention of retaining women. He sincerely believed that women deserved no claim to jobs in business or industry. "They should be forced back into the home," he told a WSS agent.[67]

Pressure from within the railroad industry to dismiss women did not come exclusively from railroad officials. Male workers whose jobs were put in jeopardy during the postwar period also conspired to get rid of women. Several men employed in the Harrisburg yards of the Pennsylvania Railroad addressed the issue of women's employment in a letter to their local boss. Identifying themselves anonymously as "some employees," the men used the standard clichés of the time to argue against women's right to work. Referring to the pin money theory, that women only worked for luxury goods, they accused women of "spend[ing] all they make on their backs," while hard-working men sacrificed their personal desires for the greater welfare of their families. Women were also blamed for adversely affecting the men's efficiency by wearing "short skirts" and "low necks," which distracted men from fully applying themselves to their assignments. In closing, they further asserted that "our men came first before the war, why not now? We will say the female help was kind to help men out, but having them two years is two years too long."[68]

Sometimes women received aid from their unions in struggles to keep their jobs. In other instances, the union allied with the local railroad officials to terminate the women's employment. The Brotherhood of Railway Clerks often intervened in cases where it was alleged that the seniority rights of women had not been recognized. When the employment situation became critical in the first half of 1919 and the union's primary concern centered on the reemployment of men who had been laid off or who had returned from active service in the armed forces, many locals nonetheless persisted in their efforts to help women clerks and occasionally car cleaners to cope with the extreme cutbacks in the work force. Such persistent endeavors educated women about their rights as workers.[69] Support for women was not, however, always forthcoming. Some clerks' locals betrayed the union oath by not actively endorsing the efforts of union women to keep their jobs.

In the case of Jeannette Miller, membership in the Brotherhood of Railway Clerks helped her to retain her job. Miller had been employed as an abstracting clerk for five months in the local freight office of the Grand Trunk Western Lines in Chicago when she was laid off in February 1919. Since employees of more junior standing had been retained at the time of her dismissal, she decided to challenge her supervisor's ruling that she had been hired only temporarily and had earned no seniority. As a member of the Brotherhood of Railway Clerks she sought the support of that organization. Together they issued a complaint to the Division of Labor within the Railroad Administration. The division ruled that Miller did indeed have seniority standing. This ruling obligated the Grand Trunk Western Lines to allow her a reasonable length of time to qualify for a new position.[70]

In contrast, Anna Crosson fought for her job in spite of the unwillingness of her local of the Brotherhood of Railway Clerks to offer support. In March 1919, following the discharge of thirty-four storeroom attendants and sixteen clerks employed at the Harrisburg yards of the Pennsylvania Railroad, Crosson complained to the Women's Service Section. She charged that the local rail officials had totally disregarded the principle of seniority and dismissed all of the women for "inefficiency." Crosson tried to get her lodge of the clerks' union to support the case, but the local union ignored her request. As Crosson explained to the investigating WSS agent, the men "want our jobs, there is no doubt about that, and if unable to do anything to get us out, they will at least do nothing to keep us there." After an exhaustive investigation, the Division of Labor decided to reinstate the women in May and give them their rightful thirty days to prove their fitness for the jobs.[71]

Reinstatement proved to be problematic. Although the clerks' rehiring transpired smoothly, "ugly" consequences resulted from the reinstatement of the storeroom attendants. Before their layoff, the stockman had praised the women's work performance. When the women were rehired, he "was furious and said [they] had no business there." Women attendants resigned one after the other as their workload was redefined upwards. For the first time they were expected to carry brake shoes weighing close to seventy pounds and valves weighing between forty and seventy pounds. Formerly, the men had assisted the women in their assignments, but after the women were rehired, "they refused even to tell [the women] where things were located and filed complaints against them for their mistakes." One woman lasted a month on her new job during which time she became completely "used up and discouraged [with] no spirit left." Another woman resigned because she had, in her own words, been "treated like a *beast*."[72]

The Brotherhood of Railway Clerks often supported women's right to employment after the war, but a very different approach was taken by the Brotherhood of Railway Carmen. This group directly requested the replacement of women workers by men. In February 1919, 104 men and women employed at the Greenville yards of the Pennsylvania Railroad in Jersey City were temporarily laid off because of demobilization. In April, as workers were recalled according to seniority, ten women were rehired. The local chairman of the Brotherhood of Carmen complained that this procedure amounted to giving women an unfair preference over "his" men. In June 1919, the general chairman of the brotherhood announced his union's objections to the employment of women as car oilers, storehouse attendants, and laborers in the Greenville yards. When the union chairman's requests went unheeded by the local foreman and the general manager of the Pennsylvania Railroad, the union took its request to the Division of Labor. The Women's Service Section investigated the case and found no evidence to support the union's complaints. The final WSS report on this matter charged the Brotherhood of Railway Carmen with sex discrimination.[73]

The International Association of Machinists went much further than other unions in the postwar period to reassert control over the labor force and slow the trends towards both the dilution of labor and the employment of women. After a national strike in August 1919, shop craftsmen negotiated a new national agreement with the director general of the Railroad Administration, an agreement which effectively tied the hands of management in a number of ways. Of most importance to the future employment of women, the agreement limited the supply of labor by carefully defining who would be eligible for mechanics' work. The agreement bound the management to permit no one but mechanics or their apprentices to perform shop work. Only males between the ages of sixteen and twenty-one could be apprentices. In the selection of regular apprentices preference had to be given to the sons of railroad employees. This restriction of the recruitment base for the work force was coupled with a new detailed job classification for each craft and for each grade of employee within each craft. By defining carefully what each worker could and could not do and which workers were eligible for employment, the shop craftsmen took many decisions over labor out of the hands of management. As long as there was no national emergency or a severe labor shortage of males, the new rules and regulations made it virtually impossible for the railroads to hire women for machine shop work.[74]

It is difficult to assess fully how women reacted to losing their jobs. As evident in some of ninety-nine formal complaints initiated by women or others on their behalf and investigated by the Women's Service Section, women workers were primarily concerned with job retention.[75] Complaints about dismissal comprised fully 25 percent of these cases. Wage disputes made up 14 percent, while complaints about protective legislation and abusive treatment by male supervisors composed 6 and 7 percent of the cases respectively. The total number of complaints should not be given more weight than their limited number merits, but these grievances provide some insight into women's feelings about demobilization. Even though economic necessity and the prospect of decent wages had induced women to take railroad jobs in the first place, they believed that they had truly done their share for the war effort and had therefore earned job security. They accepted the practice by which returning soldiers might rightfully replace them, but they felt outraged when men with no prior service on the roads were hired to do their work.

Sensitive to the labor market's manipulation of their lives, the railroad women expressed resentment at being courted at first and then discarded. The women's reactions speak clearly of their dilemma. Upon being discharged from her work as a common laborer in a machine shop, one woman wrote to the director general of the Railroad Administration,

We are women that needed the work very much one woman gave her only support to the army one has her aged Father another has a small son and I support my disabled Sister. . . . We never took a soldier's place, a soldier would not do the work we did . . . such as sweeping, picking up waste and paper and hauling steel shavings. . . . We are . . . respectable but poor women and were liked and respected by all who knew us. . . . Womens work is so very hard to find that time of year and expences are so high with Liberty bonds and insurance to pay and home expences it is hard to get by. We like our job very much and I hope you will do for us whatever you can and place us back at the shop. . . .[76]

Another woman told a WSS agent, "Of course, [the work] would have broken us all down sooner or later, but I believe we would all have stuck at it if we hadn't been laid off."[77] Like the women truckers in Pitcairn, Pennsylvania who were laid off from their jobs as warehouse laborers, many women railroad workers were "loath to go and wept bitterly."[78] Much to the women's dismay, the WSS could do little about dismissal if local officials argued that the work in question did not suit women, that returning soldiers requested the women's jobs, that a budget cut necessitated a reduction in force, or that the women were less efficient than the men. In the end, those women who wanted to retain their wartime jobs had no effective weapons with which to fight their forced departure from the railroads.

It appears, then, that by the fall of 1919, women's role in the railroad work force had decreased considerably from its wartime peak. The Railroad Administration's postwar austerity program, the reinstatement of servicemen formerly employed by the railroads, the illegal practices of local officials to get rid of women, and the enforcement of state protective laws, as well as the WSS regulatory policies, combined to reduce the female work force by 19.6 percent between October 1, 1918 and October 1, 1919. Within twelve months, the number of women railroad employees fell from 101,785 to 81,803. Of the three groups of women railroad employees, the female shop workers lost the most ground. Their number dropped 33 percent between October 1918 and October 1919, whereas the ranks of women clerical workers were thinned by only 12.2 percent and those of cleaners were reduced by 15.4 percent.[79] With demobilization, women lost their new common labor jobs on scrap docks, at freight transfer stations, and in supply departments. Women employed in craftsmen's work in machine shops almost totally disappeared from such railroad work. Women maintained their hold on clerical and cleaning jobs.

CONCLUSION

This survey of women's clerical, yard, and shop employment in the railroad industry has portrayed both the separate and common experiences of three groups of women wage earners. The case study results in a complex balance sheet of the positive and negative aspects of women's work experiences. Certainly women who worked for the roads during the period of federal control benefited substantially from the improvements in wages and working conditions that were given to all railroad employees by the Railroad Administration. The combination of decent base wages plus time and one-half for overtime work gave women an excellent opportunity to improve their economic status. In addition, the extension of seniority benefits to women made it possible for women who had worked many years for the railroad to apply for more responsible, better-paying jobs. Exposure to more remunerative occupations offered women a new reference point from which to evaluate their previously limited options. The official recognition of the right to bargain collectively gave women a chance to join the labor movement. The creation of the Women's Service Section provided women with a special government agency to safeguard their rights as wage earners. In these several ways the railroads under the governance of the Railroad Administration recognized the importance of women's work to the efficient and smooth operation of the roads during the national emergency.

At the same time, organized labor, local supervisors, and in some instances the Women's Service Section agents made it difficult for women railroaders to take full advantage of their new opportunities. Skilled male office and machine shop workers often organized against the introduction of women into their jobs. The men not only objected to the women but also to the changes which accompanied women's admittance to their work. In the case of claims adjustment work the preferential treatment of women was at issue. In the case of welding and core making the dilution of labor and the women's work practices triggered hostile reactions from craftsmen. Women found the path to nontraditional jobs blocked by the individual and collective actions of these skilled men.

Trade union protection was also not a simple matter for women. Carmen refused to accord black and white women the same treatment as white men. Molders had no intention of admitting women into their organization. Ironically, the war brought many women their first contact with highly organized, militant workers from whom they might have learned about the advantages of trade union protection. Instead, the opposition of some labor organizations to women's membership taught these women to think of trade unionism and sex and race discrimination synonymously.

Other men who thwarted women's opportunities were local supervisors, chief clerks, foremen, and master mechanics. Instead of upholding either the spirit or the letter of the Railroad Administration orders granting women equal rights with men, local managerial personnel did whatever suited them. The takeover of the railroads by the federal government was meant to insure a nationwide system of labor standards. In practice, the implementation of the government's policies depended on the good will and integrity of the men in charge at the local level. Consequently, women's opportunities for advancement, correct job classification, and job retention varied from one local office, yard, and shop to another.

While women might have expected less than fair treatment from male co-workers and male superintendents, they were surprised to have their job opportunities restricted by the Women's Service Section agents. Unlike the local male supervisors, the WSS agents acted with the full authority of the Railroad Administration. Their decisions were not arbitrary or capricious, but they nonetheless barred women from jobs which many women wanted to perform. Whether protective legislation was supported by male craftsmen or middle-class reformers, its effect was the same. It protected men's jobs from the competition of women.

In the end, women railroad workers lost their nontraditional jobs as a result of the various objections of skilled clerical workers, shop craftsmen, and Women's Service agents. The limits of women's wartime opportunities in the railroad industry were clear. Women made lasting gains only in those fields of work which had become accepted as women's domain. In railroad offices women continued to operate typewriters, card punching machines, and comptometers, take dictation, answer telephones, and file correspondence. In railroad yards, shops, and offices, women kept the premises clean and tidy. They also continued to earn their living as railroad matrons, janitresses, and laundresses. The war essentially accelerated the concentration of women in these fields of employment. Between 1917 and 1930, the number of women railroad employees dramatically increased by 75 percent—from 31,400 to 54,994.[80] As they had before the war, women continued after demobilization to provide the essential support services that enabled men to run and repair the trains.

4 The right to wage labor: women as streetcar conductors

> Lightest work I ever did and best pay. Have worked at housework, done clerical work, and [labored] as a telephone operator. Had to do heavy lifting when I checked orders in the drug company; filled a man's place at $15.00 a week, while men beside me got twice that. Do you wonder I appreciate being treated as well and paid just the same as a man?
>
> Anonymous Woman Streetcar
> Conductor, 1919[1]

Conspicuous among the occupations first opened to women during World War I was the job of conductor on street and elevated railways. While women had been ticket agents for many years before the war, the woman streetcar conductor was a complete innovation. Transit owners, beset with financial and labor problems, used the wartime labor shortage as a convenient excuse to hire hundreds of women conductors in 1917 and 1918 and thus simultaneously trim their expenditures and strengthen control over their work force. In twelve cities across the United States, waitresses, sales clerks, telephone operators, domestic servants, and factory operatives, discontent with their dead-end and low-paying jobs, seized this opportunity to improve their economic status. They rallied to end the war-caused labor shortage, echoing the patriotic call to service at new tasks. However, economic incentives were the women's prime motivation in initially seeking the work and later struggling to hold onto it.[2]

Figure 22. Women streetcar conductors employed by the New York Railways Company in 1917. Hundreds of women in twelve cities across the United States first became trolley conductors during the war. Resistance to their employment by male transit employees led to acrimonious conflicts in several cities. *War Dept. No. 165-WW-595-E-13, National Archives, Washington, D.C.*

Like laboratories running the same experiment under different conditions, streetcar firms had widely varying results from the introduction of women. Historians have noted, but previously not explained, the dissimilar responses to women by male streetcar employees in different communities. Three major factors determined male-female work relations in street transit: the existence of a streetcar union and its ability to define and defend the conditions of labor; the intentions of women to work as conductors on a permanent basis; and the extent of solidarity between men and women wage earners within a community.

Where motormen and male conductors were unorganized or only weakly organized into trolley unions, carmen offered no collective resistance to the introduction of women conductors. In communities with strong transit unions, the simple shift of women's employment became a contest of power and principles. The presence of smartly uniformed female conductors touched off a series of acrimonious battles for job control between streetcar unions and streetcar companies. To the Amalgamated Association of Street and Electric Railway Employees, the hiring of women was synonymous with economic competition and union busting. The title of a carman's poem, "Keep the Girls Off the Cars," aptly captured the Amalgamated's sentiment toward female conductors.[3] In only one instance—Kansas City—did a trolley local pursue a policy contrary to the Amalgamated's national opposition to women. In this lone case the union actively sought the cooperation of the new women conductors, recruited them into the local, and demanded equal wages and benefits for them as part of its concerted endeavor to deal with a citywide employers' offensive against organized labor.

The women responded in kind. They worked without incident or rancor where their employment was accepted. Where their right to work became a matter of dispute, they mobilized to protect their jobs, often with the aid of middle-class female supporters. Angered by the unexpected hostility of union carmen and encouraged by the enthusiastic assistance of women's groups, the female conductors became dedicated advocates of women's right to work at jobs of their choice. Their political consciousness as women developed through the employment disputes.

The particular way that economic, social, and local factors shaped the association of women and men in municipal transit from 1917 to 1919 can be best examined by a careful reconstruction of the patterns of response and the course of events in several cities. Because of their contemporary prominence, the experiences of women conductors in Cleveland, Detroit, and Kansas City are especially important. Since the political economy of streetcar transit set the stage for women's entrance into conducting, a capsule history of the development of the street railways industry provides the essential backdrop against which the wartime emergency hiring of women conductors became such a contested issue.

THE ECONOMICS OF URBAN TRANSIT

The wartime labor shortage served as the immediate catalyst for the employment of women conductors by streetcar companies. For years economic trends had been forcing managers to consider technical and social innovations for the operation of their transit systems. Between 1890 and 1920 street railway transit went through the same phases of charter and franchise battles, financial promotion, fortune building, and political maneuvering as the mainline steam railroads.[4] In a manner reminiscent of earlier railroad tycoons, the promoters and speculators in the electric street railway industry built their empires on very shaky economic foundations. By World War I municipal street transportation was in deep financial trouble.

With the introduction of electrification in the 1890s, huge quantities of watered stock were sold to the public to finance the development of trolley lines. This procedure artificially stimulated credit and enabled certain companies to obtain capital for construction and improvement, but it made for unsound finances. Stocks and bonds which represented little intrinsic value ultimately weakened the base of secure credit needed for the industry's further development, especially in conjunction with financial management designed for maximizing the short-term return on investments. Trolley owners who neglected long-term depreciation costs found their firms' credit ratings jeopardized while their physical assets deteriorated. In a similar fashion, short-term depreciation reserves earmarked for maintenance were often diverted into dividends instead of being used to assure the continuation of safe, adequate electric railway service. Companies reduced their level of maintenance on the assumption that the payment of dividends would better insure their credit rating and make possible the sale of more new securities to investors. They expected that the future growth of business earnings would be sufficient to cover replacement and renewal costs. In reality, inadequate maintenance and poor credit ratings of financially milked enterprises could not be redeemed indefinitely by further improper practices.[5]

Overbuilding street railways weakened the industry even more. Since the days of horsecars, competing firms had tried to create and secure urban mass transit markets. The introduction of electricity gave rise to even higher expectations and more intense speculation. In addition, railway design changed periodically, demanding the investment of large amounts of capital in new rail outfits. Heavy expenditure went at one point into increasing the size and weight of cars and rails as well as into the larger power plants required to run the heavier equipment. Then a changeover to better-built light cars necessitated still more capital to replace the outmoded heavier rolling stock.[6]

The uniform five-cent passenger fare, adopted by most companies, also proved to be a problem. This flat fare did not correspond to distances passengers travelled and had no fixed relationship to the cost of service. In view of frequent fiscal mismanagement in street transit companies, the uniform and inflexible fare became a detriment to companies in need of credit. The fare was fixed by law in many railway franchises, making it very difficult for companies to change the rate when the cost of goods, labor, or money rose appreciably, as each did during the war.[7]

Taxation policies by which local public treasuries sought a regular share of company revenues often compounded the industry's problems. Although the taxes themselves were not usually excessive, they reduced railway companies' net earnings and diminished their financial flexibility. Public regulation of stocks and bonds was not highly developed early in the twentieth century, but it attempted to insure that new securities represented new money earmarked for legitimate purposes. Such efforts at least combatted some tendencies toward speculation, but since public utility commissions generally lacked powers to compel the financial reorganization of street railway firms or the restructuring of existing capitalization, investors remained wary of the industry.[8]

Especially after 1910, street railways faced increasing competition from jitneys and private automobiles, while public demands for better service prompted regulatory agencies to pressure transit companies. Jitneys were inexpensive, often second-hand touring cars whose routes usually paralleled streetcar lines. Since local authorities did not monitor jitneys, the touring cars could use the roadways without paying anything for the mandatory maintenance provided by streetcar companies. Private automobiles began to drain passengers and revenues from the street railway services. While there were only 2,300,000 private cars on American roads in 1915, a mere five years later the presence of 8,200,000 such vehicles signalled the vastly increased importance of automobiles as a common means of transport.[9]

Discontent among street railway workers surfaced when financial concerns forced urban railway companies to attempt to curtail labor costs. Unionism among transit employees remained brief and sporadic until the founding of the American Federation of Labor in 1886. At the suggestion of the AF of L, a national organization of various local streetcar unions, known as the Amalgamated Association of Street and Electric Railway Employees of America (AASERE), was founded in 1892. The Amalgamated grew rapidly, reaching a membership of 70,000 in 250 locals in 1917. Its success varied considerably from city to city, but the union did win recognition and collective bargaining agreements from many companies. Its strength could be seen in the degree to which wages absorbed a steadily rising proportion of the industry's revenues. In 1912, wages accounted for 30.8 percent of revenues, while in 1917 they had risen to 32.8 percent.[10]

As wartime inflation increased the cost of living for streetcar workers, the employees fought more strongly for wage increases and reduction in work hours. Due to fixed transit fares and monthly jumps in operating costs, streetcar companies—often near the point of receivership—could not keep pace with labor demands and wartime inflation. Since many workers depended on trolleys to take them to work each day and uninterrupted service was essential to the business community, the street railways constituted an essential wartime industry. Transit strikes, which had always been considered troublesome, assumed the character of public catastrophes during the wartime emergency. Consequently, the federal government intervened to settle labor-management disputes, often to the advantage of streetcar unions.[11]

Although the financial status of urban railways varied from city to city, generally the margin between solvency and bankruptcy significantly decreased between 1900 and 1920. Months before any women were hired, the Cleveland Railway Company began to feel the adverse effects of wage increases, payments for injuries sustained by workers and passengers, damages to equipment from accidents, and costly increases in fuel charges. Although the company had operated under the terms of a city franchise which guaranteed a six percent dividend to stockholders and a regulated fare scale, this much heralded innovation did not adequately meet the company's financial obligations during the war. By 1917 the Cleveland Railway could not assure both a decent dividend and adequate service.[12]

In mid-June 1918, several hundred miles northwest, the Detroit United Railway (DUR) operated under a debilitating deficit of $925,000. With pressures for wage increases the company faced a possible additional burden of $2,500,000. Because the DUR teetered on the brink of bankruptcy, its president proposed that the federal government assume control of the company. In the Middle West, Kansas City Railways, a reorganized version of the bankrupt Metropolitan Railways, was rapidly following in its predecessor's footsteps. By October 1918, President P.J. Kealy was ready to relinquish authority over his company to the mayor of Kansas City.[13] Despite their hopes that government would bail them out, the city rail systems remained locked in their financial predicaments.

The troubled transit systems had to meet financial and labor pressures by raising new revenues or lowering expenses. In their search for economic redemption, many companies came to see the introduction of women as a means of meeting the dual challenge of wartime inflation and labor militancy. From the very moment the

United States officially entered the war, the urban transit industry launched local campaigns to prepare the public for the impending introduction of women conductors. A central news bureau served the needs of the industry by circulating many lavishly illustrated stories for local newspapers in 1917 and 1918, the thrust of which was the appropriateness and importance of hiring women conductors to help win the war.[14] Patriotism, the labor shortage, and economic incentives combined to open the way for women into this new area of work.

COOPERATION OR CONFLICT IN
WORKER RELATIONS

From late 1917 through the fall of 1919, women conducted trolleys in Brooklyn, New York City, St. Louis, Camden and Elizabeth, Newark, Baltimore, Milwaukee, Los Angeles, Duluth, Cleveland, Detroit, and Kansas City. The reception women received from carmen varied from one community to another, but two basic patterns characterized work relations in seven cities for which information could be found. In most places, carmen presented no collective challenge to the employment of women conductors. Where harmony prevailed, conductors and motormen were not members of transit unions or had only recently organized collective bargaining units. Possibly these men could not muster the necessary group unity to resist their employers' new hiring policy. More likely, they did not perceive women conductors as an economic threat because many of the female recruits were related by blood or marriage to their male co-workers and intended to work as conductors only for the duration of the war.

In sharp contrast, conflict distinguished worker relations where well-established union locals firmly determined the conditions of transit employment. Fearful of economic competition and a challenge to union authority, Amalgamated members fought the introduction of women conductors. In these cases, the women recruits and the union carmen shared no family ties. The hostility of Amalgamated members to the employment of women on streetcars eliminated streetcar conducting as a viable job option for female relatives of union carmen. Instead, the women who became conductors for union-controlled transit firms were new to the industry and looked upon transit employment as a permanent alternative to their former wage labor.

In unorganized settings, daughters, sisters, mothers, and particularly wives of streetcar workers responded to the call for trolley conductors. They were among the hundreds of women workers employed in 1917 by the Brooklyn Transit Company and the New York Railways. In Kenosha, Wisconsin nine of the twenty-six women hired in December 1917 were the wives of motormen. A majority of the twenty women recruited in St. Louis in January 1918 also came from carmen's families, and five of the seventy-five women hired ten months later in Duluth were motormen's wives.[15]

The recruitment of women who were related to carmen in military service made sense to all concerned. Companies advertised for women whose male relatives had been drafted into the armed forces during the war in order to reduce the potential for conflict between women conductors and carmen. Preferential hiring of family members also served to demonstrate to the men that it was the war-caused shortage of white male workers that was forcing the railways to hire women. When transit managers had to fill job vacancies with women unrelated to streetcar employees, the managers could forestall workmen's opposition by honestly claiming that they had done their best to keep the jobs within "the family."[16]

In similar fashion, carmen likely reasoned that they could more effectively control their jobs if they taught and worked alongside the female relatives of their male co-workers instead of other women. Equally important, the men could assume with considerable confidence that female relatives of carmen in military service would conduct trolleys only for the duration of the war or until their male kin returned home from the armed forces. The pattern of family hiring preference acted as a kind of job security system for male workers.

Conducting might have appealed to these women for a number of reasons. Practically speaking, the job provided regular income with which to cope with wartime inflation. The women's stint as conductors could also be understood in terms of a family tradition of protecting their men's livelihood during labor crises. In the street railway industry, women had achieved notoriety for their enthusiastic support of their male relatives during labor-management conflicts. For women whose world revolved around family loyalty, the shift from fighting scabs and strikebreakers under certain circumstances to conducting streetcars under altered conditions of labor took no great leap of imagination. By temporarily filling vacancies in conducting, the women were, in effect, holding jobs for men who intended to return to transit service after the war. Equally important, these women could be trusted to maintain the wage level ordinarily paid to men. For example, the carmen and the new family recruits looked favorably upon the Kenosha carmen's wives who struck with other women conductors and motormen in June 1918 for wages equal to those paid in Milwaukee and Racine by their common employer, the Wisconsin Gas and Electric Company.[17] Worker solidarity triumphed, even without the presence of a union.

Congenial relations between men and women streetcar employees did not necessarily guarantee decent working conditions and wages. The united struggle in Kenosha found no counterpart in New York, where women relatives of carmen also became conductors during the war. The lack of organizational strength of the local transit union, either to bar women's employment or demand higher wages for them, left the New York Railways Company a relatively free hand in defining the conditions of labor. A 1918 grand jury inquiry into the employment of women conductors in New York confirmed the Amalgamated's charges. The state investigation found low wages, long hours, and excessive night work among the women streetcar conductors, who were granted only inadequate rest and hygiene facilities at carbarns of the New York Railways and the Brooklyn Rapid Transit Company. The report compared the cost of living to wages paid by the New York companies and found ample grounds for worker dissatisfaction. Although living expenses had risen 44 percent from 1914 to 1918, the highest increase in wages was not quite 26 percent for employees who had worked sixteen years and more. First-year surface conductors were earning only twenty-seven cents per hour.[18]

The New York inquiry revealed that the Brooklyn Rapid Transit Company was hiring fifteen- and sixteen-year-old girls and was paying them such meager wages that a number of them felt constrained to supplement their incomes by turning to prostitution. Given the depressed wage scale, the union's weakness, and the exploitative policies toward labor on the part of the street railway companies, it followed that the hiring of women, whether or not they were related to carmen, might mean additional exploitation of the male transit workers. It was this kind of "equality" which the union carmen seemed to dread most.[19]

Because working conditions could deteriorate in proportion to the number of women conductors employed by a company, the Amalgamated Association of Street and Electric Railway Employees reacted viscerally to any change in its members' traditional men-only work settings. It launched a nationwide campaign against the employment of women as car conductors. At the same time the union made a concerted effort to organize the remaining unorganized male streetcar workers. As a further step, regulatory agencies governing street transit or industrial labor were pressured by the Amalgamated either to prohibit or restrict women's streetcar employment. Lastly, the union adopted a new wartime policy governing women's membership in the Amalgamated.

As soon as women were introduced in New York City in the fall of 1917, the Amalgamated branded the practice a "profiteering subterfuge for patriotism." At the annual convention of the American Federation of Labor in 1917, the carmen first publicly denounced the employment of women as motormen, brakemen, or conductors on United States or Canadian street railways. Throughout 1918 the *Union Leader*, the local Chicago transit union newspaper, and the *Motorman and Conductor*, the national organ of the Amalgamated, accused street railway companies of an orchestrated campaign to drive men and the Amalgamated from the industry.[20]

Just as the machinists, boilermakers, and molders had reacted to the introduction of women in the railroad industry, the union carmen were concerned most with changes in employment practices which would follow the establishment of a mixed work force of men and women. The companies were suspected of pursuing two main strategies in hiring women conductors. The first involved the employment of as many women as possible at wages equal to those of men in an effort to tip the gender balance in women's favor. According to this scenario the women would necessarily be indebted to the firms for such treatment and would willingly serve their bosses by breaking the unions during strikes.

The second presumed strategy involved the establishment of a two-track force—one for men and another for women. Under this plan, the companies would hire women at lower than ordinary wages and give them favored work schedules normally reserved for senior employees. The women's introduction would supposedly be accompanied by an acceleration in the use of technical innovations for the performance of streetcar operation. Instead of the conductor personally collecting fares, pay-as-you-enter boxes would be installed. Air-pressured folding doors would replace manually operated doors. Automatic lights, rather than the conductor's call, would signal motormen to start their trains. All these changes would significantly alter the conductors' responsibilities and ultimately lead to a sharp decline in the number of workers needed to handle trolley traffic. Both strategies, of course, would threaten union control of working conditions.[21]

As further justification for its opposition to women conductors, the Amalgamated beat the moral drum in expressing fear that unsavory passengers might take advantage of female conductors. The *Union Leader* declared that it would be nothing short of criminal for the companies to "expose young women of immature experience, or even women of mature age, to the insults, profanity, and vulgar jibes of the drunk, the enticing snare of the moral leper, and the hammer-and-tongs abuse of that element among the riding public that makes the employees suffer for the shortcomings of traction companies. . . ."[22]

With an air of chivalry the Amalgamated righteously claimed that women should not be subjected to the job's excessive physical dangers, particularly the large number of accidents to which streetcar trains were prone. The union also argued that women should be protected from the high risk of tuberculosis and liver and kidney ailments among the streetcar men, ailments attributable to the carmen's exposure to inclement weather and the continuous vibrations of trolleys. As proof of its claims, the Amalgamated pointed to the higher cost of workmen's compensation premiums in the transit industry as compared with those lines of work with more obvious dangers, such as bridge construction, carpentry, oil refining, and turpentine manufacturing. Voicing a prevalent view of the times, these arguments suggested that such occupational health and safety hazards were considerably more detrimental to "mothers of the race" than to "fathers."[23]

The following excerpts from a carman's poem capture the essence of the Amalgamated's opposition to the employment of women as conductors.

> We wonder where we are drifting, where is the
>   freedom of the stripes and stars
>
> If for the sake of greed and profit we put
>   women conductors on the cars.
>
> When our dear brothers left us, shouldered
>   their guns and went to war,
>
> Little did we think street railway kings
>   would use a woman like a squaw.
>
>   *   *   *
>
> To the street railway kings patriotism came
>   second; first came greed for gold.
>
>   *   *   *
>
> Woman is God's most tender flower, made to
>   blossom and to bear
>
> To keep our homes, raise our children, and
>   our joys and sorrows share.
>
> She was made by God the weaker, like a vine
>   on man to lean;
>
> She was meant to work like her nature, tender,
>   sweet and clean;
>
> How, when the Railway Kings for greed and gain
>   would cover womanhood with scars
>
> We pray God to protect and keep our women off
>   the cars.[24]

To protect itself from accusations of misogyny, the ASSERE publicized its efforts on behalf of women in other branches of street transportation. Much was made of the newly improved wages and working conditions for female collectors, receivers, coil winders, and office personnel in Boston and Chicago. Women, it was clear, could be tolerated, and at times even championed, as long as they maintained non-competitive positions appropriate to their status as women.[25]

As part of its strategy for protecting the union and women workers from exploitation, the Amalgamated launched an organizing campaign to establish locals in cities where women conductors were employed. Between April and September 1918, organizations were founded in Camden and Elizabeth, Newark, Milwaukee, and Los Angeles. Elsewhere, the Amalgamated pressured state industrial agencies and public service commissions to prohibit the employment of women conductors. In January 1918, the Public Service Commission of Washington responded favorably to the Seattle Amalgamated's plea for a strict prohibition against the employment of women conductors. After public hearings on the issue of women's streetcar work, the Wisconsin Industrial Commission decided in June 1918 to limit the work hours of women transit employees. Likewise, protests from the Central Labor Union of New York City encouraged the New York State Legislature to curtail women conductors' employment schedules.[26]

After exhausting these avenues for defending itself from the influx of women conductors into street transit, the Amalgamated took one further step. In September 1918, the union temporarily altered its official position on the question of women conductors. For the protection of its regular members, the Amalgamated instructed its locals to accept women for the duration of the war and grant them all the benefits and conditions that men received. This policy entitled women to men's pay scales and a seniority position at the bottom of the extra list.[27] This short-term concession did not fundamentally modify the union's basic stand that conductors' work belonged solely to men. Even with a national policy mandating the acceptance of women, many local unions concluded from the New York experience that the employment of women as conductors should be fought with all vigor from the very outset. Such was the case in Cleveland and Detroit, where strong union locals marshalled their full strength against the employment of women conductors. In stark contrast, the Kansas City Amalgamated's initial opposition to women conductors yielded before the greater challenge of class conflict.

PROFILES OF WORKERS IN CONFLICT

Despite the national controversy surrounding the employment of women in the street railway industry, in Cleveland and Detroit women conductors were surprised by the outbreak of major union-management confrontations, which ultimately required not only city, but also state and federal intervention. In contrast to the kin of male employees hired in such cities as Kenosha and St. Louis, the new conductors in these cities were strangers to the economics and labor relations of urban transit. When Detroit and Cleveland women climbed aboard their trolleys, they were more aware of the battles raging in foreign lands, which endangered the lives of their loved ones, than of the intense local conflicts their employment would set off. The unions' antagonism triggered an immediate gut response from the offended women, who rose to defend their economic need to work, their sense of patriotism, and an unshakable belief in the individual's right to paid employment. From fragments of information in local newspapers, trade journals, and government studies, a portrait of the experiences and expectations of approximately one hundred of these women can be pieced together. The collective biography of the new women transit workers reveals a complexity of motivations for entering urban train service and militantly defending this choice of work. The hostility they encountered can be better understood by comparing these women with their male antagonists.

Single, widowed, divorced and married women with prior work experience entered the field of urban transit in order to escape more limited, low-paying employment. As seasoned wage earners, they well knew the advantages and disadvantages of different jobs. In their former work, most women had been subjected to rigid schedules and the performance of closely supervised, routine, repetitive tasks. Streetcar conducting looked quite attractive in comparison to labelling biscuit boxes all day, making silk braid in humid quarters, working as ladies' maids, checking coats in restaurants, answering telephone calls at a furious pace, waiting on disgruntled department store customers, or doing any one of the other jobs typically known as women's work.[28]

Like their previous employment experiences, conducting was technically easy for women, although it was often exhausting and sometimes dangerous. A conductor collected fares, informed passengers of transit routes, insured riders a safe entry and exit, and kept cars free of debris. The work could be learned readily by almost any minimally educated and able-bodied person who could speak and read English and count accurately. The job's most important characteristic was its public function. Many of the rules which defined conductors' work concerned appearance, deportment, and other personal matters, rather than technical training, knowledge, or skill. Applicants were screened for intelligence, alertness, punctuality, efficiency, courtesy, and honesty. Based on these social characteristics, the job suited women well.[29]

The ease with which women could learn their new work was only one of its several special attractions. In interviews with government investigators, female conductors listed more than a dozen reasons for their interest in the job. The most obvious working conditions were important to them. They repeatedly mentioned opportunities for arranging time off for rest and for personal matters, for alternating sitting and standing during work hours, for changing surroundings regularly, and working outside. Some women attributed a weight gain of several pounds to their more healthful and relaxed work environment. Even the sheer novelty of dressing in tailored uniforms and performing men's work appealed to a few women.[30]

The new conductors' own words attested to their genuine enthusiasm for the job, especially in comparison to other kinds of wage labor.

No one who has worked in a factory can fail to appreciate or understand why we prefer this outdoor work. I have tried driving a taxicab, but found that too cold. This is not work, it's being on duty without special exertion, . . . under pleasant conditions with constant change of scenery. . . .[31]

Another confirmed that

it [is] so much better than anything I ever did. The wages are good, it's outdoor work, and a million times easier than washing. . . . Laundry work . . .
means new bosses every day and often unpleasant matters come up. Here
no one bothers us if we attend to our job.[32]

Higher wages and steady work made conducting especially
desirable. Wages for conducting averaged about a third more than
those of traditional female jobs. A former janitress who could not
support her eight children on thirty-five dollars a month cleaning
buildings eagerly turned to conducting during the war. In contrast,
her hourly conductor's wage of forty-three cents brought her an
income of between seventy-five and eighty dollars a month. With
her husband's intermittent wages as a coal wagon driver, the family
could once again make ends meet. Like so many women conductors, she wanted to retain her street railway job permanently
because the wages were so agreeable to her.[33]

Most of the women faced needs as pressing as those of the
Detroit janitress-turned-conductor; they worked because they had
to, not because they wanted to escape their home routines or earn
pocket money for personal luxuries. The women required living
wages to meet real responsibilities. Of thirty-three Detroit women
interviewed by Department of Labor investigators in December
1918, thirteen were single, ten were married and living with their
husbands, six were widowed, three were divorced, and one had
been recently deserted by her husband. Eighteen of the thirty-three
women supported dependent parents, husbands, or children. In
another Detroit survey, it was found that 120 women conductors
supported 154 dependents. As experienced workers and the sole
support of many people, these women closely resembled the typical
male wage earner. Unlike the majority of the white labor force,
which sought employment only until marriage, these women represented a minority who were committed by necessity to steady, long-
term employment. They were all acutely aware that their weekly
wages kept a roof over their heads, supplied food, and bought
necessary clothing. In short, the quality of their daily lives depended directly on their jobs.[34]

Many women conductors brought to their work a keen sensitivity to the war's effect on family life. Laura Prince, a former waitress from Cleveland, worried not only about her ability to pay her bills, but also about her family's present and future safety. Because her husband was serving as a soldier in France, her immediate kin had become directly affected by the international crisis.

To many women conductors the war meant a new employment opportunity compounded by new family responsibilities. More than ever before, these women experienced the double burden of paid employment and household duties. Moreover, women like Prince had to face the possibility that they might suddenly be widowed and have to raise their children alone. The women conductors who suffered extreme personal hardship during the war believed that their sacrifices were "borne in equal measure" to those of their husbands, brothers, and fathers. Even without the clash of armies on U.S. soil, the war had a frightening and cruel effect on many families.[35]

The women's domestic responsibilities and wartime concerns gave them a feeling of legitimacy in asserting their right to conductors' jobs. When their employment in Cleveland and Detroit was contested, women in both cities mounted collective efforts to retain their transit employment. During the course of the disputes they became outspoken guardians of women's rights in general. The women conductors organized clubs to define and defend their rights as workers and as women. As eloquently stated in the founding document of the Detroit Women Conductors' Association, the belief in political and economic rights of women was the cornerstone upon which they hoped to build.

Our contention is based upon sound logic and reason. In this state women have been given equal rights with men, and that right was recognized and approved by the vote of the electors on November 5th, 1918. We are charged with the duty and responsibility of carrying our defensive action to a successful issue, and it is our purpose to permanently see the right of women to be employed and retained in the service of electric railway companies as conductors.[36]

Compared to the principle of equal rights, trade unionism had a more limited meaning to these women. Given their previous work in the fields of sales, manufacturing, telephone operating, and domestic service, into which trade unionism had barely penetrated, they were likely to know little about union policies or practices. Laura Prince, who led the Cleveland fight for the women's right to work at their chosen occupation, was an exception. She came to streetcar conducting already familiar with the principles and operation of collective bargaining. As secretary of the Cleveland Waitresses' Union she had held a responsible union post in a field of work which claimed few labor movement participants. Understandably, she also expected the benefits of union protection in the streetcar industry. Even though the other women did not share Prince's anticipation, they actively sought membership in the Amalgamated locals so that their wages might be protected along with men's. Trade unionism was synonymous to them with wages, pure and simple. Not having participated in the Amalgamated's Cleveland or Detroit fight for recognition of collective bargaining, these women could not fully fathom what union affiliation meant to their male co-workers.[37]

Men approached street railway work from a different vantage point. Few of the men followed the occupation of conducting by choice. They were not especially attracted by the outdoor nature of the job, the opportunity to alternate sitting or standing, the relative ease of the work, or its wage scale. Usually men entered the industry out of necessity to see them through a period of idleness. Until the 1920s, streetcar companies drew their labor supply from young rural males or foreign-born men who could speak English; for them the work served as a transition between their former employment and other urban occupations. The job's steadiness and the hardwon opportunity to bargain collectively for conditions of labor attracted them.[38]

Although streetcar men had no craft tradition involving skill, training, or pride of accomplishment, they did have a tradition of white male domination of transit occupations and a history of violent labor-management conflicts over employment conditions and union recognition. In contrast to transit employers, who maintained that conductors and motormen could resign one day and be replaced the next by fully competent personnel, Amalgamated members held that the ability to transport passengers safely from one place to another constituted a valuable skill. As loyal trade unionists they firmly believed that only the collective bargaining procedure should effect any changes in the nature and terms of their work. They militantly enforced this principle by using the power of collective action, even when they had to paralyze the operation of their communities and incur the wrath of employers, local politicians, and transit riders. Since such confrontations often placed them at the center of controversial urban issues, such as municipal ownership or government regulation of public transportation, they were keenly aware of the larger dimensions of their labor struggles.[39]

Even though streetcar service was short-term employment for many male conductors, union members expressed strong exclusionist attitudes toward their jobs. They had learned through painful experience that the American economy did not normally provide enough work for men who needed employment. They understandably feared that once the usual imbalance of fewer jobs than job seekers returned after the war, women's competition would become yet another obstacle to men in the labor market. Since women conductors were introduced only a few months before the Armistice, streetcar men would soon face the prospect of competition for jobs from both women and returning soldiers.

In order to make the most of the draft-induced labor scarcity and the importance of urban transit to the war effort, the Cleveland, Detroit, and Kansas City unions negotiated changes in wages, hours, and terms of employment. Having won substantial improvements in their union contracts, the men responded hostilely to the introduction of women who would, in the words of one union official, undeservingly "reap the benefits" sown by the Amalgamated.[40]

While battles raged in Europe, the new labor situation created in the United States by the war brought two very different groups of workers into bitter conflict. Women burdened with family responsibilities who had traditionally accepted restrictive, low-paying jobs now clashed head-on with staunch trade unionists who were trying to strenghten their control over working conditions. Following the introduction of women conductors in Cleveland and Detroit, women learned that they had much more to fear from their male co-workers' threats than from the "jibes of the drunk," "the snare of the moral leper," or the "hammer-and-tongs abuse of the public." In Kansas City unusual circumstances transformed the Amalgamated's initial resistance against women conductors into a policy of cooperation. Unfortunately, Kansas City's unique experience became the exception which, by contrast, only served to "prove the rule" of discrimination against women.

THE CASES OF CLEVELAND AND DETROIT

In April 1918, five months before Laura Prince was to become a Cleveland conductor, the president of the Cleveland Railway Company, John Stanley, proposed terms of an agreement to the Amalgamated local which would create an open shop, permit the wartime employment of white women and black men, and allow a rearrangement of the seniority lists and work schedules. The union successfully rejected these proposals and not only maintained its closed-shop contract in May 1918, but also won new hour, wage, and schedule concessions from the company. The Amalgamated only agreed to discuss the matter of employing female and black labor in the event of a severe labor shortage.[41] Unsatisfied by this turn of events, the company consciously violated the new contract on August 31, 1918, when it began the hiring of 150 women conductors without consulting the union. Because the Amalgamated viewed the women as unionbreakers, it threatened to strike unless the company immediately dismissed the new female conductors. Then the union backed down and agreed with the company to a U.S. Department of Labor investigation to determine whether the war-induced local labor shortage made the employment of women absolutely necessary.

Labor investigators responded promptly to Cleveland's call for help. In the course of September the federal agents decided that the company had intentionally created its own labor shortage and recommended the discontinuance of women conductors as of November 1. The government investigators based their conclusion on the railway company's wartime policy of offering special inducements to women, such as a paid ten-day training period, while denying male applicants the same incentives.[42]

Since neither the company, union, nor federal government had given the women any chance to speak as yet in their own behalf, the women were forced to create new channels for voicing their own opinions. Immediately after the unfavorable Department of Labor decision, Laura Prince and the other women conductors established the Association of Women Street Railway Employees, hired the noted Ohio suffragist Florence Allen as their lawyer, and sought the aid of women's rights groups. The organization's sole raison d'être was to protect the women's jobs by making their collective sentiments known. From the dispute's very beginning the women firmly believed in the justness of their cause and the importance of legal recourse through channels of the federal government. They promptly collected the signatures of 35,000 Cleveland residents on a 446-foot long petition asking the Department of Labor to reopen the case. Confident of success, Florence Allen appealed the government's ruling to Secretary of Labor Wilson and to the president of the United States.[43]

In this period of vigorous feminist activity, the importance of the case to the women's movement became immediately evident. All during the war, women had become accustomed to daily newspaper accounts of women's feminist or patriotic activities. Few days passed without a report on one of the militant marches in Washington, D.C. of the National Woman's Party, which as an organization pointedly compared the government's commitment to democracy abroad to the disenfranchisement of women at home. Locally, newspapers such as the *Cleveland Plain Dealer* included a regular column entitled "What Women are Doing to Help Win the War," which effusively praised and documented women's many wartime activities. Such publicity accustomed women to a widespread recognition and discussion of their political, social, and economic roles. As soon as the Cleveland conductors' case became public, various civic, business, and wartime government organizations concerned with women's rights rallied to their cause with a sense of urgency and agitation. The Ohio Woman Suffrage Association, the Woman Suffrage Party of Cleveland, the Ohio Women in Industry Committee of the Council of National Defense, and the Cleveland Federation of Women's Clubs joined in asserting that the women conductors deserved a "square deal."[44]

At this point in the controversy the railway company defended its employment of women conductors on the grounds that a real labor shortage existed. Later, however, the company would find it in its own best interests to reverse its position and side with the Amalgamated. Frightened by the adverse implications of the government's ruling for the entire business community, the chamber of commerce also appealed the decision on its own behalf to the Department of Labor. Speaking for all its members, the chamber's secretary, executive committee chairman, and labor relations vice-chairman complained that women's dissatisfaction with being alternately courted and fired would probably discourage them from entering male-dominated industries despite patriotic or economic inducements. They urged the secretary to reopen the case, so that women would continue to seek jobs in fields which had formerly excluded them and so would dare to face union antagonism. The issue especially worried the chamber because local employers had been preparing since midyear to substitute women for men wherever possible. The chamber feared that effective resistance by the union to female conductors would discourage citywide employer interest in the use of unskilled, unorganized women workers in new positions. In the chamber's broad perspective the case meant much more than the employment of a few hundred females in the transit industry.[45]

As a result of these diverse protests the women won a momentary victory when Labor Secretary Wilson granted a deferment of the women conductors' dismissal until December 1, despite opposition from the Amalgamated, the Cleveland Building Trades Council, the Cleveland branch of the International Brotherhood of Electrical Workers, and the Ohio State Federation of Labor. Even more encouraging, the National War Labor Board (NWLB) agreed to hear on November 8 the complaint filed by the women conductors and issued an order prohibiting the Cleveland Railway Company from discharging the women until the board had rendered its decision.[46]

Despite their temporary success, a sense of futility marked the women conductors' efforts to obtain a favorable decision from the government because the union officially refused to acknowledge the jurisdiction of the NWLB in the case. Without prior jurisdictional agreement by the contending parties, the NWLB could make no enforceable ruling but merely recommend that its judgment be considered final. Legal representatives of the company, union, and women conductors nevertheless assembled before the NWLB on November 8 for a preliminary hearing on the case. The union's respected and well-known lawyer, James Vahey, matter-of-factly claimed that the employment of women concerned only the railway firm and the Amalgamated, because the union had contracted with the company to prohibit women's employment in certain job classifications. Since according to this view the women had been engaged in contravention of a valid contract to which they had not been party, Vahey could directly challenge the women's *prima facie* case and hence the propriety of NWLB jurisdiction in the matter. For the union the issue was settled and required no further action.[47]

Florence Allen thought otherwise. She charged that the company and union had illegally conspired against the women conductors when they first submitted the question of continuing the women's employment to Department of Labor arbitration in September 1918 without having consulted the women conductors. Allen stated that the company had engaged the women to work during continued "good behavior" and to discharge them only for incompetence, insubordination, or unsatisfactory service.[48]

The women remained on the job while the NWLB delayed its decision in the case almost a month. On December 2, the union resolved to settle the case itself by demanding impatiently that the women be discharged, and a day later struck to enforce its demand. The strike severely hampered the city's operation. Hayricks, limousines, cars, and five-ton trucks were recruited to transport people to work while thousands of others simply walked or stayed home. Mayor Harry L. Davis of Cleveland anxiously appealed to the NWLB for a prompt decision, pleading the gravity of the city's transit situation. He openly echoed the union's argument, noting that men were immediately becoming available for streetcar work by virtue of the reduction in wartime industry and the return of men from the armed forces. The employment of women could therefore be terminated. Grudgingly moved to action, the board eventually held that the company should employ no more women and that within the next thirty days all of the women currently employed as conductors should be replaced by competent men. This hasty decision was made without informing the women conductors, who immediately protested on procedural grounds.[49]

Even with a ruling favorable to its cause, the union continued to deny the NWLB's jurisdiction in the case. The organized motormen and conductors decided, instead, to hold the railway company directly and solely accountable to the union's wishes. The Amalgamated pressed the company hard through its strike action by persuading streetcar dispatchers and inspectors to support its position. Despite the union's firmness the Cleveland Railway refused to yield to the striker's demands and outrightly dismiss the women.[50]

Caught in the middle, the women conductors felt torn between their wish to struggle for their jobs and their wish to maintain domestic peace. As the strike proceeded, intense pressure for settlement came from all sides. In an effort to resolve the matter, the city council pleaded with the women to surrender their jobs as conductors for the sake of public convenience and civil order. There is only sparse evidence with which to reconstruct the women's reactions to the strike, but daily newspaper accounts suggest that the confrontation over their employment had become much larger and more bitter than the women had ever imagined. Their martial spirit of "fighting to the finish" faded gradually but significantly when the full force and acrimony of the power struggle became apparent to them. The women could accept harassment on the job but not a full-scale labor-management dispute which paralyzed the city's public transportation and mobilized the sentiments of different groups against them. For a loyal trade unionist like Laura Prince, whose commitment to her work vied with her loyalty to the labor movement, the confrontation probably posed other difficulties as well. At one point in the conflict, the women conductors became so discouraged by the situation that they considered leaving their streetcars in a body, thereby literally removing themselves from the center of the struggle. In order finally to break the deadlock between management and labor, the women accepted the city council's plea that they step aside and allow the company and union to settle the strike. The women promised to abide by the terms of such an agreement. It was a foregone conclusion that the settlement would then favor the union. As a gesture of fairness the union promised to look for vacancies for the women in other branches of transportation. Despite their discouragement the women maintained the hope that the federal government would later reestablish their right to jobs as conductors.[51] In removing themselves from this stage of the conflict, the women did not abandon the field entirely.

The women's action hurt the company's effort to win the dispute. The Cleveland Railway failed to dissuade the women from publicly relinquishing claim to their jobs at this time. When the company further failed to stop its dispatchers and inspectors from supporting the strike, transit president Stanley had no alternative but to accept the union's demands. On December 5, the Amalgamated obtained a new labor agreement by which the company pledged not to hire women again nor to keep those presently employed after March 1. The case appeared closed as headlines in the *Cleveland Plain Dealer* proclaimed that "Carmen Agree to Work Again, Women to Go." With the loss of this battle, the company's long-term strategy of challenging the union with the employment of females was defeated. Furthermore, during the strike the transit company lost revenues which amounted to $100,000. The Amalgamated scored an immense victory, while the women won only a vague promise of possible employment elsewhere.[52]

The day after the new company-union agreement, the women conductors assembled at the Superior Avenue carbarn to discuss whether they would make a national issue of the strike resolution. Rose Moriarty, a feisty Irish Republican, whom the press variously identified as "petticoat mayor of Elyria," assistant secretary of the Champion Stove Company, an authority on municipal law, and a suffragist of fifteen years' standing, urged the disappointed women to let the National Women's Trade Union League appeal their case to the National War Labor Board. The women feared the negative consequences to themselves of renewing the hostilities between the union and the company. Honor-bound, they remained steadfast to the principle of keeping their promise to accept the terms of the new company-union settlement, even though they regarded the labor-management agreement contrary to the laws of Ohio and the United States. Still, their loyalty to their word did not extinguish their intense desire for justice. Cautiously, they finally accepted

Moriarty's position that the government did indeed have a distinct obligation to inform women, particularly during wartime, what work was open to them and what was not. Without a fair evaluation of their experience, they feared further exploitation of themselves and other women in similar employment circumstances. By the meeting's end, the women had come to view their case as a national test of women's right to work.[53] The notions of contractual and social justice would go on trial.

Following the women conductors' decision to pursue the matter further, various women's rights and middle-class women's reform organizations began to wage an intensive campaign on their behalf. From the perspective of the women the case had more to do with the *social* right of women to work at employment of their own choice than with the *legal* right of the trade union to determine hiring practices. The National Women's Trade Union League, the Young Women's Christian Association, the National American Woman Suffrage Association, and the Women's Association of Commerce each stressed separately that the Cleveland streetcar case established a dangerous precedent because the women conductors were being denied the right to earn their living in a particular occupation merely on the grounds that male workers demanded the exclusion of women.[54]

Support for the fired women conductors came from still another quarter—from within the federal bureaucracy itself. The administrative procedures of the National War Labor Board outraged Mary van Kleeck and Mary Anderson, director and assistant director of the Women in Industry Service of the Department of Labor. This organization was mandated to advise the Secretary of Labor on labor standards for women wage earners. Although van Kleeck and Anderson ordinarily remained silent on matters outside their immediate jurisdiction, they angrily protested to the NWLB in this case. They considered the board's ruling a dangerous precedent which denied the women even an opportunity to present their side of the story. The two administrators charged that the NWLB decision implied "that the federal government will not only permit but direct [the] dismissal of an entire group of women from an occupation as a means of settling an industrial dispute in which apparently there was no issue of strike-breaking or lower wages involved."

They asserted that such arbitrary discrimination against women by the board undermined the Women in Industry Service's efforts to establish a fair postwar reconstruction policy for women workers.[55]

Anderson and van Kleeck could readily agree with Rose Moriarty's view of the matter. The home-front battle uniting female wage earners and middle-class suffragists and reformers ought "to make America safe for working women."[56] On the other side of the battle line, the union viewed these advocates of women's rights as nothing but "sensationalists, sentimentalists, anti-unionists, and low-wage advocates" whose "half-baked equality chant" was aimed at destroying one target—the labor movement.[57]

In an effort to moderate the growing hostility between organized labor, on the one hand, and women workers and middle-class feminists, on the other, the National Women's Trade Union League sought a meeting with leaders of the American Federation of Labor. On December 16, 1918 members of the AF of L executive committee and representatives of the NWTUL met in Washington, D.C. The discussion between the two groups followed a familiar pattern. AF of L president Samuel Gompers flatly insisted that the central issue of the Cleveland case was female competition. He argued categorically that streetcar work was unsuitable employment for women. Florence Thorne of the News Writers' Union responded that women could perform streetcar conducting as well as men and deserved the opportunity to do so. With the two sides polarized from the outset, nothing positive came of the meeting. At the conclusion of the conference, Gompers warned the women against "attempting to make a national issue of this for it would arouse bitterness and antagonism which would take years to allay."[58] The representatives of the NWTUL decided they had no alternative but to disregard Gompers' admonition.

By mid-December 1918, when women privately and publicly pressed for a reconsideration of the Cleveland case, the National War Labor Board's first hearing concerned with the Detroit dispute over the employment of women conductors had already been convened. The Detroit affair coincided with the more dramatic events in the Cleveland transit case, thus heightening tension among the Detroit participants. Two hundred sixty Detroit women conductors who wanted to keep their jobs permanently were locked in battle with a strong, hostile Amalgamated local. With the turn of events in Cleveland, both the Detroit Amalgamated and the women conductors each sensed the larger implications of winning their dispute.

While the Cleveland union had substantial legal grounds for resisting the introduction of women conductors, the Detroit union did not. Its situation rested on a fundamentally different legal premise. In July 1918 the Detroit Amalgamated and the Detroit United Railway had formally agreed to the employment of "women and colored men" if the necessity arose. In September 1918, the DUR began hiring women. Because the Amalgamated objected more to the employment of black men than to white women, the company hired hundreds of white women conductors and only a few black motormen between September and December. According to the union's closed-shop contract, every worker was required to apply for union membership. Following its policy, the Amalgamated issued permit cards allowing the women to train, practice, and work for three months, at the end of which time—if their work proved satisfactory—the union meant to take them into the organization as "fellow" members. In a three-month period the Amalgamated issued 260 permits to women.[59]

Company-union and co-worker relations appeared to be operating smoothly until the beginning of December, when the transit local demanded the termination of women's employment by January 1919. The union took the initiative. It began eliminating women conductors' jobs by refusing to issue union permits to a group of fifteen female trainees. In a countermove against the union, the company refused to grant an expected pay increase to the men. Significantly, the Amalgamated took its action precisely at the time when the women conductors who had been hired in September should have been accepted as regular members of the union. By then, women comprised eleven percent of the company's conductors and motormen.[60] The National War Labor Board's first decision on Cleveland's female conductors encouraged the Detroit union to challenge women's presence in Detroit transit.

The union's sudden change of policy was also prompted by labor struggles in Detroit which went beyond the streetcar industry. A citywide antiunion campaign led by Detroit employers was threatening to destroy labor's collective strength. Well known for its unscrupulous use of power, the Employers' Association of Detroit (EAD), founded in 1902, steadfastly defended its businesses against the trade unions. By 1910 the EAD had acquired a notorious reputation for its antagonistic attitude and its often brutal treatment of labor. In October 1918 the Detroit labor movement issued an emergency call for worker solidarity in the face of employer abuses. The trade unions publicly accused business of collusive discrimination against organized workers, such as boycotts of employers who hired union members, evasion of the federal eight-hour law, refusal to meet minimum shop conditions set by the National War Labor Board, the use of bonus systems in lieu of standard wage increases, and the systematic imposition of unnecessary overtime. The unions also accused Detroit employers of failing to raise wages to meet increased wartime living costs, manipulating military draft deferments, and using promises of military exemptions to induce workers to accept jobs at reduced wages. Organized labor particularly resented employers' hostile attitude toward unions, their complete domination of patriotic activities, and their coercive methods of selling Liberty bonds and war-savings stamps. Last but not least, the unions charged business with the unfair substitution of lower-paid women workers for men.[61] Although the women streetcar conductors were in fact doing equal work for equal pay, the Amalgamated feared that women would become company pawns and eventually destroy the union's effectiveness. Since Detroit was the home of the Amalgamated, the impulse to protect itself was even more pronounced in Detroit than elsewhere.

In handling the Detroit case, the National War Labor Board concerned itself primarily with determining the status of Detroit's labor supply. From that standpoint, it was a foregone conclusion that the women had been hired because of labor scarcity, since the issuance of union permits to the women had certified that a demand had indeed existed for women conductors. On January 8, 1919, the board decided that the Detroit United Railway could retain women conductors and receive fifteen women into its regular service. Because of the already apparent postwar surplus of male workers, no more women were to be hired by the Detroit street railways. All parties accepted the decision.[62]

The board's verdict in the Detroit case accorded the women conductors a real victory on several levels. Those women employed by the Detroit Railway Company at the time of the board's ruling won the right to retain their employment. By giving the women some measure of job security, the decision recognized that they had to work for a living just as men did. The decision implicitly challenged the labor movement's traditional mistrust of women's motives for working outside the home and its disregard for women's right to paid work and union protection. Furthermore, the case had a positive influence on the board's reversal of its original decision in the Cleveland dispute.

While the Detroit conductors' case was being deliberated, the National War Labor Board reluctantly agreed to convene another hearing on the Cleveland case as a gallant and courteous gesture "to the ladies."[63] The board conveniently delayed the new hearing until March 13, 1919, by which time all of Cleveland's female conductors had been dismissed according to the December company-union agreement. The firing of the women engendered further discord and made the new hearing a feminist *cause célèbre*. Prominent national figures in the women's movement lent their prestige and influence to the conductors' cause by attending the hearing. Among these were Ethel Smith, the "watchdog" secretary of the Washington Committee of the NWTUL, and Anna Howard Shaw, eminent Methodist minister, suffragist, and head of the Woman's Committee of the Council of National Defense. Former NWLB member Frank P. Walsh, a noted labor lawyer, had not participated in the board's initial decision, although he agreed in private with his male colleagues that streetcar work was inappropriate employment for women. No longer a board member, Walsh now agreed to represent the women conductors before the board.

Walsh's acceptance of the case followed his recent resignation from the board. Privately he had confided to a close friend that the NWLB's potential as a "forum for justice" for wage earners had become "a disappointing mirage." He resigned before the board's actions had tarnished his own reputation as a champion of justice and fair play for working people. He confessed to his friend that he could not idly sit by and watch the employers on the board "pounce" upon workers like "hawks." Despite the fact that his representation of the women conductors embittered some male trade unionists, he took the case on its merits after Ethel Smith and Rose Moriarty had persuaded him of the gross injustice perpetrated against women by the ruling in the Cleveland case.[64]

The highlight of the women's presentation to the board was Reverend Shaw's eloquent speech, which figuratively placed the board, the union, and the company on trial for oppressing women. Her commentary echoed the Declaration of Rights and Sentiments of 1848, the founding document of the American women's rights movement. With the intensity and emotion which had become her hallmark, the elder stateswoman of the feminist movement asked for liberty, justice and freedom for women. In her own inimitable style she demanded an end to patriarchy.

As I sat here and looked at this board which has been appointed by the Government to decide on these cases and then heard the reports of the committee that men had been consulted . . . but . . . the women had had no opportunity to speak for themselves, I could not help feeling that it was impossible to understand that sort of serfdom or slavery on the part of one half of the people of a country. . . . Why should we have men decide for us what is good for our morals and bad for them and what is good for our health and bad for it? We are adults. . . . Let me say that the time has come when it is neither the right nor the duty . . . nor justice for men to decide these problems for women. . . . [L]et us be tested by our act to render good service and our act to be faithful to that service. . . . I claim that our time has come now when we women have a right to ask that we shall be free to serve in the capacity for which we are fitted. . . . These women in Cleveland on the street cars have proven themselves able to do the work.[65]

Comforting as Shaw's speech was to the advocates of female emancipation, it did not sit well with the board's all-male labor representatives. They shared the prejudices, fears, and outlook of the Amalgamated members and steadfastly believed women belonged in the home, not on streetcars competing with men for jobs. To persuade the board to reverse its previous ruling, Walsh delivered a carefully prepared defense of the women conductors' case. He emphasized the women's efficiency as conductors, their willingness to join the transit union, the essentially clerical nature of the job, the availability of streetcar work for both women and men, and finally the jurisdictional powers of the NWLB to reinstate the women since the original appeal had been submitted before the Armistice.

The final NWLB award, handed down on March 17, 1919, affirmed Walsh's view. According to Basil M. Manly, Walsh's NWLB replacement and very close friend, the labor members of the board "didn't have the nerve" to reject Walsh's plea.[66] The board directed the company to reinstate the sixty-four women conductors who had been discharged.[67] The women conductors and their supporters were jubilant. In a letter from Moriarty which Walsh characterized as "wild," "exuberant" and "enthusiastic," she wrote, "Wasn't it a great victory? And to think the opinion was rendered on St. Patrick's Day. I was so pleased with the combination that I have not gotten down to a normal state yet."[68]

The glorious taste of victory turned sour overnight. The company, which had refused to participate in the hearing, also refused to adhere to the new NWLB decision unless the local union consented. The decision suggests that the Cleveland transit company could not marshal the necessary strength to challenge the streetcar union. The Amalgamated renewed its threat to strike again, eliminating any possibility that the NWLB award would be implemented. Since the board itself would expire in mid-1919, nothing but the power of public opinion remained to enforce its decision. The fired women conductors had no further legal remedy.[69]

While employer defiance of NWLB awards was commonplace by the spring of 1919, the Cleveland streetcar union's refusal to abide by the board's decision represented one of the very few instances in which a union defied a government ruling. The Amalgamated staunchly defended its position because it firmly believed that the company had no other motive in hiring women than to dislodge the union. The weight of the evidence substantiated the Amalgamated's suspicion. The women conductors were caught in the middle, with the company's manipulations on one side and the government's vacillations on the other.

For the women conductors, the consequences of the war, of streetcar employment, and of their labor struggle were frequently bitter. When, for example, Laura Prince lost her job as a street railway conductor on March 1, 1919, she again sought work as a waitress but was refused reinstatement in the Cleveland Waitresses' Union of which she had formerly been secretary. She could only surmise that behind-the-scenes union decisions were responsible. Could it be mere coincidence, she wondered, that the very man who, as business agent for the Amalgamated had personally refused women admission to the local street railway union, was simultaneously serving as secretary of the waitresses' union. For Prince, the personal and economic hardship of finding work after her dismissal from the transit industry was further compounded by the recent knowledge that her husband had been seriously wounded in France. In many ways the war had permanently scarred her life.[70]

The Detroit women fared better than their Cleveland "sisters." They got to keep their jobs as conductors, but their co-worker relations remained strained. These Detroit women publicly agreed to vacate their jobs for soldiers who had risked their lives in "no man's land," but they branded as illegitimate anyone else's claims to their jobs. Remaining true to their ideal of cooperation between men and women wage earners, they supported the Detroit Amalgamated's June 1919 strike for better working conditions. Unfortunately, this act of solidarity did not persuade the union to abandon its view of the women as economic competitors. The Detroit Amalgamated continued to protest the women's employment and to bar them from union membership. The Detroit contest of power and principle ended in a stalemate.[71]

THE EXCEPTIONAL CASE: KANSAS CITY

In striking contrast to the situations in Cleveland and Detroit, in Kansas City, Missouri the Amalgamated eventually accepted and maintained its commitment to the employment of women. The pattern of struggle over working conditions in Kansas City took a very different course because of several factors unique to the local situation. First, a thoroughly organized citywide employer effort to dislodge trade unions forced cooperation among male and female workers, both unionized and unorganized, who might otherwise not have been inclined toward unity. Secondly, the introduction of women conductors occurred after a general week-long strike of Kansas City workers. The intensity of class struggle expressed during the strike left a strong impression on the city's wage earners. Thirdly, the presence of an effective citywide women's labor organization acted as a catalyst in uniting labor across gender lines.

To organized labor, Kansas City represented a business fortress controlled from without by Chicago meat magnate J. Ogden Armour and dominated from within by four powerful business-men: W. T. Kemper, R. A. Long, J. J. Heim, and Walter Dickey. According to the Kansas City commissioner of conciliation, "every source of labor unrest unerringly revert[ed] to [this local] quartet." Colleagues of the "big four" controlled the Employers' Association, which secured a fund of five hundred thousand to one million dollars specifically to combat workers' militancy. As in Los Angeles, San Francisco, Omaha, and Detroit, where employers' associations had undertaken well-organized campaigns against unions since the official entry of the United States into the war , the Kansas City employers' association purchased large newspaper ads criticizing labor, hired special police to patrol workers, and employed professional strikebreakers. Employers in Kansas City inaugurated a particularly aggressive antiunion policy in the summer of 1917 after street railway and packing-house workers struck for union recognition and higher wages. Those employers who dissented from the dominant policy of the association suffered reprisals and other harassments.[72]

By the time women were introduced as streetcar conductors in Kansas City, a pattern of labor cooperation had emerged from a laundry workers' struggle for union recognition which began in July 1917 and climaxed in February and March 1918. The laundry workers' dispute clearly revealed the employers' special exploita-tion of laundresses, but served a positive function by suggesting how much might be gained if women and men showed a willingness to fight together for better conditions. In July 1917, laundry drivers formed a union, which by December of that year achieved a mem-bership of 125 men or 38 percent of the Kansas City drivers. Most of the city's remaining 200 drivers joined the union when laundry employers refused to grant a wage increase in February 1918. The organization of laundry drivers encouraged laundresses to comple-ment the men's efforts by seeking a wage increase of their own. By mid-February, all of the city's 1800 laundry workers had gone on strike. The militancy of the unorganized, poorly paid laundresses captured the sympathy of Kansas City residents.[73]

All the prominent women's civic organizations in Kansas City backed the laundry workers. The Jackson County branch of the federal government's Woman's Committee of the Council of National Defense, which was largely composed of newspaper journalists, magazine writers, settlement workers, factory inspectors, employment officers, and women labor leaders, held a hearing on the laundry strike. The laundry workers reported intolerable conditions. In the Fern Laundry, one of the largest in Kansas City, the women's committee learned that "horses were stabled in the basement, and the stench of the stable mingled with steam, escaping gas, and bad air. . . . Floors were wet, filth was everywhere. . . . The building [was] a firetrap. . . ."[74] The exposure of such primitive conditions won further public support for the strikers.

Commercial laundries in Kansas City were dominated by a cartel of nine large laundries run by F. W. Porter, a staunch opponent of organized labor, who prohibited any meeting with a committee of employees. The laundry employers even refused to meet with federal Department of Labor conciliators. Repeated violence by the laundry employers' specially hired police worsened labor relations. The Jackson County woman's committee chairman, Mrs. G. W. Addison, accused the companies' police of waylaying striking laundresses in dark streets and assaulting them. Addison further reported to the government that one laundress had suffered a broken arm and another a broken wrist. The employers' obstinancy and their agents' physical cruelty and insulting language enraged the workers.[75]

For five weeks the laundry workers struggled militantly against the laundry owners. After repeated attempts by labor sympathizers among the city's clergy and prominent citizens had failed to make the employers relent, organized and unorganized workers throughout Kansas City called for a general cessation of work as of March 27, in support of the laundry workers' demands for union recognition, increased wages, and the enforcement of state legislation regulating laundresses' hours and conditions of labor. This city-wide strike lasted a full week and involved most segments of the city's working population, including street railway employees.

According to one contemporary observer, the Kansas City work stoppage was the most important American general strike of the war. Little violence occurred during most of the seven days of the strike until the Kansas City Railways Company attempted to run the streetcars with scab labor. Then rioting broke out and the city brought out the National Guard to quell the disorder.[76] At this point the mayor requested a conference of laundry owners and employees. Because the laundry owners now agreed to grant the workers the right to organize, the laundry workers agreed to return to work under conditions prevailing before the strike. A later agreement between the employers and employees increased by one dollar the weekly wages of laundresses, who were already earning more than the new minimum. The union made no progress, however, on the issue of enforcement of state statutes concerning women's hours and working conditions. Worse still, even these few gains proved illusory when the laundry owners subsequently refused to pay the promised wage increases.

In reaction to their own bitter disappointment, the laundry workers of Kansas City began to prepare for future encounters with management. A major result of their efforts was to plan a merger between the laundry drivers' union and the new laundresses' union.[77] These events in turn illustrated to the streetcar employees how the Kansas City Railways Company would greet their own request for a wage increase. The laundry workers' saga taught the transit workers how very crucial their own labor solidarity would be in meeting their employer's challenge.

In January 1918, the Kansas City transit company attempted to win the approval of the city's residents for the introduction of women street railway conductors by appealing to the growing war-time sentiment in favor of hiring women for new occupations. Clyde Taylor, acting president of the company, first tried to obtain an endorsement of the idea from the city's association of middle-class women's clubs known as the Round Table. He believed that middle-class women would be apt to accept his sales pitch uncritically. However, the company studiously avoided notifying the Kansas City Women's Trade Union League (WTUL), whose commitment to fair employment practices and trade union organization was well known. One of the Round Table members spoiled

Taylor's scheme by informing Sarah Green, an organizer for the WTUL, about the forthcoming meeting. Green attended the gathering but kept her identity unknown to the company.

According to the league's report of the meeting, Taylor delivered an eloquent address "on the efficiency and capability of women" for railway work and the company's intention of hiring them soon. He told the club women that the new conductors could expect thirty-six dollars a month for full-time work and the supervision of a matron especially hired to look after them during off-duty hours in the carbarns. Taylor's audience seemed favorably impressed with the plan until Green, a former waitress and long-time enthusiast of the labor movement, rose to challenge the company's real motives for hiring women. In a manner truly befitting the daughter of a militant Welsh coal miner and a committed feminist, she exposed the company's chicanery.[78] Quoting from the streetcar union's wage scale and job contract, she showed that men earned a minimum wage of seventy-five dollars a month, more than twice the wage intended for the prospective women employees. Taylor's initially receptive audience grew restive and suspicious as Green exposed the street railway's actual intentions of reducing its net payroll by hiring women in place of men. Following Green's coup, Taylor thought it wise to adjourn the meeting promptly.[79]

In March 1918, the Kansas City Railways Company hired thirty women conductor-trainees. The Amalgamated immediately challenged the need to employ women and refused to instruct them. When the company dismissed those conductors who had refused to teach the women, the union complained to the Department of Labor. When the union threatened to strike, the company agreed to a government investigation of the city's labor situation. The Amalgamated proved to the satisfaction of the Labor Department agents that a shortage of men did not in fact exist at that time. In accord with a government ruling to this effect, the company withdrew the women and reinstated the men who had been dismissed.[80]

The second draft call of June 1918 made it genuinely necessary to hire women for streetcar service in Kansas City. In notable contrast to the practices of most other transit locals, the Amalgamated at this point opened the union to women for the duration of the war.

Unlike the Cleveland and Detroit locals, which bitterly resisted women, the Kansas City Amalgamated conducted its wartime wage struggle with women's cooperation. By mid-1918 the wartime labor shortage had grown severe and could no longer be denied by the Amalgamated, but at the same time the employers' citywide open-shop campaign substantially influenced the union to admit women. Yet a third, and exceptionally important, factor in persuading the union men to accept women was the role played by the WTUL, which explained to both sides the possibilities and advantages of cooperation between men and women transit workers.

The particular contribution made by the Kansas City WTUL to opening the transit union to women had developed from the especially cordial relationship that existed between the city's male and female trade unions. Kansas City's unions had recognized the WTUL's importance even before this women's organization had become an important force in the local labor movement and long before the city's laundry workers went on strike. Several years before the United States' entry into the war, every organization in the city's Central Labor Union had started to pay a regular per capita tax to help support the WTUL. In the fall of 1917 the league began openly to assist men as well as women in their respective efforts to improve their working conditions. The WTUL offered active organizing support to box makers, coach cleaners, canners, glove makers, film inspectors, janitors and janitresses, railroad yard laborers, laundry workers, soap makers, domestics, and not least, streetcar employees. After the August 1917 streetcar men's strike, for example, in which Sarah Green had worked as many as seventeen to twenty hours a day, not only did the streetcar men organize their own union, but their wives also applied for active membership in the local WTUL.[81]

This cooperation laid the foundation for a very solid trust between a significant portion of the city's male and female workers. When Green discussed the issue of women's employment as conductors with the Amalgamated in the fall of 1918, she was accorded the respect of a dependable colleague. She urged the male transit workers to accept women as "fellow" employees and to treat them with the same faith and consideration ordinarily accorded to men just entering the industry. A WTUL printed report on trade union organization confirms that she persuaded both the local union and the International to welcome women, if only for the duration of the labor crisis.[82]

As the Amalgamated had feared, however, the Kansas City Railways Company hired women conductors at lower than prevailing wages. Although the women were offered sixty dollars per month, a substantial improvement over the thirty-six dollars which the company's acting president had first quoted to the Round Table members, the women's wage was still notably short of the seventy-five dollars which men were earning. Instead of demanding their dismissal, as other local unions had done in similar circumstances, the union supported equal pay for women as its strategy for protecting itself. Kansas City labor had clearly learned a lesson from the laundry workers' struggle. When the union submitted a request to the NWLB in September 1918 for a cost of living increase, among other changes, it requested the same rate of payment for women. The company argued that it would only abide by a NWLB decision for a wage increase if the money for the wage increment could be obtained from a raise in customer fares. The case involved both the Amalgamated in Kansas City, Missouri and in its sister city in Kansas. After several hearings in September and October 1918, the NWLB determined on October 24 that a wage increase should be paid to the streetcar workers, that women conductors should receive equal pay for equal work, and that the money for the increase should come from a raise in fares to be determined by the respective Missouri and Kansas state authorities.[83]

The company's behavior soon belied its word. When the NWLB decided in favor of the streetcar workers, the Kansas City Railways Company quickly took steps against the wage increase. Instead of submitting a request to the state public service commissions which regulated the twin cities' fares, the company took the position that the NWLB had directed it to raise the fares itself without interference by any municipality. The company sought an injunction against the municipal and state regulatory bodies from the federal courts for the districts of Kansas and Missouri. Once the courts denied the injunction, the company appealed the decision to the United States Supreme Court as a further delaying tactic.[84]

Consequently, in early December, nine weeks after the original award, the streetcar workers had not yet received any wage increase. The company's stalling tactics finally sparked a walkout of 2,675 streetcar men and 127 of the company's 150 women conductors. Only members of the Kansas City Employees' Association, a company union, remained at work. Repeatedly throughout December, the Amalgamated tried to negotiate with the Kansas City Railways Company. Finally, the union appealed to the NWLB, but the company refused to participate in any further hearings. The board could do nothing.[85]

The company next took the issue to the Missouri and Kansas district courts to obtain a restraining order against the Amalgamated's strike. It also purchased a full-page advertisement in local newspapers which argued that the streetcar workers' strike was an act against the community of Kansas City. Despite such actions against the strikers, the workers continued to withhold their labor. The company's next move was to hire scabs. On the Missouri side, state militia protected the strikebreakers, while U.S. marshals guarded the Kansas side of the urban railways network. By April, a federal grand jury in Kansas indicted the union leaders for conspiring to obstruct a vital industry during wartime.[86]

With the law, money, and time on its side, the company won the Kansas City struggle. By May 1919, the strike had totally failed. Four hundred men and two women of the original 2802 strikers had returned to work for the Kansas City Railways, while the other strikers sought employment elsewhere. The company could report that it had almost a full quota of streetcars in operation. Because so many women had participated in the strike, the Kansas City Railways Company refused to hire them any longer as of February 1919. In July 1919, only twenty-six women, twenty-three of whom had been hired in October and had not gone on strike in December, were still employed as conductors.[87]

In contrast to the actions of other streetcar companies, the determination of the Kansas City Railways Company to break the union appeared extreme. By the end of the war most urban railway firms had become so weakened financially that they customarily submitted to a complete suspension of service when strikes occurred. The Kansas City company's absolute resistance to its striking employees was exceptional. Significantly, the company's revenue dropped 18 percent in the first nine months of 1919 as compared with the same period in 1917. A large part of the loss can be attributed to the animosity of workers toward the company. The striking railway employees used every effort to dissuade the public and returning soldiers from riding streetcars and accepting transit employment. The prolonged contest with its employees proved financially disastrous to the company. By October 1920 Kansas City Railways had become insolvent and was placed in receivership. The company resisted the union to the very end, but its victory proved to be a Pyrrhic one.[88]

CONCLUSION

Throughout the United States a severe financial crisis in the streetcar industry which began before the war induced street railway companies to move to reduce their debts. After the rapid growth of the Amalgamated Association of Street and Electric Railway Employees had compounded the firms' fiscal problems, transit management hired women during the war as a strategy both for undermining the workers' organization and for lowering labor costs.

Several responses followed the introduction of women conductors into urban transit. In cities where carmen were not organized into effective unions, the women conductors met no opposition from their male co-workers. The hiring of female kin of carmen in military service acted as a buffer against the development of hostility between the male and female conductors. Where carmen were organized into Amalgamated locals, they collectively fought the introduction of women either by striking against the employment of women conductors, by skillfully using state regulatory legislation to protect their job control, or, as a last resort, by previously admitting women into the Amalgamated for the duration of the war.

As the case studies have shown, the Cleveland and Detroit carmen regarded the women conductors only as competitors who were opportunistically advancing their economic status during the wartime labor shortage. The male trade unionists continued a long labor movement tradition of resisting their employers by rejecting women workers. So rigidly ingrained were their fears of women's economic rivalry that they were psychologically incapable of approaching women wage earners from any other standpoint. Even when the Detroit women conductors showed a strong interest in union membership, Amalgamated members were unwilling to view their presumed adversaries as union comrades. Labor market competition clearly could be as powerful a deterrent to class solidarity as any employer strategy.

Contrary to the Amalgamated's view of the Cleveland and Detroit women conductors as inefficient, immoral homewreckers who worked only to buy frivolous goods, the women conductors were responsible breadwinners who sought nontraditional employment during the war to ease their real financial burdens. Their consciousness as workers was directly shaped by their new circumstances and experiences. The war, the women's rights movement, and the streetcar disputes made them more thoughtful and aware of their place as women in American society.

With equal political rights as their reference point, they rejected second-class citizenship in industry in favor of employment equality with men. The women's responses to the Amalgamated locals were largely shaped by the manner in which the union men behaved toward them. Since the Cleveland and Detroit unions challenged the women's jobs as conductors, the women sided with the employers and mobilized in their own behalf. Although they were unfamiliar with trade union practice and labor relations in the streetcar industry, they demonstrated a willingness to join the ranks of organized carmen, if only to preserve their jobs. For these women in Cleveland and Detroit, their introduction into new work during the war held economic and social significance long after the international crisis. It is likely that the emotional legacy lingered on—of frustrated chances for higher wages and more responsible work, of impotence against an entrenched and well-organized union and an essentially manipulative industrial policy, and of chagrin over the indifferent or ineffectual efforts of government agencies.

From the point of view of the working class, the management-labor confrontation in Kansas City had some redeeming features. Kansas City showed a potential for cooperation among women workers, women labor leaders, middle-class feminists, and male workers. Throughout 1917 and 1918 female and male wage earners, both organized and unorganized, supported one another's efforts to meet the challenge of their employers' open-shop campaign. The week-long general strike of workers in support of striking laundresses was the culmination of years of cooperative labor activity. When women conductors were hired in late 1918, the Kansas City Amalgamated upheld its commitment to the principle of equal rights for women workers, forging a firm basis for labor solidarity in the transit industry. The new conductors remained with the Amalgamated throughout the struggle because the women had been accorded basic rights by the union. Equal rights in Kansas City was not simply an ideal but a reality which gained national prominence. Under the appropriate circumstances, women did not have to choose between their identification as women and their identification as workers. Their class consciousness could emerge unhindered by gender conflicts.

In Cleveland and Detroit, suffragists and middle-class reformers supported the streetcar employers precisely because labor had resisted the hiring of women. In their eagerness to protect the right of women to paid work of their choice, women's rights advocates in the two cities sided with those groups which favored women's employment. In Kansas City, however, activist middle-class women wholeheartedly supported the union. In neither Cleveland nor Detroit was there a female labor organization committed to economic advancement and equal rights for women which could mediate between members of the women's movement and members of the labor movement. In Kansas City, the Women's Trade Union League made this cooperation possible by educating middle-class women about management strategies while persuading male workers of the importance of interclass alliances to buttress intraclass solidarity.

The National War Labor Board, the highest government agency to become involved in the streetcar controversies, acted only reluctantly in cases concerning women's protests. In response to pressure from various groups, the board wavered between one or another position regarding the employment of women conductors. The board's decisions implied a profound ambivalence toward women's employment in industry.

Although the streetcar cases laid before the board the question of women's right to jobs of their choice, the wartime agency refused to pass judgment on this issue. Instead, it limited its jurisdiction to determining whether a legitimate labor shortage actually necessitated the hiring of women. In the first Cleveland decision, the board simply upheld the Department of Labor finding that women were not needed. Because the decision provoked a heated reaction from women across the country, the board grudgingly agreed to reconsider the matter. Although the second Cleveland award reversed the first, the board still refused to sanction the future hiring of women for transit work. It merely ordered the reinstatement of the female conductors engaged during the wartime emergency. The increasingly ineffective agency had, however, no power to enforce its more favorable ruling for women, and so it could not reverse the company's termination of the women's employment.

The board's first decision in the Cleveland case also had a detrimental effect on the labor movement because of its tendency to encourage gender rather than working-class solidarity. The organized carmen challenged management by challenging women, who in turn identified their cause with the feminist movement. Each group of workers came to see its economic interests as antithetical to the other's, when in fact both shared the same economic status and responsibilities. The accentuation of gender in industry had the pernicious effect of turning worker against worker.

Although the board decided in favor of the Detroit women's right to retain their jobs, several unarticulated values shaped the final outcome of the case to the women's detriment. Because the board prohibited the company from hiring any more women, the decision implied that men had a prior responsibility and need for work and so should have preferential access to jobs. The board's attitude toward women implied that they should have at best only a *limited* right to paid employment. The board's Detroit ruling thus symbolized women's dilemma as workers and confirmed the conventional wisdom about women's domestic and economic roles: they should not have to work, but if need drove them into the marketplace, then their employment should be confined to jobs traditionally sanctioned as women's work. Because those areas of work considered suitable for women paid lower wages than comparable jobs open to men, women workers were implicitly doomed by such attitudes to a lower status, lower pay, and relatively lower standard of living than working men had the "right" to enjoy.

In the Kansas City streetcar case, the board faced no dilemma over the issue of women's right to transportation jobs. Because the Missouri Amalgamated had taken women into its ranks and aggressively demanded that they be paid equally with men, the board's decision simply ratified the union's wishes. In this case the board did not hesitate to grant women unqualified wage equality, but its inability to enforce the ruling essentially nullified the Kansas City precedent.

In the end, the women conductors of these cities lost their jobs to the combined effects of the vacillation and ineffectiveness of the National War Labor Board, the street railway unions' resistance, the restrictions of protective laws, and the end of the wartime emergency. The trend was clear. By 1930, the United States Census officially recorded 35,680 men employed as streetcar conductors, but only seventeen women.[89] Women's readmittance to trolley conducting was to depend, ironically, upon another world war.

How different the outcome might have been had the Amalgamated adjusted its membership policies and aims at the outset of the international crisis to protect women by including them! As one contemporary observed,

Unless all this talk of the new democracy is sheer cant the women have earned recognition and the wise policy lies in organizing them into agencies for collective bargaining. The . . . sooner [labor leaders] gather into their organization all the employees in their industry and make conditions, physical, moral, and economic, the best the industry can afford, the more permanent will be their service and success. . . . If this cannot be done in the United States, what has this war been about?[90]

5 No service, no smile: telephone operators and the war

"Once a Bell System employee, never again a Bell System employee" is a current saying among former telephone workers.   N. R. Danielian, 1939.[1]

In the telephone industry, women workers led the massive wartime and postwar strikes. Up and down the New England and Pacific Coasts and across the South and Midwest, telephone operators struck in ricochet fashion from 1917 to 1919. With the support of repairmen, male telephone installers, and line splicers, women operators struck for union recognition, improved wages and hours, and replacements in individual supervisory personnel. The dramatic and militant entry of women telephone employees into the labor movement was stimulated primarily by the new business practices of the early twentieth century. As a relatively new American industry, telephone communications entered its adolescence at a time when corporate consolidation, efficiency schemes, and the open-shop movement were gaining popularity in the business community. The Bell System was in the very forefront of the movement to reform labor relations and work performance known as scientific management. As new business methods reshaped the nature of telephone operating, militancy among women operators developed in direct response.

Wartime federal control of the telephone and telegraph wires from August 1918 through July 1919, played a secondary but nevertheless important role in sparking working-class action. As a direct result of federal control, telephone company officials obtained significant new power over telephone workers. Under the direction of Postmaster General Albert S. Burleson, the Wire Administration consciously stripped workers of rights won through collective bargaining before the war. Telephone operators frustrated by their poor working conditions doubly resented such abusive treatment at the hands of the government agency and began to take direct action.

The workers' challenge to corporate power, however, was short-circuited by weaknesses in the telephone union and by the superior strength of the Bell System. The women telephonists' new militancy as well as their organizational shortcomings must be examined against the background of the growth of the telephone industry into a major American business and the impact of scientific management on telephone operating. The government's operation of the wires must in turn be considered in relation to the industry's management practices and labor policies. The histories of several telephone strikes can serve to illustrate these relationships among women workers, the telephone industry, the federal government, and the new "scientific" methods of management.

THE GROWTH OF A CORPORATE GIANT

As a product of the twentieth-century revolution in American business organization, the telephone industry came to exemplify the new model of "industrial conquest."[2] From 1880 to 1930 the industry grew rapidly, from crude single-line systems, each connecting two stations, to clusters of exchanges controlled by local operating companies, and finally into a corporation with connecting service throughout the nation. In the short span of fifty years, the telephone industry, led by the pace-setting Bell System of the American Telephone and Telegraph Company, consolidated its financial operations, standardized its equipment and methods, and centralized its administration. From whatever perspective the telephone industry has been examined, the particular contributions of the Bell System have assumed central importance. American Telephone and Telegraph's financial arrangements and technological innovations, as well as its management, labor, and public relations policies outstripped all other voice communications companies. While the early development of the telephone company involved competition between Bell companies and independent firms, AT&T alone dominated this branch of voice communications by 1930.

From its founding in 1879, the Bell Telephone Company was in the forefront of innovative strategies for corporate development. Bell won control over the telephone industry by acquiring controlling shares of stock in susidiary operating companies, by establishing a vertical monopoly in telephone equipment manufacturing, and by constructing its own interconnecting long-distance lines. Throughout the 1880s, Bell expanded by means of contracts with local licensing companies authorized to operate under Bell patents in return for a percentage of their stock. The operating companies gradually became a part of the Bell System as the parent company, then called American Bell, acquired sufficient capital to purchase majority holdings in the stock of its licensees. In 1882 Bell bought the majority of the Western Electric Manufacturing Company's stock from Western Telegraph. This acquisition allowed the company to standardize and control the production of telephone apparatus. In 1908 Bell began to allow Western Electric to sell equipment to independent telephone companies, thus further insuring that Bell's standards would become those of the entire industry. At the same time, Western Electric became the sole purchasing agent and storekeeper for the entire Bell System. With the founding in 1885 of the American Telephone and Telegraph Company in New York, where favorable laws welcomed corporate enterprises, Bell embarked on the systematic construction of toll lines. To forestall future competition, Bell looked toward control of long-distance operations as a significant advantage over other companies. By 1894 AT&T had already connected the exchanges of twenty-six licensee companies along the New England Coast and as far west as Ohio.[3]

Between 1894 and 1902, when Bell was beset by competition from independent rural and urban telephone firms, it met their challenges in part through the procedure known as association, which in turn prepared the way for later direct absorption. Bell entered into agreements with small independent rural companies which permitted the independents to use Bell instruments and connect with the adjacent Bell Company. Bell also practiced sublicensing through which agreements were made with companies that had developed territory in which Bell had no substantial interest. Since many of the independents were beset by financial difficulties, Bell was also able to purchase many of them. Finally, it captured even the smallest remaining market by aiding farmers' associations which installed telephone lines in extremely rural locations.[4]

More than any other person, Theodore N. Vail has been credited with Bell's successful growth and consolidation. From telegraphy operator in 1864 at the age of nineteen, Vail quickly progressed to the position of clerk for the U.S. Railway Mail Service in 1869, and then to the rank of general superintendent under the postmaster general. In the late 1870s, Alexander Graham Bell hired Vail as an executive for his new firm. When the company changed hands, Vail continued under the new owners as general manager and in 1885 became president of the new long-distance company, AT&T. When in 1887 he was denied the presidency of the parent company, American Bell, he resigned and spent the next twenty years in South America and Europe developing utilities and cultivating relations with important banking houses. In 1907, Vail returned to the Bell System as a management expert for the banking group which had come to dominate AT&T, the corporate entity that had become the parent company of the entire Bell System. As president of AT&T from May 1907, Vail trimmed competition from independent companies by nurturing new investments from New York banking firms, rationalizing his company's structure, actively promoting public relations, and inaugurating new labor policies.[5]

Vail's organizational genius soon made AT&T the corporate giant in voice communications. By the end of the industry's "great rate war," which lasted from 1894 to 1910, the Bell System could flex its muscles freely against the remaining telephone companies. The increasing need for raw materials, transportation facilities, buildings, and personnel taxed the capability of independent firms to compete with so powerful a corporation. From the turn of the century, Bell controlled the local companies on the Pacific Coast through the Pacific Telephone and Telegraph Company. It had connections from San Diego, by way of San Francisco, to Portland, Oregon, and through the Rocky Mountain Telephone Company to Salt Lake City. It controlled New England Bell, which, in turn, governed practically all the Bell companies of Maine, New Hampshire, Vermont, and Massachusetts. Bell possessed the New York Telephone Company and the Bell Telephone Company of Philadelphia, with which American Bell controlled the other Bell companies in New York and Pennsylvania. It also held the majority of shares of all the licensed firms from New York to the Gulf. These companies, in turn, held a controlling interest in Central Union Telephone, which operated in Indiana, Illinois, Missouri, Kansas, Colorado, and Nebraska. In 1911, the Mountain States Telephone and Telegraph Company was incorporated as a consolidation of the Colorado Telephone, Rocky Mountain Bell, and Tri-State Telephone and Telegraph companies. By 1916, Southern Bell also controlled the entire Bell System operating in Alabama, Florida, Georgia, North Carolina, and South Carolina.[6]

The dominance of Bell could be measured in other ways as well. The federal government's 1917 Census of Telephones reported 2200 telephone systems with annual incomes of $5,000 or more. Of this number, 145 comprised Bell Telephone. Although the number of exchanges operated by Bell only slightly exceeded the total reported for the larger non-Bell organization, the private branch exchanges connected to the Bell System brought AT&T's service to almost 90 percent of the country's telephone exchanges. This extended Bell System controlled more than 80 percent of the total mileage of telephone wire in the United States, and it represented more than 70 percent of all the telephones in operation. The annual revenue of the Bell System in 1917 was five times greater than all non-Bell telephone systems together. Bell's assets exceeded the others' by a factor of four, while Bell's total dividends were seven times greater than the collective dividends of the independent organizations.[7] By 1930, AT&T exceeded all other American corporations in total assets and in the number of its investors, employees, and customers. As a publicly owned, privately managed institution it projected an image of democratic control, while in fact it operated as an autonomous self-perpetuating financial oligarchy.[8]

THE SHIFT TO CORPORATE
TELEPHONE OPERATING

The consolidation of the Bell System into a powerful monopoly resulted in important changes in the customary working conditions of its growing number of employees. A highly bureaucratized, rigid, routinized, and impersonal system of relations quickly developed with the industry's surge of growth. In the earliest days of telephone companies in the 1870s, exchanges were tucked away in corners of offices, back rooms of general stores, attic lofts or railroad stations. Boys served as the first telephone operators, a carryover of their employment in telegraph offices. In addition to servicing a switchboard, the telephone operator's job initially included sweeping the office, keeping coals on the fire and carrying out ashes, running errands, collecting bills, throwing wagon spokes at crossed phone lines, and even keeping taxi drivers informed of calls for customer service.[9] Because boy telephone operators reportedly often tended to treat telephone patrons with impatience and impudence, companies soon looked elsewhere for a more reliable and disciplined labor force. Females with grammar school educations appeared to be more patient, docile, and agreeable than boys.[10] According to the United States Census in 1900, telephone companies hired almost exclusively native-born white women of either native-born or foreign-born parents.[11] Initially, companies could only employ females for the daytime weekday shift because parents objected to night and Sunday work for their daughters. Resistance to night work for females soon gave way to acceptance and by 1900, only three years after the Bell System decided to substitute female for male operators, women tended telephones during the day and evening.[12] The United States Census of Telephones records the rapid replacement of boy by women operators: by 1917 females accounted for almost 99 percent of the nation's more than 140,000 switchboard workers.[13]

In the 1880s and 1890s, working for telephone firms was relatively attractive employment for females. The companies had long waiting lists of female applicants who had had experience as cashiers, bookkeepers, and clerical workers. Some girls even used aldermanic influence to obtain a coveted operator's position.[14]

Figure 23. Teenage boys operating an early telephone switchboard. Teenage boys operated the first switchboards. The boys employed in this telephone exchange office in 1879 had to leap from one board to another to make connections. They were also required to sweep the office, keep coal on the fire, run errands, and sometimes even collect bills. *Courtesy American Telephone and Telegraph Photo Center, New York City.*

Figure 24. Male and female operators in a New York City exchange in 1885. Telephone companies hired females because boys reportedly often tended to treat telephone patrons with impatience and impudence. By contrast, females appeared to be more patient, docile, and agreeable than boys. *Courtesy American Telephone and Telegraph Photo Center, New York City.*

Figure 25. An all-female telephone operating staff. By 1917 females accounted for almost 99 percent of the nation's more than 140,000 switchboard operators. Supervisors monitored the operators who were in turn supposed to supervise one another. *Courtesy American Telephone and Telegraph Photo Center, New York City.*

Compared to other occupations available to women at the time, telephone work offered some particularly appealing features. In the industry's first decades, informality and personal contact marked the operators' relationships with each other and with individual telephone subscribers. Since each operator regularly serviced a single set of customers, all of whose calls required operator assistance, personal relations were not uncommon between callers and operators. The operator could inform, advise, or joke with a customer as the occasion dictated. In her personal capacity she gave news of fires or accidents, sporting events, and elections. She often provided subscribers with the correct time of day. For such services subscribers customarily rewarded operators with gratuities.[15]

Jessie Mix, a pioneer operator, remembered the atmosphere of the Southern New England Telephone Company as casual, sociable, and pleasant.

In those days the board had drops (annunciators) that fell down when people called. You put the plug in, and said hello, and asked who they wanted. The subscribers usually gave the name of the person they wanted, instead of the number, so we had to remember every name and number in the whole exchange and had to shout the number to a girl at the other board if the connection were not on our own. . . . Since there were sometimes ten girls shouting numbers back and forth, you can imagine what a confusion it made.

It was a lot of fun, however. We weren't busy all the time, and there were yards of crocheting and knitting done in that office between calls. We were a regular family, the girls in the office and even the subscribers. They used to send us boxes of candy and flowers and drop in to see us from time to time, and on occasion some of the livery stables . . . would put a horse and carriage or sleigh at our disposal, and take the girls on a picnic. We also used to play a few harmless pranks. I remember Louise Spang particularly. On rainy days when the girls' shoes were wet, and they were sitting on the high chairs with their feet on the brass rail, Louise used to connect one of the plugs to the rail and put the buzzer on it and give the girls a shock.[16]

Another characteristic of the work women and men performed for the new telephone companies was flexibility. While the first exchange divided labor along gender lines, a rigid sex-segregation of work had not yet become common. Operators often supervised their offices, personally collected bills from subscribers, and repaired their switchboards. In the small Canaan, Connecticut office where Ellen Considine worked, for example, the manager, service person, and operator routinely performed one another's jobs.

It was not unusual for the repairman to start at 7 a.m. and not return until late in the evening. When he was busy on outside work, he would relieve me at the switchboard, and, in turn, when he was busy or out of town, I would visit a subscriber's station and repair any trouble I was able to locate, or change "bobbins" . . . on the main frame of the switchboard. . . . After a week's instruction I was expected to be capable of handling the office alone. . . . In the early days we collected from both subscribers and pay stations quarterly and deposited weekly. . . . I recollect taking home at night several hundred dollars after a quarterly pay station collection. I was paying office expenditures from my personal account and being reimbursed each month by the company.[17]

The careers of pioneer telephone operators suggest that women could expect telephone operating to lead to better-paying, higher-level positions within their companies. Emma M. Nutt, the first female telephone operator in the United States, worked continuously for New England Telephone and Telegraph for thirty-three years, first as an operator, then as a chief operator, and finally as a matron responsible for the health and welfare of hundreds of operators. Katherine M. Schmitt, one of New York's first female operators, stayed with the New York Telephone Company for nearly forty-seven years. Hired in 1882, she rose to the level of chief operator in 1896 and was selected to be the first manager of her company's training school for telephone operators in 1902. Schmitt holds the honor of having designed the system of training switchboard operators that the Bell System later adopted throughout the United States. While Jessie Mix worked as an operator, she studied typing and shorthand at night school. When she completed her studies, she became the private secretary to the president of the Southern New England Telephone Company in New Haven. Thirty-four years from the start of her employment, she became an assistant librarian and then, just before her retirement, a librarian for the firm. Similarly, Ellen Considine entered the employ of the

Southern New England Telephone Company as an operator-clerk in the Canaan exchange in 1887. For many years she was the only operator for the community's eighty-seven telephones. According to her own recollections she became an indispensable member of the village, a friend and counselor to many telephone subscribers, and an inexhaustible source of local information. In 1911 the company promoted her to manager of the same exchange, which had in the meanwhile grown considerably. The lifelong telephone company careers of these women suggest that telephone operating initially offered women an unusual employment opportunity.[18]

With the expansion and consolidation of voice communications, the introduction of new telephone technology, and the systemization of business methods, the very nature of telephone operating in urban exchanges changed dramatically in the first decade of the twentieth century. Whereas the operator in the early days learned on the job and exercised some control over her work, the application of twentieth-century scientific management techniques to urban telephone work brought new training programs aimed at eliminating operator initiative. Additionally, the technical improvements which made the telephone more convenient, as well as the increasingly complex apparatus needed to handle the growing number of subscribers, increased the demands and pace of telephone operating. The introduction of traffic engineers, supervisors, and chief operators further stratified and homogenized the work. Even the smallest decisions disappeared from the operator's sphere. Superiors regulated her entire workday and enforced a fixed number of work operations per hour, a number which had been determined by experts in the company's traffic department. The increased number of workers contributed to the need for regulation of meals and even rest breaks. Everything became subject to coordination and regulation, from the day a prospective operator applied for a job until her voluntary or mandatory severance from the company.[19]

A candidate for telephone operating in the Bell System had to pass many requirements before becoming a member of the company's labor force. Often she had to secure two letters of recommendation from businessmen testifying to her good character. If her credentials were in order, she then faced a battery of tests to determine whether she possessed the attributes Bell found most desirable. Like an obstacle course, the applicant confronted a number of restrictions, including those of age, size, and ethnicity. She could not be too old, too young, too small, Jewish, or black. Any hearing or sight defects, a slovenly appearance or an unpleasant-sounding voice meant automatic rejection. To be seriously considered for telephone operating the applicant usually had to be a native-born white woman between the ages of fifteen and eighteen with at least six years of grammar school education. According to the 1910 guidelines furnished to an employment officer in one telephone company,

An individual who . . . is perfect physically, that is, not crippled, and who has (1) a calm, clear eye and steady gaze, (2) steady hand and firm set jaws, (3) weight proportional to height, (4) good appetite, [and] (5) healthy, rosy complexion . . . can usually withstand the wear and tear of . . . exhausting work, such as telephone . . . operating successfully.[20]

If an applicant met such standards, the personnel manager urged her to take the job by extolling the virtues of training with pay, automatic wage increases, and profit-sharing through stock ownership. The sales pitch also included information about company medical services, lunch provisions, and rest rooms. To a novice in need of work, Bell sounded like a company with humane concerns.[21]

The structure and content of the training school revealed another side of AT&T. Instruction consisted of drills on the most common types of calls with coaching and close guidance, first at a dummy and then at a real switchboard. The female applicant learned to obey directions given to her by supervisors and to parrot on command appropriate responses for a variety of circumstances. Lessons in telephone operating included directions for such contingencies as local calls, delayed connections, wrong numbers, busy signals, messenger and toll service, manager, hospital, police and fire calls, as well as out-of-order tone tests. Every occurrence had a well-defined procedure of its own. Lesson number one of the 1910 Chicago telephone operator's manual suggests the degree to which conformity was demanded.

Description of a Completed Local Connection:

1. When a subscriber takes the receiver off the hook of his telephone, the line and pilot lamp signals light up in front of "A" operator.
2. She picks up an inside cord, known as the answering cord, inserts the plug in answering jack above the line lamp signal, and at the same time throws the corresponding listening key toward the face of the switchboard. The plug puts out the lights, and the key enables operator to talk to subscriber.
3. In a clear, distinct tone with the rising inflection on the word "please" she says, "Number please?" to be repeated if no response is received the first time. If subscriber cannot be heard operator will say, "Please come closer to your telephone." If subscriber fails to give name of the exchange wanted operator will say, "What exchange please?"
   If subscriber gives name of exchange but omits number, operator will say, "What number please?"
4. The subscriber gives number wanted, "Central 128." Operator repeats it back to subscriber, separating the figures, as "Central one-two-eight."
5. She then picks up outside cord, known as the connecting cord corresponding to answering cord in use, locates jack of Central 128, and lightly taps the tip of plug against the outer rim of multiple jack three times, resting on the last stroke.
6. If no sound is heard, connecting cord is inserted in multiple jack.
7. [The operator then] ring[s] the bell on the called party's instrument . . . [and] leav[es] the line clear for both parties to talk. . . .
8. When both parties are through talking and hang receivers on the hooks . . . operator then disconnects. . . .

In addition, Bell insisted that the operator always deliver service "with a smile."[22]

The telephone trainee soon learned that a pleasant performance could prove to be especially trying. After a short time, the new operator also found the long working days, the intense rate of speed, and the system of surveillance exacting and oppressive. Since telephone companies required operators twenty-four hours a day, 365 days a year, three separate work shifts—day, evening, and night—were needed to provide round-the-clock service. To handle calls during the particularly busy periods, the telephone system had a division of hours known as the "split trick" which demanded that women work nine hours extended over a fifteen-hour period. As might be expected, operators particularly disliked working from late evening to early morning or arriving in the morning only to take four hours off and return later in the day for another several hours. Company policy demanded that new operators be assigned first to the less agreeable shifts. Although in time each operator transferred to the regular day hours, she sometimes had to wait as long as two to four years for the change. By turning night into day, the unusual hours circumscribed the ways an operator could use her free time. Bell further insisted that each operator be available to work during her day off, if for any reason the company required her services.[23]

The new operator found her hours and the work itself disagreeable. Seated at the long switchboard with the constantly flashing lights, she had to reach from side to side and overhead to connect and disconnect her prescribed load of 250 to 350 calls an hour. She had only a few seconds to answer each signal. Always nervous, always on edge, the operator suffered from headaches, backaches, arm and eye strain. She knew that at any time she or one of the other operators might faint from exhaustion and be fired. Regulations prohibited her from responding to customers with any except the company-prescribed statements or questions. No matter how pleasant or unpleasant the customer, the operator had to treat each person with the same standardized civility. She could neither chat for a moment with an operator sitting next to her nor leave her post without permission, which was seldom granted promptly.[24] As one operator noted, "It gets to be [so] mechanical, after awhile, you become a part of the machine."[25]

A highly refined system of surveillance, known euphemistically as "team work," constantly reinforced the stresses and strains of telephone work. Presumably, team work was designed to lighten an operator's work load by dividing her calls among other operators. Part of each operator's job entailed handling calls made to the person on either side of her and being ready at all times to assume the work of another operator farther down the line. Each supervisor walked up and down behind her charges seeing that they properly attended to their duties. Out of sight, behind the supervisor, sat a monitor who had an observation board connected to every position in the exchange; from here the monitor could listen to any operator and follow her work in detail. As an additional control, many companies maintained a corps of "service testers" whose job it was to make calls from various public and private telephones in order to evaluate the condition of the lines as well as the service. On the basis of the errors recorded by the "testers," companies compiled a monthly service report with an assessment of each operator. For good work the company issued service awards.[26]

Like every other worker who joined the Bell System, the young female trainee soon learned her place in the company structure. The operator joined the bottom rung of one part of an inflexible, hierarchical scheme of administrative organization. She learned to account for her performance to a chief operator, just as that person paid allegiance to a supervisor, who, in turn, answered to a manager, and so on up to the company president. After having worked for a Bell company for many months, one operator likened switchboard operating to "working on a chain gang."

"Hustle up and pick up those calls!" ordered the supervisor angrily. The lights were flashing all over, and I hustled, all right, but I didn't know what she got so mad about it for. Later I found out that the supervisor is directly responsible for the way girls under her work. If they loaf it shows on their record and she gets called to account by her chief supervisor, who has charge of a division of the board. The chief supervisor has to keep jacking up all the supervisors in her division because if the division doesn't make a good record, she gets called on the carpet by the chief operator. That's the way it is, everybody watching somebody else and the whole gang watching the poor operators and trying to get more speed out of them. It's the greatest speed-up system in the world.[27]

Pay scales for telephone operating did not provide sufficient compensation for Bell's demands. The 1910 U.S. Senate investigation of telephone companies found, for example, that Bell paid telephone operators rather meagerly. Of 16,258 operators for whom payroll cards could be obtained, 13,268 or more than 80 percent earned between twenty and forty dollars a month. Within this range, the largest cluster of operators included 4,562 women, or 28 percent of the total, who made between thirty and thirty-five dollars per month, about the same amount as women earned in manufacturing.[28]

While companies attracted workers with the prospect of quick promotion, mobility was usually possible only within the traffic department where telephone operators worked. Any woman could theoretically become a chief operator, supervisor, senior operator, monitor observer, or information operator. The pay scales were generally so low and the work of telephone operating so exacting and nerve-wracking that, in practice, most operators did not remain in the employ of the telephone industry long enough to secure substantially better positions. Women disliked the system of surveillance so much that they did not want to become its paid agents.[29]

As a result of the application of new twentieth-century business methods to telephone operating, employment that had been extremely desirable for women in the 1880s and 1890s became increasingly undesirable by 1910. In an era of limited work opportunities and high unemployment, telephone operating remained a valuable option for many women. Few other industries guaranteed females year-round employment.[30] Women's initially positive image of telephone operating usually faded once they acquired direct experience with the intense rate of speed, the oppressive system of supervision, and the long irregular hours. Steady work in a clean environment did not long outweigh the disadvantage of employment in a scientifically managed industry. Dressed for work in her finest shirtwaist and long skirt, the telephone operator may have occupied a higher social niche than the factory operative, but her working conditions and income evoked little envy from those women who had experienced corporate telephone operating.

As a result of the intense surveillance of telephone operators, the women had little opportunity for sabotaging work regulations in the manner of laborers and operatives in manufacturing. Telephone operators could not easily act as "a submerged, impenetrable obstacle to management's sovereignty," as unskilled workers characteristically were doing in the early twentieth century. It was typical of pieceworkers to control their own work pace regardless of company production goals.[31] Since telephone operators could not organize themselves against prescribed work rates as pieceworkers could, they had only two alternatives other than suffering in silence. They could either quit telephone work altogether or they could organize themselves into trade unions. Despite the apparent contradiction, increasing numbers did both—they quit *and* they organized.

OPERATORS' ACTIONS AND CORPORATE REACTIONS

As modern management changed the nature of telephone operating, women looked elsewhere for employment and labor turnover became a critical problem for phone companies. A 1920 survey of New York State telephone service, which starts with the war years, reported that of every three trainees, one dropped out during the training, the second left within the first year of work, and the third stayed only a little over a year. Furthermore, the report contended that women operators gained no marketable skills from telephone operating other than disciplined deportment. The small percentage of trainees who stayed with the company longer than twelve months reached their maximum pay scale after six years.[32]

Part of the high labor turnover stemmed from the obstacles confronting operators' efforts to deal collectively with their working conditions. According to the militant organizer and first national president of the telephone operators' union, Julia O'Connor, the industry's policy toward her organization was one of "extermination." She recalls that "[t]he organization of an operator's union was a signal for swift and sure hostilities on the part of the company. Discrimination ranging in refinement from enforced signing of 'loyalty' pledges to summary dismissal for union membership or activity was the universal fate of [a] new organization."[33] Despite such opposition some telephone operators continued their attempts to organize.

The trade union organization of telephone operators must be understood within the context of the widespread class conflict which characterized the period from 1909 to 1922. In these years, as David Montgomery has shown, "large scale strikes erupted whenever the level of unemployment fell off sufficiently to give the strikers a ghost of a chance of success."[34] Labor discontent grew principally in response to management's introduction of new efficiency schemes, such as premium pay plans, time-and-motion studies, personnel record keeping, and speed-ups. The spontaneous uprisings of unskilled workers from traditionally unorganized industries spread rapidly from workplace to workplace. Like the garment, meat-packing and textile employees who wrested concessions from their employers between 1909 and 1922, telephone operators also reacted to the increasingly oppressive working conditions in their industry.

Telephone operators' efforts to organize also reflected a dramatic change in the consciousness of women as wage earners. The labor revolt throughout the United States and the existence of a large-scale, well-coordinated feminist movement encouraged the women to create new options for themselves. In order to challenge managerial authority effectively, the women had to overcome a number of tangible and intangible obstacles. As females they had to dispossess themselves of the stereotypic view of women as docile, emotionally dependent, and incapable. As workers they had to find ways to communicate with each other. Pinned to a switchboard day in and day out, with supervisors watching over their shoulders and enforcing a no-talk rule, they had to make a special effort to develop trust and solidarity with one another. Since AT&T cultivated an image of telephone operators as public service employees, "heroines" who stayed on the job during all national or local emergencies, the women had to divest themselves of allegiance to the company and emphasize the primacy of their own needs. Of equal importance, they had to acquire new organizational skills and establish contacts with groups outside the telephone industry which might sympathize with them and help their cause.[35] Much to the employers' surprise, the women proved to be able bargaining agents for their own demands.

The successful union organization of telephone operators also depended on the development of effective leadership. Little is known about the many women operators who devoted themselves to organizing Bell employees. Forgotten are women such as Mary Quinn of Springfield, Massachusetts; May Matthews, Rose Sullivan, Mary E. June, Helen Moran, Mary Curley, Maude Foley, Grace Scribner, and Birdie Powers of Boston, Massachusetts; Rhoda Kerr, Irene DeLaney, Margaret Odlin, Blanche Johnson, and May Duffy of Seattle, Washington; Laura Polland of Grand Rapids, Michigan; and Kathryn McGovern of Providence, Rhode Island. Their names can be found in the occasional reporting of union elections and strike activities in various local newspapers of the day.³⁶ Their commitment, know-how, and spirit turned many an uncertain situation into a victory for striking switchboard workers.

Fortunately, by piecing together fragments of existing information, a portrait can be assembled of the most prominent woman in trade union organization efforts among telephone operators in the early twentieth century. Born in 1890 in Woburn, Massachusetts, Julia O'Connor had worked as a telephone operator for four years when in 1912 she and her co-workers took their first decisive steps toward improving their working conditions. Disgusted by the intensely nervous pace of her nine and one-quarter hour workday, O'Connor wanted to "humanize" telephone operating by redefining work schedules and shortening the length of the workday. From 1912 until her retirement in 1958, she devoted herself to trade union organizing. She headed the telephone operators' department of the International Brotherhood of Electrical Workers (IBEW) from 1912 to 1938. While serving the IBEW, she also worked actively with the National Women's Trade Union League, a feminist organization known for helping women wage earners to better their working conditions. According to newspaper accounts of early twentieth-century telephone strikes, O'Connor was an able, principled leader who courageously stood her ground in negotiating strikers' demands with presidents of Bell companies and with secretaries of executive departments of the federal government.³⁷

In 1912 O'Connor and her co-workers began their assault on the Bell System in Boston, the city of its origin. Angered by the adverse effects of the "split trick" and the bureaucratic complications of working through company channels, O'Connor and a group of toll and senior operators consulted with the Boston Women's Trade Union League (WTUL). As older, well-seasoned employees, the operators were sensitive to their rights as workers. The league put O'Connor and the other women in touch with the International Brotherhood of Electrical Workers, which had until that time organized only highly skilled male telephone workers. In five months the IBEW successfully enrolled 2200 operators into Sublocal No. 1 and submitted a list of hour, wage, and procedural grievances to New England Bell. In June 1912, after waiting two months for a response from the company, the operators decided that unless their demands were met they would walk off their jobs during the busy summer months. The company immediately agreed to an eight-hour day and the transfer of employees from the split trick to a regular evening or daytime shift after eighteen months of service.[38]

In March, 1913, eight months after the original agreement, the company had still not implemented the promised improvements, and the operators decided that a show of strength might be most likely to bring results. They appealed to local labor unions, the WTUL, the chamber of commerce and the mayor of Boston, as each had reason to sympathize with their efforts. Because of outside pressure, the company agreed to arbitrate the disputed issues but armed itself against a possible strike by importing 1200 strikebreakers from Midwestern and New England Bell exchanges. Guarded by detectives and company officials, the out-of-town operators were escorted to the most expensive local hotel, the Copley Plaza. With the strikebreakers comfortably housed, fed, and entertained at Bell's cost, public opinion noticeably favored the telephone operators' demand for a wage increase. Meanwhile, the Boston operators held to their agreement not to strike during the arbitration. Since company efforts to weaken the women's organization did not succeed, Bell was forced to grant the operators a wage increase and equal representation with the company on a labor adjustment board.[39]

With union recognition the women gradually obtained other improvements. In the first five years of their organization, they won an eight-hour day, two-week vacation, standardized pay scales with automatic increases, modification of the "split trick," and clearer grievance procedures. These Boston successes triggered rapid unionization among the telephone operators in Lynn, Springfield, Worcester, New Bedford, Framingham, Fitchburgh, Salem, Lowell, Lawrence, Haverhill, and a number of other Massachusetts cities. The struggle for telephone operators' rights also moved northward to Maine, New Hampshire, and Vermont, and as far west as the Rocky Mountain states.[40]

The new consciousness among women operators and their support from male workers, middle-class feminists, and the general public deeply concerned Bell. In order to preserve its monopolistic control of voice communications, Bell constantly needed capital

Figure 26. Julia O'Connor, trade union activist on behalf of telephone operators. Disgusted with the working conditions she experienced as an operator, O'Connor joined the union movement in 1912. She headed the telephone operators' department of the International Brotherhood of Electrical Workers from 1912 to 1938. *Courtesy International Brotherhood of Electrical Workers, Washington, D.C.*

for expansion, repair, and improvement of its nationwide service. The corporation, therefore, had always chosen to sacrifice employee salaries for the regular payment of a high dividend to its thousands of stockholders. The ground swell of operator discontent before the war, however, prompted Bell to initiate several new labor policies aimed at promoting good will, efficiency, and loyalty.

In 1912, Theodore Vail introduced a pension and disability plan and three years later a profit-sharing program. The pension plan was designed to give workers the illusion of future security while benefiting them as minimally as possible. Although the company did provide some coverage for sickness and retirement, the plan gave management discretionary power over the allocation of resources. The employees acquired no rights under the plan until management deemed them qualified. Typically the program favored officers over employees and men over women.[41] Similarly, Bell designed its stock program to promote a friendly spirit among workers by offering them a personal monetary investment in the company. According to AT&T's annual report in 1916, 43,000 employees held stock in Bell, but, like the other thousands of small stockholders, they lacked any effective voice in the corporation's affairs.[42] Bell also established a bonus plan which paid workers a set sum at the end of each year for outstanding service. By offering workers bonuses rather than wage increases, AT&T hoped to compensate for increased labor costs with higher productivity. While Bell employees saw some advantage to their first two programs, they categorically rejected the bonus system whenever they could.[43] By the time the United States officially entered the First World War, the struggle between welfare capitalism and trade unionism that had become so characteristic of other industries came to define labor-management relations in the Bell System as well.

THE WAR'S EFFECT ON THE BELL SYSTEM

The war had an immediate impact on the telephone industry, straining both its financial resources and its labor relations. With national focus on the development of human and material resources for wartime use, communications between Washington, D.C. and the rest of the United States assumed new importance.

Extensive toll lines had to be established quickly between the nation's capital and other major cities. Existing communications between Army and Navy headquarters and cantonments throughout the country had to be strengthened. Firms engaged in vital war material production needed supplements to their telephone equipment. Cables, poles, wires, switchboards, and associated apparatus had to be provided to the American Expeditionary Forces. As the telephone exchanges expanded, the need for telephone operators, engineers, and skilled workers grew rapidly. Consequently, prices for raw materials and labor soared.[44]

As service expanded and prices rose, Bell required additional capital to meet the wartime requirements which compelled company growth. Rising interest rates resulted in a poor market for both bonds and stocks, which corporations like AT&T ordinarily used to finance their operations. To meet this new situation AT&T issued short-term—rather than long-term—notes at high interest rates with the hope of refinancing at a later time at lower rates. In this way the company protected itself against unnecessary interest charges in the event of a subsequent decrease in the interest rate. Also, as the result of the war, the quoted value of AT&T stock dropped, reflecting general declines in all investment stocks. Since Bell companies had difficulty securing increased rates for telephone service from state regulatory commissions, net earnings of the operating companies declined all over the country. The newly increased rates on the money market prompted AT&T to examine carefully ways of raising capital internally by holding down current labor expenses.[45] When in the interest of wartime efficiency Postmaster General Albert Burleson assumed control of the telephone service in the District of Columbia, AT&T's board of directors began to give serious consideration to federal control as a vehicle for stabilizing Bell's financial situation during the inflationary period.

Both labor turnover and militancy grew during the war because telephone companies did not meet the market price for salaries during the high-wage period. The appeal of higher wartime wages in war-related industries made it virtually impossible for telephone companies to keep their exchanges staffed with experienced operators. Despite some increases in wages, premiums, bonuses, and free lunches, telephone operators nevertheless earned lower incomes than workers in other vital industries. Consequently, they turned a deaf ear to telephone company appeals to patriotism. The workers' eagerness to secure better-paying jobs elsewhere caused normal telephone service in most large cities to break down.[46]

The New York Telephone Company, for example, one of the largest and most important subsidiaries of American Telephone, could not keep its switchboards adequately staffed during the war. High labor turnover led the company to establish a separate employment department to secure operators. A special recruitment staff of over sixty persons even visited former operators and prospective recruits at home, but the number and quality of applicants decreased nonetheless. New York Telephone spent more than $37,000 on employment advertising for three months in 1919. Operators received bonuses to enlist new employees. During these same months 1,549 operators joined the company while 956 left its employ, resulting in a net gain of 592 workers. In the judgment of a New York Department of Labor report, such intensive recruitment was overly expensive. Of 19,862 applicants for the entire year of 1919, only 7,810 even qualified for work. During the war the company even operated a dormitory at its own expense to attract women workers. This experiment failed despite an expenditure of $33,000 for housing repairs and a maintenance cost of $67 per month per woman resident. Only 145 women actually took advantage of the free housing. From a financial standpoint, operators cost the company money until they had been employed at least a year. Few women remained in telephone operating that long.[47]

The composition of the female labor force in telephone work also changed during the war, as wartime employment opportunities opened for women in other fields. Although the majority of telephone trainees had always been young—single native-born women between the ages of sixteen and twenty-four—their average age reached an all-time low during the war. Of 816 female applicants in New York during December 1918 and January 1919, for example, 40 percent were sixteen and seventeen years of age and 71 percent were under twenty-one. These applicants included fifty-five children with working papers who were only fourteen and fifteen years old. While 77 percent of these young women had been employed previously, their industrial experience had been short and intermittent, the largest portion having had some office or factory experience. Fifteen percent had worked as sales clerks, elevator operators, or domestic servants. Twelve percent had had some previous experience in telephone operating. Their youth, their limited work experience, and their residence at home with their families made them poor candidates for the rapid pace and long hours of telephone work. Most young girls at New York Telephone sought employment elsewhere within twelve months of their hiring. Some left work to marry or quit in direct response to the overly strict discipline imposed by their female supervisors. Those who stayed with the job frequently disobeyed the instructions of company officials and often the orders of union officials as well. The absenteeism and even deliberate inefficiencies which plagued many industries during the war were particularly widespread, although sporadic, among women in telephone operating.[48]

Increasingly, worker dissatisfaction also found expression in direct action. The first strike of any magnitude involving telephone operators occurred in November 1917, when 3200 linemen and 9,000 women operators employed by Pacific Telephone, a Bell subsidiary, withdrew their service in California, Oregon, Washington, Idaho, and Nevada. As skilled workers the men had been unionized for some time, whereas the women had no union affiliation prior to the summer of 1917. The major challenge to the company came when the men requested a wage increase for the women in conjunction with a renewal of their own agreement. The men called the strike, which the women promptly joined when the company refused to recognize their new operators' union.[49]

The government's wartime labor machinery responded to the Pacific Telephone strike. The President's Mediation Commission endeavored to obtain a postponement of the walkout pending its effort to resolve the dispute. The California workers obeyed the request for a delay, but those in Oregon and Washington struck. Misinformation about the President's Mediation Commission, suspicion of the company, and a radical labor atmosphere encouraged the Northwest walkout.[50]

Some of the company's subordinate officials attributed unpatriotic motives to the strikers, a charge which only added to the workers' bitterness.[51] Charges of disloyalty on the one side were matched by accusations of profiteering on the other. An investigation by the President's Mediation Commission of the lumber, telephone, meat-packing and copper-mining industries in the Middle and Far West found that national disaffection was widespread among workers. The report stated that

it is difficult for the workers to appreciate fully that the war is being prosecuted for democratic ideals when many industries at home resort to such Prussianisms as deportations, hanging, horse-whipping . . . and the government not only fails to prosecute such acts but also resorts to suppression of labor movements, IWW prosecutions and . . . arrest without trial of other workers. It is somewhat difficult for workers to appreciate the call to loyalty when their strikes to achieve industrial justice, following employers' refusals to arbitrate, are condemned in the name of patriotism and employers organize so-called 'loyal leagues' to defeat the workmen's organizations.

The report concludes that workers would not allow employers to continue reaping huge profits without gathering a portion of the harvest for themselves.[52]

Fearful of the potential power of the women operators' movement, Pacific Telephone refused to recognize the operators' union and tried to compel its employees to withdraw from it. The company offered male workers a separate contract without the women. In response, the men's locals along the entire Pacific Slope and the organized telephone operators of the Northwest struck jointly against Pacific Telephone. The workers finally won a combined settlement involving the International Brotherhood of Electrical Workers, Pacific T&T and the federal government.

Although the telephone workers won significant wage increases, the heart of the agreement proved detrimental to the operators' interests because it failed to provide a direct and workable method for resolving grievances. The company took advantage of this situation by instructing its supervisors to harass members of the operators' union as an example to other would-be members.[53] Resentment against the company smouldered at Pacific Telephone and Telegraph until the workers spontaneously struck in 1919, when they crippled phone service for six weeks.

GOVERNMENT CONTROL OF PHONE SERVICE

Bell subsidiaries like Pacific Telephone and Telegraph soon welcomed government operation of their wires because of the financial benefits and improved leverage for coping with labor difficulties that federal control provided. In effect, government control meant corporate self-regulation under the protection of the Wilson administration. Federal control of the wires from August 1, 1918 until July 31, 1919 allowed the telephone industry to increase its revenues and to use the coercive powers of the government to challenge the International Brotherhood of Electrical Workers. In short, federal control guaranteed to the industry the kind of stability which it could not easily obtain on its own.

In many ways the operation and impact of federal control of the telegraph and telephone wires resembled government operation of the railroads during the war. In both industries, established officers of the companies acquired official status as representatives of the federal government, while the government assumed all financial obligations for the firms. While the rail executives used their new positions to achieve industrywide standardization and rationalization, federal control of the wires permitted Bell telephone executives to increase their financial control of the industry. In both the railroad and telephone fields, federal control overrode local regulation. In the case of telephone service, this change eliminated a factor that had helped keep down costs. Just as the Railroad Administration forced railroad shippers to absorb the war-generated cost increases, the Wire Board put the same burden on individual and commercial telephone subscribers.[54]

The joint resolution of Congress placing telephone operation under federal control left the financial negotiations completely up to Bell officials and the postmaster general. N. T. Guernsey, general counsel of AT&T, pronounced the final contract obtained from the federal government a "distinct triumph for Mr. Vail."[55] According to economist N. R. Danielian, the wartime arrangement accommodated Bell's needs very well.

The Federal government . . . agreed to pay AT&T 4½ percent of the gross operating revenues of the telephone companies as a service fee; to make provisions for depreciation and obsolescence at the high rate of 5.72 percent of plant; to make provision for the amortization of intangible capital; to disburse all interest and dividend requirements; and in addition, to keep the properties in as good a condition as before. Finally, AT&T was given the power to keep a constant watch on the government's performance, to see that all went well with government operation, by providing that the books of the Postmaster General would be at all times open for inspection.[56]

While telephone officials publicly called the agreement with the government "fair," they might more honestly have called it extremely advantageous. Officials from the telephone companies were able to get Postmaster General Burleson to institute service connection charges which the Bell System had been trying to obtain for a number of years from state regulatory commissions. At Vail's urging, Burleson raised long-distance rates by 20 percent. The postmaster general also increased local telephone rates during the period of federal control. When local authorities balked at the new charges, the federal government banded together with AT&T to defend them. Federal control provided for the secure maintenance of the Bell System and, more importantly, legitimated the rate structure that had made AT&T so enormously wealthy. Bell thus achieved under the aegis of federal control a number of objectives which private operation had not been able to accomplish. When the Bell Company resumed control of its telephone system, the federal government absorbed a $13,000,000 deficit which had accrued during the period of federal control. The company also gained a $42,000,000 annual rate increase.

In one respect, government operation of the rails and wires differed significantly. While railroad labor found William McAdoo's administration sympathetic to the efforts of trade unions to exercise control over their working conditions, Albert Burleson's board fought against collective bargaining for telephone workers. Although railroad workers were never fully satisfied with their wartime wage increases, they did achieve national wage standardization and full implementation of the eight-hour day with time-and-one-half for overtime as well as permanent labor relations machinery for settling disputes. Far from providing guarantees of the right to organize and bargain collectively, Postmaster Burleson suspended these rights even where they had been explicitly accepted by the telephone companies before the war. He administered the wires the way he moved the mails—with an autocratic hand. While workers looked to the federal government for a guarantee of their industrial rights, telephone officials, secure in the approval of Postmaster General Burleson, inaugurated more destructive tactics against the labor organizations than they had dared to employ while under private control. As one observer noted, Burleson's rule was one of "terror" against workers.[58]

The labor policies of the Railroad and Wire Administrations represent opposite sides of the same coin. Government labor policy varied according to the importance of the industry, the strength of the union, and the outlook of the government official. The enormous importance of the rails to the successful prosecution of the war, and the railroad workers' fifty-year tradition of trade union organization and militancy, forced the government to cater to rail workers' interests. In contrast, the Wire Administration's hostility toward organized labor reflected the traditional antiunion sentiments of the Bell Company and took advantage of the relative weakness of the International Brotherhood of Electrical Workers. As a young union with strength mainly in the building trades, the IBEW could not easily match the strength of the telephone companies.

The particular role of Postmaster General Albert S. Burleson in the Wilson administration also contributed to the abuse of telephone workers during federal control. By the time that Burleson, a lawyer and large cotton plantation owner, assumed responsibility for operating the telephone service, he had earned a reputation as a controversial politician. After serving fourteen years as a U.S. Congressman from the Austin District of Texas, Burleson became postmaster general in 1913 and devoted his considerable energies to reorganizing the Post Office Department.[59] Soon after Burleson took office in the Wilson government, his policies embroiled the Post Office in conflicts with many groups. He expanded parcel post facilities, forcing many express companies out of business. His readjustment of the cost of second-class mail brought him into conflict with newspaper and magazine publishers. His relations with organized labor became charged when he refused to allow postal employees to affiliate with any labor organization and had those workers who threatened to strike promptly indicted and prosecuted. Burleson's antiunion sentiment so incensed organized labor that in 1917 the AF of L passed a harshly worded resolution condemning Burleson for his "unpatriotic" and "oppressive" labor policies.[60] As a superpatriot, Burleson vigorously enforced and defended censorship of the mails during the war. Nothing pleased him more than pursuing dissenters. During the international crisis he assisted the Department of Justice, the Bureau of Intelligence of the Army and Navy, and the Department of Labor in collecting information about labor activities.[61] As he publicly admitted after the war, his aim had been to "destroy all evils at one time."[62] Burleson's attitudes foreshadowed the antilabor and antiradical sentiments which would sweep the country in the 1920s.[63]

Given Burleson's attitudes toward labor, it is easy to understand why the Wire Administration operated so very differently from the Railroad Administration. Most importantly, it allowed labor no real voice. To manage the telephone and telegraph wires during the war emergency, the Post Office Department established a Wire Control Board, which consisted of three government officials plus AT&T president Vail as an advisor. The department also established an Operating Board of four telephone and telegraph officials. Labor relations were relegated to a third body, the Commission of Inquiry, whose five members were mandated to investigate the working conditions and wages of telephone and telegraph employees. Only one member of the commission, Julia O'Connor, represented workers, while two members represented the companies and two supposedly neutral government appointees represented the public interest. Neither the Wire Control Board nor the Commission of Inquiry seemed to know its respective duties and jurisdictions. Each offered only bland assurances of good will to workers without establishing machinery for resolving grievances. Unlike the Railroad Wage Commission, which thoroughly investigated wages and working conditions and recommended the establishment of railroad adjustment boards to hear specific cases, the Commission of Inquiry failed to act decisively. Without funds and authority, the commission held only a few meetings and made a few weak attempts to accumulate and analyze wage data on the pretense of developing a plan. Frustrated and angry with this affront to wage earners, Julia O'Connor resigned from the Commission of Inquiry in March 1919 and called for a Congressional investigation of the Wire Administration. She faulted Burleson for prohibiting companies from negotiating directly with their employees, allowing the Pacific Telephone and Telegraph Company to break its 1917 agreement with the IBEW, and actively discouraging workers from joining trade unions. In her parting statement O'Connor publicly declared that "to remain longer on that commission would be a betrayal of the interests of the workers."[64]

The Wire Administration's attitude toward telephone operators' problems was incendiary. It was not until June 1919, almost a year after government control had begun, that the postmaster general directed each telephone company to designate an officer to hear labor complaints. The local companies' authority to make adjustments remained vague, while many local officials refused in any case to adjust serious grievances. Under such circumstances labor unrest and dissatisfaction grew to crisis proportions.[65] Although Burleson broke most of the strikes by using the force of federal command, the labor revolt testifies to the women's audacity. Burleson usually warned the strikers that if they failed to return to work within twenty-four hours they would not be reinstated. He demanded from the companies the names and addresses of the strikers, presumably to be used for a blacklist. His threats worked until New England telephone operators resisted such intimidation in April 1919. Some examples from the immediate postwar period, drawn from the records of the Post Office Department, illustrate the kinds of problems which operators faced.[66]

MILITANCY AMONG OPERATORS

In December 1918, Kansas telephone operators struck in support of a fired Wichita supervisor who had circulated a petition requesting increased wages. One hundred forty-two striking operators and supervisors claimed that the firing was unjustified, even if the supervisor, Waity Lela Phipps, had committed an infraction of the company rules by leaving her post to circulate a petition. Far more important to the strikers was Phipps' membership in the operators' union and the fact that she had two brothers fighting abroad and a mother who was dependent on her support. The strikers collectively demanded her reinstatement. A committee of operators admitted to the district superintendent that Miss Phipps had indeed broken the rules, but they demanded her reinstatement nonetheless. The women argued that while the company did not ordinarily allow operators to leave their posts without permission, it had been customary for operators to leave their stations at the company's behest to circulate petitions pledging money for war funds or for other causes sanctioned by company officials. The company wanted to discipline the supervisor, they argued, only because her petition demanded a wage increase.[67]

Expressions of sympathy for the Wichita women came from widely diverse groups, including the Council of Churches, the Brotherhood of Railway Clerks, the Boilermakers' Union, and one hundred local businessmen who were anxious for a quick settlement. The issues of union recognition and increased wages assumed the greatest importance because of the threat of a citywide strike by organized labor which would endanger the community's normal operations. Burleson sided with the company in the interest of maintaining discipline among the telephone operators. He refused to investigate the situation until pressed to do so by the telephone operators' union and government officials who sympathized with the women—Felix Frankfurter, Mary Anderson, and William B. Wilson. Burleson's Wichita investigator, however, confirmed the postmaster general's judgment.[68]

Not all the Wichita operators agreed with the strikers. Eighty-nine of the two hundred thirty-one operators, a little over 38 percent, stayed at work during the dispute. The strike leaders from the women's union had been employed by the telephone company for two to eight years. Over that time they had grown increasingly dissatisfied with supervisory personnel and low wages. Other workers who had been employed just as long, however, felt indebted to the company for its welfare benefits, particularly its sick pay, vacations, and steady employment, and showed little interest in union membership. Since discontent over working conditions had grown from the inception of the union, potential members feared that the union might take direct action to change working conditions and that all members would consequently suffer dismissal.[69]

The Post Office inspector who investigated the Wichita situation concluded that the supervisor had willfully committed an infraction of the rules, that the union organizer had used the situation to further the recognition and growth of the newly organized telephone operators' union, and that two labor leaders, members of the typographical union employed by Wichita's two leading newspapers, had systematically manufactured sympathy for the strikers in the columns of daily papers. The inspector argued that the mayor, chief of police, and city attorney took the operators' side in the dispute because of the threat of a strike by all the city's labor unions. The Southwestern Bell Telephone Company remained adamant against the strikers. The company even had to hire a private detective agency to protect old and newly hired nonunion operators since the local police refused to offer their services to the company. With the power of federal sanction and the absence of the threatened citywide strike, the union operators lost their struggle.[70] Only four months after the Wichita defeat, operators on the East Coast would prove to be a more equal match to the Bell System and the Burleson administration.

When the New England Union of Telephone Operators set a strike vote for the morning of April 15, 1919, they had behind them eight continuous months of efforts to avoid a strike. For the previous seven years they had been able to settle every dispute without a strike. Unlike other telephone companies, New England Bell had also been able to control its rate of labor turnover. The company's conciliation machinery, which included labor representatives, had defused worker dissatisfaction and had ably averted crises. Nearly a decade of relatively smooth labor-management relations had developed a partnership capable of withstanding even the economic strains of the world war.[71] New England Bell proved receptive to the use of arbitration machinery because the telephone operators' organizational strength centered in New England. It is quite possible that the East Coast branch of Bell feared a series of strikes similar to those which had crippled New England's metal trades during the summer of 1915. From New England Bell's standpoint, workers' representation was a small concession to ensure production.

Burleson's federal policies upset normal telephone operations in New England by eliminating the successful machinery for resolving disputes. The general manager of New England Bell, in the fashion of telephone managers throughout the country, informed the workers that their requested wage increase could not be negotiated because of federal control. From September 1918 until April 1919, New England telephone operators sought some method of securing consideration for their proposed new wage schedule, but Burleson's antiunion policies made the fundamental right of collective bargaining an overriding issue. It took a crippling five-day, five-state strike by nearly all of New England's telephone operators, and denunciation of Bell and Burleson by business and political leaders, before Burleson conceded the employees' right to be heard.[72]

Most of the nine thousand New England strikers had never experienced a protracted work stoppage, but they early demonstrated their militancy by taking a strike vote in February 1919. In one local, three thousand women voted for the strike, opposed by only twenty-eight dissenters. On April 13, the New England operators met in Boston's Faneuil Hall and set the strike date and time. Even though their male co-workers tried to discourage them on the grounds that women would get hurt in a strike, they proceeded with their plans. Promptly at seven a.m. on April 15, the night shift operators left the exchanges to strike. According to May Matthews, a dedicated and highly spirited union organizer for the telephone operators, labor solidarity carried the strike to a successful conclusion. The women acted as one. At a mass meeting the first day of the strike,

[a] crowd was coming downstairs and in that crowd one person caught my eye, a woman who had been in the [telephone] service thirty-eight years. She was surrounded by a lot of kids who were laughing and thought it the greatest joke in the world, but her face was serious and set. We had to win—not for the kids, but for women like this one who had given everything. As she came close to me I said, "Oh, I think it is wonderful for you to be here!" She said: "No more wonderful than the other girls. I am satisfied my fate is in good hands." A woman who could have been my mother satisfied to leave her fate in our hands! Those are the things that made us fight.[73]

The big Boston organization, Local 1A, boasted a regular attendance of four thousand girls and women at its daily strike meetings.

In turn, New England's male phone workers from the IBEW joined the strike two days after it began.

In Washington, Postmaster General Burleson accused the women of disloyalty to the government in time of international crisis. To this charge the women indignantly replied that almost each of them had a loved one in the armed services, that they all belonged to the Red Cross, and had all purchased Liberty bonds. When Burleson threatened to replace the women with soldiers, one hundred women picketed the telephone exchanges accompanied by male relatives, who appeared in armed forces uniforms. The head of the procession carried a military service flag. The soldiers declared that they had not expected to come home to fight against women.[74]

In other ways the picket line itself demonstrated community solidarity. Boston policemen served the pickets instead of the company. Not a single arrest occurred throughout the strike. When it rained, policemen gave their coats to the strikers. When women wanted lunch, the policemen fetched food for them. Such unusual cooperation may well have stemmed in part from the operators' and police officers' common Irish heritage, in some instances from their common family ties, and from their mutual interest in trade union organization. The unity of these working people also derived from their shared animosity toward the Burleson administration and the Bell System. When the postmaster general actually brought strikebreakers into Boston, hotel waiters and taxi drivers refused to serve them. Janitors, watchmen, and elevator operators employed at one of Bell's Boston exchanges decided to strike in solidarity with the operators rather than perform any services for the strikebreakers. Office boys detailed to act as night operators also quit the company's employ. Students in the telephone company's school for operators, although unorganized, joined the strike when they were asked to enter telephone exchanges as strikebreakers. Operators reported that their success at Boston's South Station exchange was due to the help of the New Haven Railroad employees who "tipped off" the pickets about the arrival of strikebreakers. Boston firemen extended moral and financial support to the strikers, while women doctors volunteered free medical service to the striking telephone operators. Any person who entered Bell's employ as a telephone operator in local exchanges during the strike met the disapproval of neighborhood residents. One lone strikebreaker in South Boston was followed home from a telephone exchange by a crowd that grew to 250 children and adults. All along the way the young woman was greeted with hisses and jeers that could be heard for blocks.[76]

Elsewhere in New England, support was showered upon the strikers. In a Lynn, Massachusetts telephone exchange, a boy scout who insisted on working as a strikebreaker was stripped of his uniform and expelled from the organization by a chief scout master. In Brockton, Massachusetts, union labor cheered the strikers and sent them money. In the Bangor, Maine business office of New England Telephone and Telegraph, unorganized clerks and stenographers publicly declared their sympathy for the telephone strikers. Noticeable exception to this community support for the strikers included several Boston society women and a number of Smith College students who wanted to express their allegiance to the government, as well as antifeminists like the president of the Massachusetts Anti-Suffrage Association.[77]

Merchants also rallied to the operators' side. In Boston's Chinatown, restaurant owners fed three hundred women strikers at tables behind the local telephone exchange for five days in a row. In Plymouth, Massachusetts, businessmen treated the girl pickets to boxes of chocolates and warm drinks. Further north in Nashua, New Hampshire, prominent merchants and citizens flooded the strikers' headquarters with gifts of ice cream, cake, fruit, and candy. The daily newspapers recorded the strikers' side of the story. When the strike finally ended, even bankers and brokers showered the women with confetti.[78]

The postmaster general's plan for resolving the strike provided that requests for wage increases first be submitted to the general manager of the company; he, if he saw fit, could submit a secret recommendation to the operating committee, a group made up exclusively of AT&T and Western Union officials. This committee, in turn, would submit a recommendation to the Wire Control Board and ultimately to Burleson for his approval. Under this plan the workers would have had no opportunity to air their grievances. On behalf of the operators, Julia O'Connor rejected this proposal and on the fifth day of the walkout the strikers forced the post-master general to send his first assistant to Boston.[79]

On the afternoon of April 19, a committee representing all of New England's telephone workers went into conference with the superintendents of plant and traffic, the general manager, and the president of the New England and Providence Telephone Companies. The postmaster general had been forced to permit his representatives to deal directly with labor union representatives. The union emerged from the negotiating session victorious. The final settlement provided for a restoration of the principle of collective bargaining and a wage increase retroactive to January 1, 1919. In contrast to other telephone strikes during Burleson's rule, all the strikers regained their former positions without loss of seniority rights. Most importantly, Burleson's power had been effectively challenged for the moment. Julia O'Connor pronounced the strike a complete success.[80]

While the New England strike had been a rebuke to governmental maladministration and a wage victory, it had an even broader significance. It clearly demonstrated to telephone workers throughout the country that it was possible for them to win some modifications in their working conditions through collective action; in effect, it set a successful precedent and as such, it encouraged remarkable trade union growth among southern telephone operators in Louisville, Atlanta, and Norfolk, and among midwestern operators in Cleveland, Youngstown, and St. Louis. The International Brotherhood of Electrical Workers chartered more than one hundred locals in the course of 1919, effectively tripling its membership in the telephone operators' department. Previously, it had taken seven years to establish one hundred locals.[81]

Before the return of the wires to private control, telephone operators successfully wrested one major concession from their adversary Albert Burleson. The telephone companies' and the government's joint resistance to unionization engendered mounting bitterness among operators, repairmen, and linemen—a bitterness which manifested itself in a call for a general strike of all telephone workers in June 1919. The Post Office Department became truly alarmed. In a last-minute effort, the brotherhood requested that the American Federation of Labor Convention, then in session, send an official delegation to meet with Burleson. To avert the general walkout, the postmaster general reversed himself and now guaranteed to telephone workers every basic right for which they had struggled. Order 3209 defused the impending strike. Its issuance on the very eve of restoring the wires to private control, however, lacked the force it might have carried earlier.[82]

THE REASSERTION OF CORPORATE CONTROL

Telephone companies in the Midwest, South, and Far West responded to the successful New England strike of April 1919 by disregarding Burleson's new policy of union recognition for telephone operators and by immediately increasing their antiunion efforts. In June 1919, for example, Bell Telephone of Cleveland used harassment and bribery to prevent women from joining the telephone operators' union after six hundred women signed membership cards at one union meeting. The Cleveland Telephone Company used its chief operators and supervisors to obtain union resignations from the operators, threatening to dismiss any woman who refused to withdraw from the union. The Cleveland commissioner of conciliation reported that

in one exchange there were about 15 [operators] mostly imported from Chicago, who would take their seats, one at a time, alongside of a girl who had refused to resign her membership in the union, and they would [each] call . . . the foreman in charge of that branch and talk loud enough for that girl to hear, and say they did not want to sit beside her because she belonged to the union. This was done in numerous cases, as many as 19 of them doing it within an hour to one girl.

At the same time, company officials asked the operators to join the company employees' association, promising them a dinner date with their new membership.[83]

In another instance, three sixteen-year-old operators in St. Louis testified to a Post Office inspector in June 1919 that they had been harassed by their chief operator for participating in a one-day strike for higher wages. In sworn testimony before a notary, one of the girls reported that the chief operator had offered her a free room at a local hotel and a twenty-five dollar bonus if she did not strike. When the young operator refused, the supervisor fired her.[84]

In the summer of 1919, a wave of trade union enthusiasm swept practically every state in the southeastern United States. Southern telephone operators had grown dissatisfied with their wages and had been inspired by the victories of organized labor in other industries. While the growing southern labor movement supported the telephone operators' efforts, company officials, acting with the tacit support of the postmaster general, nipped the new worker organizations in the bud by harassing individual union members and forcing premature strikes. In Atlanta and Macon, Georgia telephone company officials ordered workers' pay envelopes stuffed with a leaflet which denounced unions and implied that dismissal would soon be the fate of union members. Like the August 1919 Jacksonville, Florida walkout, where operators and craftsmen had to return to work on an individual basis with forfeiture of all seniority rights, practically all the southern telephone strikes ended in defeat for the workers. Embittered by such treatment, employees with the most seniority, who had usually been the strongest union advocates, refused to return to work after the strikes. Their decision to leave their companies considerably weakened the future reconstruction of the unions.[85]

The six-week Pacific Coast strike—from June until August 1919—accomplished no more than the southern strikes of the same period. The telephone workers in California, Oregon, and Washington weakened their own position by failing to ratify an agreement granting a retroactive wage increase and union recognition that had been worked out between representatives of the Pacific Telephone Company and the IBEW. Suspicion, bitterness, and dissension among the workers and the inexperience of telephone operators worked to their disadvantage. Without an agreement, the strikers were left to the mercy of the company. While the workers struck, the company made a concerted effort to establish company unions in place of the IBEW locals. The company lured the strikers back to work with a guarantee of their seniority rights in exchange for a forfeiture of their union membership. Bell sealed its power by demanding that former and new employees sign a company loyalty pledge.[86]

Although the operators' union grew steadily in the first two years after the resumption of private control of the wires, the union's officers spent most of their energies trying to protect their organization from company penetration and outright competition by company-sponsored unions. By late 1921, with two hundred locals and twenty-five thousand women in the United States and Canada —slightly more than one-sixth of all telephone operators—the union claimed its highest membership.[87] By 1924 the large wartime and immediate postwar membership had dwindled to a mere twelve hundred.[88] Weaknesses in the telephone union and the superior adaptability of corporate power short-circuited the operators' challenges to managerial authority.

The International Brotherhood of Electrical Workers must ultimately share some responsibility for the weakness of the women operators' organization. Telephone operators had remained outside trade union protection until unionized men in the industry felt their own interests threatened by the unorganized status of their female co-workers. As telephone switchboard work became increasingly female, the industry's skilled mechanics could no longer afford to ignore the organization of women. In 1909, when the Commercial Telegraphers' International Union began to organize women telephone operators, the IBEW first asserted its claim to represent them. Since a strike of operators often involved the sympathetic support of linemen, telephone installers, cable splicers, and switchboard men, the IBEW justified its claim over operators. Despite their gesture, the men had feared that women's numerical strength would lead to "petticoat rule" of the union. The women did in fact present a challenge to male power; the Boston operators' local alone had a membership of 2,500 within a year of its organization and ranked third numerically among all the locals of the brotherhood. At the insistence of men who opposed the admission of operators' locals on the grounds that the telephone operators had no place in an organization of skilled men, women's telephone locals were restricted in 1918 to a separate department of the union. The women interpreted the indefinite powers and purposes of the

department as an attempt to deny them the right to participate in
the brotherhood's deliberations while still requiring them to submit
to the brotherhood's laws. The operators fought the creation of the
department as they previously had fought limited voting rights and
representation, until the international's vice-president accorded the
department full self-government and turned over all operators'
dues to the women's department.[89]

Women operators thus found themselves a part of the union
while remaining separate from it, an arrangement which turned out
to be a mixed blessing. On the one hand, the women's organization
gained some trade union protection from an established union. On
the other hand, separatism in practice allowed the women the
opportunity to establish their own policies, but it also limited them
to insufficient financial resources. A policy of charging lower dues
for women, which initially enabled women earning low wages to
join the union, provided only meager resources for sustaining the
organization. The telephone operators' department sank into debt
as the large number of wartime and postwar strikes, both authorized and unauthorized, drained its funds. While the IBEW promised
to allocate ten thousand dollars to the telephone operators' department in 1920, the IBEW's own financial and administrative difficulties prohibited it from paying the money. The lack of funds
severely damaged the department's organizational efforts. With
only one paid organizer, the large wartime membership could no
longer be adequately served.[90]

To the problem of union structure and finances must be added
the special difficulty of organizing girls and young women who
thought of themselves as temporary workers. As young unmarried
workers, most telephone operators had no abiding interest in a
union which concerned itself with dues, meetings, rules, and regulations. To temporary workers, temporary measures seemed most
appropriate. In contrast to the rank-and-file operators, the female
strike leaders and ardent union enthusiasts were senior members of
the operating force and were several years older. Thousands of
women and girls followed their lead because they agreed that their
working conditions needed to be changed. Since operators faced
similar conditions throughout the United States, one strike easily
sparked a nationwide chain reaction. Women eagerly participated

in strikes to win immediate improvements, but they did not appreciate the need for sustaining their union in calmer periods. Locals grew steadily from 1913 to 1920, but they never coalesced into a strong national trade union. Membership expanded dramatically during the war, but due to a decided lack of follow-through, the strength of numbers was not translated into a solid structure of national organization and local chapters. In the end, only a significant minority of operators ever joined the IBEW.

Internal strife in the Brotherhood of Electrical Workers further injured the women's locals. In the summer of 1920, after failing to gain separate departmental status within the IBEW, the New England telephone men seceded from the IBEW and set up the International Brotherhood of Telephone Workers. Leaders of the new organization then attempted to lure rank-and-file operators away from the parent organization. Since the Boston telephone operators' local ranked first in the country, the secession of the New England men struck at the heart of the department. Riddled with factionalism of its own, the telephone operators' department could not maintain its loyalty to the IBEW.[91]

The telephone companies struck the final blow to the telephone operators' organization. Through the introduction of company unions and technological changes, as well as the continued use of a spy system and severe discriminatory tactics, Bell finally won its struggle for unionism without unions.[92] In June 1919, in the face of a coast-to-coast strike wave, Bell established its first company union with the encouragement of Albert Burleson. At the 1927 American Management Association Conference, E. K. Hall, vice-president of AT&T, recalled the origins of his company's plan.

Where did we get this idea . . . of improving relations? Well we got it when the industry woke up . . . right after the war and realized the extent to which the human element in industry in this country was indifferent to the job; seething with unrest; lacking interest in the job; suspicious of the management; and in many cases literally hostile to the industry. . . .[93]

Eight years after the introduction of employee representation Hall could proclaim that the new management policy had successfully eliminated the threat of strikes in the telephone industry.

From the very beginning, the plan was carefully orchestrated and executed. After management experts diagnosed labor disaffection as a reaction against the rigid application of scientific management policies, they designed employee representation as an antidote to the corporation's almost single-minded emphasis on productivity. According to Hall, the new management-labor relations acted as "a supplementary form of organization for reviewing and correcting the mistakes which have been made in the fast work of the production organization."[94] In an effort to decrease workers' antipathy towards the inflexible, hierarchical system of corporate organization and control, Bell mobilized its employees in a new way. It began to focus more attention on the worker instead of the design of the work. Since labor discontent had been effectively expressed through trade union activity, Bell developed a scheme to replace labor organizations based on class identification and conflict with cooperative associations founded by management for its own benefit. The first employee representation committees were, therefore, introduced into strongholds of IBEW organization. As a substitute for unions, Bell built an organizational pyramid which distributed responsibilities among branches, districts, divisions, departments and general boards. Members paid little or no dues and held no membership meetings of their own. The various Bell companies paid the organizations' operating expenses and reimbursed appointed officers for time spent in association functions held on company premises. They also regularly convened meetings to discuss matters of concern to workers, such as wages, work practices, carfare, and improvement in tools and methods, as well as subjects of interest to the company, such as general reviews of business conditions, company welfare programs, accident prevention, thrift, and ways of increasing revenue through employee effort. This two-tract system, as Hall called it, doubly served management's needs. It functioned as a safety valve for employee grievances, and it gave management a chance to mold workers' attitudes toward their employer.[95]

Bell applied the insights of group psychology to the development of its plan. Management was particularly interested in using such means to help reduce the high turnover and militancy among telephone operators. The company was eager to secure the operators' participation in employee representation conferences. To help overcome the women's mistrust and reticence, managers were told to maintain at least a two-to-one ratio between operators and company representatives. This ratio would "help" operators express their thoughts about wages, hours, and supervision. In his instructions to corporate executives, the general traffic manager of Bell of Pennsylvania warned that

a management chairman should be careful not to twist a representative's remarks so as to make it appear that she said something which she does not mean. The way a representative expresses her thought may imply an attitude on her part which is far from her intention. The fault may be with the way the idea is expressed, and the management chairman should help her to express it better rather than to take advantage of the inadequate expression to place the representative or her constituents in a false light.[96]

By subtly reformulating an operator's comments, the management representative tried, in effect, to reshape the woman's feelings toward her job. Such thought control even extended to the official version of conference minutes which management took responsibility for issuing to all operators.

Bell did not confine employee representation to its internal operation. Part of the new labor policy involved the enlistment of workers to serve their employer as public relations agents in their leisure hours. (No doubt Bell learned a lesson from the bitterness expressed toward the corporation by entire communities during the postwar strikes.) This policy had two broad aims: to provide employees with a closer company identification and to secure workers' assistance in the political efforts to create a sympathetic response for company policies from the general public, courts, commissions, and legislatures. AT&T invited its employees and officers to join business, social, scientific, professional, and athletic associations to further company involvement in local affairs. The Bell subsidiaries paid all membership fees for their employees and computed these as operating costs. It particularly encouraged participation in chambers of commerce, farmer and labor organizations, civic associations, improvement societies, church clubs, neighborhood groups, and consumers' leagues.[97] In practice, then, employee representation meant company representation inside and outside the workplace.

It is difficult to assess the effects of company unionism on telephone operators. From the point of view of a dedicated trade unionist like Julia O'Connor, employee representation "cost the operators nothing in time, in thought, in effort, in study and [was] worth exactly that amount in results."[98] From the point of view of AT&T, the new management plan enabled the company to curb labor militancy and develop better public relations. While the employee representation committees provided an opportunity for workers to discuss their views about working conditions, wages, and company policies, the management's perspective often dominated the conferences. As Hall informed other corporation executives, "The more we take time to explain to our people what orders mean, why they are issued, where they fit into the general scheme of things, the more intelligent acquiescence we get in the orders."[99]

John Schacht has recently rendered an appraisal of company unionism. He believes that company unionism did indirectly benefit labor. By bringing workers from different departments together, imbuing them with a sense of interdependence, and providing them with a forum for developing leadership and organizational skills, Schacht argues that the employee representation committees offered "an institutional base capable of transformation into a viable industrial union movement." At the same time he admits that company unionism also served for fifteen years to reinforce workers' subservience to Bell, to discredit action as a means of bargaining for changes, and to retard self-conscious working-class organization.[100] That social gatherings like beach parties symbolized the new labor relations of the 1920s and early 1930s is itself a telling commentary on the effectiveness of company unionism. Not until the passage of the National Industrial Recovery Act in 1933 did employee representation begin to lose its grip on the industry.

Bell did not depend solely on company unions to meet the challenge of telephone operators' wartime and postwar mass insurgency. As a result of high labor turnover, deteriorating service, and the increasing use of telephone service in daily American life, AT&T accelerated the introduction of labor-efficient dial methods for placing telephone calls. Technological innovations thus became yet another means of stabilizing the work force. From 1925 to 1940, the number of employees required to service a thousand telephones decreased 36 percent. The number of operators dropped more sharply than the number of other personnel. In 1940, only 60 percent as many women were needed per thousand telephones as in 1925. Since the number of telephones and the number of telephone conversations, however, increased more than 50 percent between 1925 and 1940, the greater volume of telephone business absorbed most operators affected by the advent of dial equipment. Nevertheless, the number of women employed in Bell's traffic departments decreased 10 to 15 percent in the fifteen-year period. The change signalled possibilities for ultimately replacing a still larger portion of telephone operators with machines.[101]

CONCLUSION

This analysis of the rise and fall of the telephone operators' militancy suggests the need to examine carefully the underlying as well as immediate causes for changes in workers' attitudes toward their employment. Rationalization of telephone communications initially set in motion telephone operators' direct challenge to managerial authority; later it made possible a broad-ranging, nationwide labor policy which undermined unionization among the operators. By making telephone operating mechanical, routinized labor with little possibility for flexible work practices, the introduction of scientific management set the stage for women's discontent. Wartime working conditions propelled their reaction to assume forms of open, even militant expression. Because federal control of the wires during the war so thoroughly benefited telephone corporations, the standard historical judgment that World War I aided labor's efforts to organize into trade unions must be qualified. The war made Bell's monopoly of telephone communications more secure and faciliated the destruction of independent labor organizations.

Initially hired for their reliability and docility, many of the girl and women operators proved their employer's expectations wrong. These women did not willingly become cogs in the corporate wheel. Women entered telephone operating in the early twentieth century with no tradition of collective work practices or union affiliation. Their sensitivity to Bell's rigid system of work, their awareness of the larger class conflict around them, and their disgust for the state's repression during wartime encouraged them to undertake massive—although brief—opposition to one of the most powerful corporations in the United States. That women could only momentarily achieve their goals, even with the assistance of their male allies, indicates how powerful the Bell System had become. Corporate power had gained enormous flexibility over and against female employees. Although telephone operators showed few signs of militancy in the 1920s, their presence in the labor movement reappeared in the 1930s when different economic and political developments triggered the reconstruction of independent labor organizations along new lines.

6   Conclusion

The foregoing chapters study women as home-front workers during the wartime. The special circumstances of America's World War I economy can be seen to have accentuated certain trends already apparent in women's employment patterns and also to have accelerated several managerial innovations in the organization and control of work in various employment settings. The case studies reveal a variety of patterns in relations between management and labor as well as among co-workers in machine shops, foundries, railroad yards and offices, streetcar companies, and telephone exchanges. These analyses permit some generalizations about women's employment opportunities before, during, and following the war, as well as about women's attitudes toward their work and toward trade unions. Other conclusions can be drawn regarding the principal reasons for conflict and for cooperation between male and female wage earners. It can further be noted how the war emergency gave impetus both to the government and to individual female reformers—the latter sometimes acting from within the government—to redefine and defend particular aspects of paid employment for women. In sum, this study of women, war, and work provides an historical prism through which fundamental economic trends and endemic social attitudes may be refracted to reveal the color, shape, and direction of changes in the nature of work for all workers and for women workers in particular. In this way the wartime crisis allows perspective on the wider confluence of impersonal forces and personal choices which have confronted

American workers in the long era of economic rationalization that began before the First World War and has continued well beyond it.

THE WAR, JOBS, AND TRADE UNIONISM

At the time of the First World War, the American economy was undergoing dramatic changes, changes which had broad social ramifications. Business consolidation and expansion, the development of new industries, the increasing standardization and specialization of work, and the intensification of workplace supervision were changing the nature of factory, office, and other work in a manner which transformed innumerable jobs into interchangeable tasks. This development, called skill dilution, enabled employers to shift workers from one area of labor to another with unaccustomed ease. It also facilitated the introduction of more women into the work force and moved the location of their paid employment. Women were already shifting from the fields of domestic service and light manufacturing into clerical work, sales, and telephone operating when the war-induced labor shortage created a host of unprecedented opportunities for them. Native and foreign-born white women as well as black American women took advantage of the new situation to improve their economic status during the war.

Women proved themselves to be shrewd exploiters of the wartime economy. With their men away at war and while wartime inflation squeezed their household economies, women assumed new domestic responsibilities. Those single and married women who were accustomed to contributing the wages they earned outside the home to their families' welfare now actively sought better-paying jobs. A distinct minority of women wartime workers were new entrants into the labor force. Most women searched for employment in their own neighborhoods or hometowns, while others migrated alone or with their husbands and children from one region of the country to another in search of new job openings. The long-distance migration particularly characterized black women's wartime experience. For most women, wartime job changes involved a shift from one traditionally female job to another. For a significant minority of women, job vacancies occasioned by wartime economic circumstances opened male-dominated jobs for the first time. Employers had no trouble attracting females adventurous enough to enter the male work domain. For such women the war economy offered a welcome alternative to their accustomed pattern of routine, dead-end employment. They carefully weighed and evaluated their options, choosing those jobs which best suited their economic needs, family responsibilities, personal interests, and physical stamina.

Fully aware of the temporary nature of the unusual wartime conditions, women tried to make the most of their opportunities. At times, women's efforts to take full advantage of the unprecedented labor market had a decidedly self-exploitative cast. In metal-working factories women worked at break-neck speeds to earn as much as possible and demonstrate their capabilities to their employers. In railroad yards women common laborers strained themselves physically to handle "men's work." Well-paid clerical workers in railroad offices tolerated sexual harassment from their male supervisors in order to retain their high wages. Black women accepted dirty, dangerous, and physically demanding jobs in manufacturing in order to gain admittance to the world of industrial labor. Such women did what they thought was necessary to increase their pay packets.

When it seemed advantageous to do so, women joined trade unions as a way of protecting their jobs. Female trade unionists constituted a decidedly small portion of the female work force. Special circumstances shaped women's understanding of the role that a trade union could play in particular industries. Female railroad clerks had benefited substantially from their union's wage negotiations with the wartime Railroad Administration and hoped union affiliation would protect their gains in the postwar period. Women common laborers and machine shop employees in the railroad industry sought union membership to demonstrate to their male co-workers that they would not willingly undercut men's standard wages and working conditions. Women streetcar conductors followed a similar approach for the same reason. Telephone operators joined the union in their field to win a better grievance procedure and higher wages from the federal Wire Administration, which was operating the Bell System during the war emergency. Uniting all these women was a common desire to improve their wages, working conditions, and job security.

Of the women who actively sought union affiliation, those most interested in the benefits of collective bargaining shouldered substantial economic responsibilities for their families. Unlike the single telephone operators who saw themselves as temporary workers, and so had no long-term commitment to building a union at their companies, married women trolley conductors, railroad common laborers, clerks, and machine shop employees saw no end in sight to a need for their wage contributions at home. Consequently, their interest in trade union membership was directly related to their desire for decent permanent employment.

CO-WORKER RELATIONS

In addition to viewing the war from the perspective of women's employment choices and attitudes toward their work, a major part of this study has focused on solidarity and conflict between women and men wage earners. Cooperation between female and male co-workers occurred where employment was rigidly segregated along gender lines and the two sexes did not compete for the same jobs. When men did not fear losing their jobs to women and vice-versa, both men and women were more likely to see each other as allies and to cooperate for the common betterment of their working conditions. Thus, rigid work separation on the basis of gender ironically laid the foundation for employee cooperation across gender lines. Such was the case among male laundry drivers in Kansas City, who encouraged laundresses at their places of work to strike for higher wages and improved working conditions. Male telephone installers, line splicers, and repairmen throughout the country either initiated unionization campaigns among female telephone operators or supported those efforts which women began on their own. Job segregation, on the one hand, and a shared animosity towards their employers in the Bell System and the Wire Administration, on the other hand, were the principal factors which united male and female telephone employees.

Although gender-segregated employment laid the foundation for male-female cooperation, it did not guarantee worker solidarity. Cooperation was not assured wherever men and women worked in different departments or at different jobs in the same industry. The willingness of workers to join forces developed gradually and only in some fairly well-defined circumstances. During the war the high cost of living, the obvious importance of workers' efforts for meeting production goals, and the government's official recognition of collective bargaining encouraged a common identity and sense of purpose among workers, regardless of gender, ethnic identity, or skill level. An employer's decision to withhold a pay increase, refuse recognition of a union, or speed up production provided the crucial catalyst for male-female solidarity. These different developments encouraged workers to take stock of their employment experiences and financial needs. In each instance involving cooperation between men and women employees, a particular course of events had taught workers that their best strategy lay in unity, if only on a temporary basis. The changing responses of male telephone workers toward the 1919 New England telephone operators' strike illustrate this point. The men lacked confidence in the women's organizational ability and degree of commitment, so the men remained aloof from the operators' confrontation with the Wire Administration until they became convinced that the women had organized in sufficient numbers to present a formidable challenge to their common employer. Then and then only did the men lend their support.

Despite all the circumstances that might have served to unify wage earners, conflict between different groups of employees emerged in many industries during the war. General economic and social factors as well as particular local circumstances often determined worker relations. Men reacted with special hostility toward women when women were used to implement a policy for the dilution of requisite labor skill for the performance of a particular job, when women entered all-male occupations, or when women were used as scabs or as a reserve labor army which employers could call upon to force a lower standard of wages and working conditions upon male workers.

In all workplaces, the perceived threat of women's economic competition presented the most formidable obstacle to men's acceptance of women workers' introduction into new fields. The men feared that the employment of women would lead to lower wages for the entire labor force in their industries. They often viewed the introduction of women into male strongholds as sinister attempts on the part of businessmen to increase profit margins.

Intraclass conflict between men and women especially characterized those industries where trade unionism had gained a firm foot-
ing and had resulted in substantial wage increases for men.

Male hostility to women's employment went beyond the matter
of wages. Union men also worried that women's introduction
would be accompanied by changes in the nature of working conditions. Their fears were often well founded. In machine shops,
women's admittance to welding and molding metal parts was in
fact accompanied by the dilution of craft skills. In railroad offices,
supervisors set up special training programs in claims adjustment
work exclusively for the benefit of women. In streetcar conducting,
the hiring of women occurred during a period of company experimentation with technical devices to decrease the number of conductors needed to serve urban transit.

Social perceptions of women's proper work role also played a
part in shaping male-female relations. In the early twentieth
century most male wage earners believed that women should not
work outside the home, but if necessity made their paid employment crucial to family survival, they should earn their living only in
those jobs deemed suitable for women. From the men's point of
view, women did not belong in certain occupations. Common
attitudes would restrict to men such diverse jobs as welding, molding metal parts, mining coal, conducting streetcars, and investigating freight claims. Men boldly and proudly defended the tradition
that barred women from such employment.

All these factors converged to turn men and women into adversaries. Under these circumstances there was little that women could
do to convince men that cooperation might be a more effective
deterrent to the erosion of their jobs than mobilizing against
women's employment.

Men's antagonism to the introduction of women into their work
took many different forms. Men protested the hiring of women to
their employers, struck against women's employment, grudgingly
admitted women into their unions for the war's duration, and
invoked or sponsored protective legislation to bar women from
working in the same fields or on the same terms as men. In nearly
all the cases examined in this study, the men's actions resulted in
women's dismissal or an end to the hiring of women in the affected
employment fields.

Only under unusual circumstances was male antagonism towards women transformed into cooperation. As was demonstrated in the case of the Kansas City conductors and motormen, men and women could become allies when the men understood that unity with their female co-workers served their own interests. A citywide labor-management struggle demonstrated the importance of labor unity to the male conductors and motormen. But Kansas City workers were an exception to the rule precisely because men and women wage earners had developed an unusually close and congenial relationship before the war. The mutual support of male and female labor movement activists that had developed in Kansas City before the war provided a powerful precedent for local wartime cooperation, but the pattern was not common elsewhere.

THE FEDERAL GOVERNMENT

The role of the federal government in shaping women's wartime work experiences varied as much as the relations of men and women wage earners. The government's policy toward labor, regardless of gender, varied from one industry to another. Its policies toward women must be viewed within this larger context. Although the federal government assumed full control over the railroad and telephone industries during the war, the labor policies of the two responsible agencies were diametrically opposed. The one key factor which helps to explain these policy differences is the relative strength of the labor unions in each industry.

Older and stronger, the railroad unions had won considerable concessions from the federal government before the government took control of the roads during the war. Consequently, the demands of organized railroad workers for improvements in wages and working conditions during the war commanded much more weight than those of newly organized telephone employees. The very takeover of the railroads by the government had resulted in part from the threat of a nationwide strike by railroad employees. As yet but weakly organized, telephone workers did not have the same clout as their railroad counterparts. Only after telephone employees had organized more extensively during the war did the government begin to take their demands seriously.

Differences between the railroad and telephone unions had a profound effect on women's working conditions and opportunities. Women railroad employees benefited from the nationwide employment standards established by the Railroad Administration. The problems faced by these women, as individuals and as a group, focused on the willingness of their supervisors, male co-workers, and women reformers to allow women the full measure of opportunity proclaimed in the rulings of the Railroad Administration. The opposite was true for telephone operators. Their conditions of labor deteriorated during the period of federal control because the Wire Administration refused to grant them the right to collective bargaining and a responsive grievance procedure. Segregated in the telephone traffic department, women operators had congenial relations with male telephone workers in other company departments; the men's concerns were equally frustrated by the Wire Administration. Men and women telephone workers shared frustrations while men and women railroad workers shared benefits during the war.

In the case of streetcar transit, no federal takeover occurred. Instead, the National War Labor Board issued separate decisions for each complaint submitted by trolley employees. Thus, wages and working conditions differed from community to community. Women streetcar conductors received no special protection from the government during their conflicts with transit union locals. Even when the board issued rulings favorable to women, such as according them equal pay for equal work, the federal agency did not have the power to enforce its decision. Consequently, transit unions and companies set their own policies for the treatment of women employees. Under these circumstances, women were forced to rely upon the good will and public support of women's civic and feminist organizations to keep their jobs.

WOMEN REFORMERS

Women reformers played an important role in the history of women's wartime employment. On the positive side, middle-class women proved to be strong allies of wage-earning women. In the controversies over women's employment as streetcar conductors, they worked vigorously behind the scenes and in public to influence local and federal government leaders in favor of the working women's cause. The reformers' efforts on behalf of women conductors put the National War Labor Board on notice that women could not be expected to support the war effort on the one hand, while being denied the right to work at employment of their own choice on the other. At the same time, middle-class women's staunch support served to strengthen the wage earners' commitment to feminist ideals. In the railroad industry and the Ordnance Department of the Army, women reformers used their new government positions to work for the enforcement of equal pay provisions and decent working conditions for women. Along with women wage earners in the railroad and trolley industries, telephone operators received the support of women's organizations in their confrontations with the government and their companies over working conditions.

The most important women's organization from the perspective of cross-class cooperation among women was the National Women's Trade Union League. The local leagues in Boston and Kansas City each played a critical role in building a bridge between the concerns of middle-class and working-class women as well as between these two groups of women and male trade unionists.

The wartime relations of middle-class women and wage-earning women also had a less positive side. In a fashion similar to that of male workers, women reformers believed that females should be barred from certain types of employment for moral and physical reasons. Despite the sentiments of women workers to the contrary, social reformers claimed that they knew what was best for women wage earners. Middle-class women also expressed a strong class bias towards their laboring "sisters." As the case studies of the Ordnance Department and the Railroad Administration make clear, women reformers, no less than their male counterparts, expected women workers to conform to their notions of proper work habits, dress, and performance. Although the reformers' vision of the work ethic was infused with feminist ideals, it was still first and foremost a middle-class work ethic. As such it was conservative, class-biased, and manipulative.

The overall assessment of women reformers must weigh the two sides of the reformers' commitment. When the scales tipped in favor of support for women workers' job actions or women's right to nontraditional jobs, wage-earning women saw social reformers as strong allies. When the scales tipped in favor of the enforcement of protective legislation or strict work rules, distinct class concerns drove a wedge between the two groups.

THE WAR AS HISTORICAL PRISM

The study of women's work during the First World War not only illuminates many facets of the domestic mobilization, but also differentiates aspects of American economic rationalization in the period encompassing the war. In particular, the study affords perspective on the development of hierarchical work arrangements and fragmentation of the labor process. It further indicates the diverse effects of these trends on skilled craftsmen and on unskilled female wage earners. In effect, the war experience of women workers is a prism for historical vision: through it one can discern broad patterns of prewar and postwar changes in the nature of work, in labor management, and, not least, in the daily lives of both male and female workers.

Although the changing nature of work has received much scholarly attention in recent years, little has been said about its impact on women and their employment. From the point of view of skilled craftsmen, fracturing of the labor process in the late nineteenth and early twentieth centuries resulted in the degradation of work and constituted an affront to the integrity of workers. In the case of women, for whom it can be argued that wage work has been degraded at least since the introduction of the industrial system in the early nineteenth century, the nature of work outside the fields of agriculture and domestic service has, with few exceptions, been monotonous and dead-end. At the same time, women have looked upon the availability of employment in new work settings as welcome opportunities. Thus, when the wartime spurt in economic rationalization suddenly opened a multitude of new, though largely "degraded" job opportunities, women wage earners eagerly sought these positions as relative improvements over the employment previously available to them. For women, the variety of work changed more than its intrinsically degraded character, and this fact was more than compensated for by higher pay packets, the psychic satisfaction of mastering new challenges, and—during the war—the sense of patriotic service.

Through an understanding of working women's experience, it is clear that the war situation strengthened both capital and labor. Employers received federal support for employment plans to utilize women in new jobs and workplaces. When hiring women for nontraditional tasks could be justified in terms of the national emergency, employers dared to challenge craftsmen and semiskilled unionized male workers. At the same time, the federal government's official recognition of the right of workers to bargain collectively strengthened organized labor and increased its legitimacy within the American economy. The benefits to women workers in this process, however, were mixed and frequently ended upon demobilization or soon after. Organized workers encountered stubborn limits to their power in the 1920s, when management plans for employee representation stifled unions' development. A new set of relations among management, labor, and government emerged after the war.

The wartime experience of women workers had already demonstrated the possibility of work force control through management programs of economic rationalization and schemes of labor relations. The wartime stimulus to unionization did not remain unchallenged. While the war emergency enhanced labor's bargaining power and secured women new opportunities, the war's end revealed the entrenched strength of management and the relative weakness of women workers against managerial rationalization strategies, on the one hand, and the hostility of male workers, anxious to maintain their own decreasing margins of craft integrity and job security, on the other. The conjuncture of women, war, and work thus provides a mosaic of insights over time, not fixed by gender, limited to labor, or even conditioned solely by the presence of peace or war.

Abbreviations

AASERE	Amalgamated Association of Street and Electric Railway Employees of America
AF of L	American Federation of Labor
AT&T	American Telephone and Telegraph Company
B&O	Baltimore and Ohio Railroad
CPD	*Cleveland Plain Dealer*
DL	Department of Labor
DL&W	Delaware, Lackawanna and Western Railroad
DUR	Detroit United Railway
EAD	Employers' Association of Detroit
ERJ	*Electric Railway Journal*
FMCS	Federal Mediation and Conciliation Service
IAM	International Association of Machinists
IBEW	International Brotherhood of Electrical Workers
LC	Library of Congress
MFWU	Molders' and Foundry Workers' Union
M&C	*Motorman and Conductor*
NA	National Archives
NWLB	National War Labor Board
NWTUL	National Women's Trade Union League
PO	Post Office Department
RG	Record Group
RR	Railroad
SUR	*Seattle Union Record*
UL	*Union Leader*
USES	United States Employment Service
UTO	*Union Telephone Operator*
WB	Women's Bureau
WSS	Women's Service Section
WTUL	Women's Trade Union League

Notes

INTRODUCTION

1. J. Stanley Lemons, *The Woman Citizen: Social Feminism in the 1920's* (Urbana, 1973); William H. Chafe, *The American Woman: Her Changing Social, Economic, and Political Roles, 1920-1970* (New York, 1972); Peter Gabriel Filene, *Him/Her/Self: Sex Roles in Modern America* (New York, 1974); Lois W. Banner, *Women in Modern America: A Brief History* (New York, 1974); Carol Hymowitz and Michaele Weissman, *A History of Women in America* (New York, 1978).

2. Aileen Kraditor, *The Ideas of the Woman Suffrage Movement, 1890-1920* (New York, 1965); William O'Neill, *Everyone Was Brave: The Rise and Fall of Feminism in America* (Chicago, 1969).

3. O'Neill, *Everyone Was Brave*. A number of studies were published during the war and immediate postwar period about the mobilization of women for voluntary activities as well as paid labor. See Ida Clyde Clarke, *American Women and the World War* (New York, 1918); Harriet Stanton Blatch, *Mobilizing Woman-Power* (New York, 1918); Mabel Potter Daggett, *Women Wanted: The Story Written in Blood Letters on the Horizon of the Great War* (New York, 1918); Emily Newell Blair, *The Woman's Committee, United States Council of National Defense, An Interpretative Report, April 21, 1917 to February 27, 1919* (Washington, D.C., 1920).

4. Frank Grubbs, *The Struggle for Labor Loyalty: Gompers, the AF of L, and the Pacifists, 1917-1920* (Durham, 1968); Ronald Radosh, *American Labor and United States Foreign Policy* (New York, 1969); William Preston, *Aliens and Dissenters: Federal Suppression of Radicals, 1903-1933* (New York, 1966); H. C. Peterson and Gilbert Fite, *Opponents of War, 1917-1918* (Madison, 1957); K. Austin Kerr, *American Railroad Politics, 1914-1920* (Pittsburgh, 1968); Melvin Urofsky, *Big Steel and the Wilson Administration* (Columbus, 1969); Robert D. Cuff, *The War In-*

dustries Board: Business-Government Relations during World War I (Baltimore, 1973).

5. The notable exception to the traditional focus on leaders is David Brody, *Steelworkers in America: The Nonunion Era* (Cambridge, 1960), which skillfully probes the effects of technology, market structure, corporate strategy, public policy, and ethnic and class tensions on the lives of steelworkers. His analysis of the war years is a model for understanding the impact of the international conflict on the consciousness of workers in a particular industry.

6. See for example the historical investigations in Martha Blaxall and Martha B. Reagan, eds., *Women and the Workplace: The Implications of Occupational Segregation,* published as *Signs,* 1, no. 3, pt. 2 (Spring 1976): 87-179.

7. Margery Davies, "Women's Place Is at the Typewriter: The Feminization of the Clerical Labor Force," *Radical America* 8 (July-August 1974): 1-28; Susan Porter Benson, "'The Clerking Sisterhood': Rationalization and the Work Culture of Saleswomen," *Radical America* 12 (March-April 1978): 15-32; Susan Reverby, "The Search for the Hospital Yardstick: Nursing and the Rationalization of Hospital Work," in *Health Care in America: Essays in Social History,* eds., Susan Reverby and David Rosner (Philadelphia, 1979): 206-225; Barbara Melosh, "'Skilled Hands, Cool Heads, and Warm Hearts': Nurses and Nursing, 1920-1960," (Ph.D. diss., Brown University, 1979).

8. An initial version of this book's examination of the railroad industry (chapter 3) appeared as "Women Workers and World War I: The American Railroad Industry, A Case Study," *Journal of Social History* 9 (Winter 1975): 154-177. The current presentation in chapter 3 fully supersedes and corrects aspects of the earlier version.

9. David Montgomery, "Workers' Control of Machine Production in the Nineteenth Century," *Labor History* 17 (Fall 1976): 485-509; David Montgomery, "Qeul standards? Les ouvriers et la réorganisation de la production aux Etats-Unis (1900-1920)," *Le Mouvement Social* 102 (Janvier-Mars 1978): 101-127; Daniel Nelson, *Managers and Workers: Origins of the New Factory System in the United States, 1880-1920* (Madison, 1975); Daniel T. Rodgers, *The Work Ethic in Industrial America, 1850-1920* (Chicago, 1978); James B. Gilbert, *Work without Salvation: America's Intellectuals and Industrial Alienation, 1880-1910* (Baltimore, 1977); Harry Braverman, *Labor and Monopoly Capital: The Degradation of Work in the Twentieth Century* (New York, 1974). For a similar commentary on the scholarship on women and industrialization, see Thomas Dublin, *Women at Work: The Transformation of Work and Community in Lowell, Massachusetts, 1826-1860* (New York, 1979), pp. 1-13.

CHAPTER 1.   FROM AFAR AND NEAR:
             PATTERNS OF CHANGE IN
             WOMEN'S WORK

1. Richard Titmuss, *Essays on "The Welfare State,"* 2d ed. (Boston, 1969), p. 78.

2. These biographical fragments are drawn from the Records of the United States Railroad Administration, Records of the Women's Bureau of the Department of Labor, and the Records of the National War Labor Board which are deposited in the National Archives, Washington, D.C.

3. Alba M. Edwards, *Sixteenth Census of the United States: 1940, Population: Comparative Occupation Statistics for the United States, 1870-1940* (Washington, D.C., 1943), p. 92; Joseph A. Hill, *Women in Gainful Occupations 1870 to 1920,* U.S. Bureau of the Census, Census Monograph no. 9 (Washington, D.C., 1929), pp. 75-84; U.S., Department of Labor, Women's Bureau, *The Share of Wage-Earning Women in Family Support,* Bulletin no. 30 (Washington, D.C., 1923), pp. 60, 84; Caroline Manning, *The Immigrant Woman and Her Job,* U.S. Department of Labor, Women's Bureau Bulletin no. 74 (Washington, D.C., 1930), pp. 52, 56; Gwendolyn Salisbury Hughes, *Mothers in Industry: Wage-Earning by Mothers in Philadelphia* (New York, 1925), pp. 6, 22, 79-89.

4. The most recent thorough analysis of this phase of American economic growth may be found in Alfred Chandler, Jr., *The Visible Hand: The Managerial Revolution in American Business* (Cambridge, Mass., 1977).

5. Daniel Nelson, *Managers and Workers: Origins of the New Factory System in the United States, 1880-1920* (Madison, Wis., 1975), pp. 4-9.

6. David Montgomery, "Quel Standards? Les ouvriers et la réorganisation de la production aux Etats-Unis (1900-1920)," *Le Mouvement Social* 102 (Janvier-Mars 1978): 101-127; David Montgomery, "Workers' Control of Machine Production in the Nineteenth Century," *Labor History* 17 (Fall 1976): 485-509.

7. Janet M. Hooks, *Women's Occupation through Seven Decades,* U.S. Department of Labor, Women's Bureau Bulletin no. 218 (Washington, D.C., 1947), pp. 94-101, 119-123, 132-133.

8. H. Dewey Anderson and Percy E. Davidson, *Occupational Trends in the United States* (Stanford, Calif., 1940), p. 19. All of the examples of gender segregation can be found in Elizabeth Beardsley Butler, *Women and the Trades: Pittsburgh, 1907-1908,* The Pittsburgh Survey, ed. Paul Underwood Kellogg, vol. 1 (New York, 1909).

9. Grace Coyle, *Present Trends in Clerical Occupations* (New York, 1928), pp. 11, 14, 33; Elizabeth Kemper Adams, *Women Professional Workers* (New York, 1921), pp. 233-235; Lee Holcombe, *Victorian Ladies*

at Work (Hamden, Conn., 1973), pp. 142-149; Margery Davies, "Women's Place Is at the Typewriter: The Feminization of the Clerical Labor Force," *Radical America* 8 (July-August 1974): 1-28.

10. Hooks, *Women's Occupations through Seven Decades*, pp. 74-79.

11. Coyle, *Present Trends*, pp. 13-14. See Michel Crozier, *The World of the Office Worker*, trans. David Landau (New York, 1973), p. 17 for a similar observation about the impact of mechanization and specialization on French clerical workers in the 1950s.

12. Susan Porter Benson, "'The Clerking Sisterhood': Rationalization and the Work Culture of Saleswomen in American Department Stores, 1890-1960," *Radical America* 12 (March-April 1978): 41-55; Elizabeth Beardsley Butler, *Saleswomen in Mercantile Stores: Baltimore, 1909* (New York, 1912); Hooks, *Women's Occupations through Seven Decades*, pp. 83-87.

13. U.S., Department of Labor, Women's Bureau, *The Change from Manual to Dial Operation in the Telephone Industry*, Bulletin no. 110 (Washington, D.C., 1933), p. 1; Marion May Dilts, *The Telephone in a Changing World* (New York, 1941), pp. 101-105; John E. Kingsbury, *The Telephone and Telephone Exchanges: Their Invention and Development* (New York, 1915), p. 318; U.S., Bureau of the Census, *Census of Electrical Industries: 1922, Telephones* (Washington, D.C., 1922), p. 52.

14. Hill, *Women in Gainful Occupations*, p. 36; David M. Katzman, *Seven Days a Week: Women and Domestic Service in Industrializing America* (New York, 1978), pp. 44-94.

15. Hill, *Women in Gainful Occupations*, pp. 33-34.

16. William H. Chafe, *The American Woman: Her Changing Social, Economic, and Political Roles, 1920-1970* (New York, 1972), p. 135; Mary V. Dempsey, *The Occupational Progress of Women, 1910 to 1930*, U.S. Department of Labor, Women's Bureau Bulletin no. 104 (Washington, D.C., 1933), p. 7.

17. Alexander Bing, *War-Time Strikes and Their Adjustments* (New York, 1921), pp. 6-7; Preston William Slosson, *The Great Crusade and After, 1914-1928* (New York, 1930), pp. 12-21; Paul H. Douglas, *Real Wages in the United States, 1890-1926* (New York, 1930), p. 178.

18. U.S., Department of Labor, Women's Bureau, *The New Position of Women in American Industry*, Bulletin no. 12 (Washington, D.C., 1920), pp. 37-142; Consumers' League of the City of New York, *A New Day for the Colored Woman Worker: A Study of Colored Women in Industry in New York City* (New York, 1919), pp. 5-6; Consumers' League of Eastern Pennsylvania, *Colored Women as Industrial Workers in Philadelphia* (Philadelphia, 1920), pp. 8-10; D.N. Crosthwait, Jr., "Making up the Labor

Shortage," *Industrial Management* 55 (May 1918): 412-413; Women's
Trade Union Conference, 4-5 October 1918, U.S. Department of Labor,
Women in Industry Service, Record Group 86, National Archives, Washington, D.C. The transcript of the Women's Trade Union Conference contains information from trade unionists about the recruitment of women in
different parts of the United States.

19. The files and transcripts of the National War Labor Board hearings
involving the employment of women indicate that women were acutely
aware of wartime job opportunities. For example, see Dockets 19, 20, 130,
233, 258, 265, 444, 491, NWLB, RG 2, NA, Washington, D.C. Information about black women's efforts to secure better employment can be
found in Amy Hewes, "Employment of Women in the Clothing Factories
of the Charleston Navy Yard," Committee on Women in Industry of the
Advisory Board of the Council of National Defense, 10D-B1, RG 62, NA,
Washington, D.C.; Mary Roberts Smith, "The Negro Woman as an Industrial Factor," *Life and Labor* 8 (January 1918): 7-8; Forrester B. Washington, "Reconstruction and the Colored Woman," *Life and Labor* 9 (January 1919): 3-7; Lula McCalep to Mr. George J. Kleffner, 22 September
1918, Office of the State Director, 1917-1919, Omaha, Nebraska, Box 24,
File M, United States Employment Service, RG 183, NA, Washington,
D.C. McCalep's letter of inquiry to the U.S. Employment Service about
new work opportunities is one of the very few letters from wage earners to
the government employment service still in existence. Only the Omaha,
Nebraska records have survived the disposal of the USES records by the
National Archives.

20. Women's Bureau, *The New Position of Women*, p. 77.

21. Ibid., pp. 93-116.

22. Dempsey, *The Occupational Progress of Women*, p. 19.

23. U.S. Railroad Administration, *Annual Report of Walter B. Hines,
Director General of Railroads, 1919* (Washington, D.C., 1920), pp. 77-79;
Mary B. Cleveland, "Women Stenographers for Government Service,"
Committee on Labor, 10A-C3, Council of National Defense, RG 62, NA,
Washington, D.C.

24. Dempsey, *The Occupational Progress of Women*, p. 8; U.S., Department of Labor, Women's Bureau, *Negro Women in Industry*, Bulletin
no. 20 (Washington, D.C., 1922), p. 5.

25. Peter Gottlieb, "Making Their Own Way: Southern Blacks' Migration to Pittsburgh, 1916-1930" (Ph.D. diss., University of Pittsburgh,
1977), pp. 129-130; Chicago Commission on Race Relations, *The Negro in
Chicago: A Study of Race Relations and a Race Riot* (Chicago, 1922), p.
392. In 1910, 54.7 percent of black women worked for wages as compared

to 19.2 percent of native-born white women and 21.7 percent of foreign-born women. The 1910 figures are drawn from U.S., Bureau of the Census, *Fifteenth Census of the United States: 1930*, vol. 5: *Population: General Report on Occupations*, Table I: 74.

26. Hill, *Women in Gainful Occupations*, p. 114.

27. Consumers' League, *Colored Women as Industrial Workers*, p. 38; Gottlieb, "Making Their Own Way," pp. 124-131; Smith, "The Negro Woman," pp. 7-8.

28. Chicago Commission on Race Relations, *The Negro in Chicago*, p. 387. See also Consumers' League, *Colored Women as Industrial Workers*, p. 29.

29. Women's Bureau, *Negro Women in Industry*, pp. 34-35, 37.

30. Consumers' League, *A New Day* underscores both the positive and negative aspects of black women's wartime employment in factories.

31. Women's Bureau, *Negro Women in Industry*, p. 17.

32. Consumers' League, *Colored Women as Industrial Workers*, pp. 13, 27.

33. Ibid., p. 23.

34. Ibid., p. 22; Helen Ross, Supply Department, Missouri Pacific RR, Kansas City, Missouri, 29 October 1918, File 148, WSS, RG 14, NA, Washington, D.C.

35. George E. Haynes, *The Negro at Work During the World War and Reconstruction: Statistics, Problems, and Policies Relating to the Greater Inclusion of Negro Wage Earners in American Industry and Agriculture* (Washington, D.C., 1921), p. 125.

36. Consumers' League, *Colored Women as Industrial Workers*, pp. 21, 29, 40-41; Consumers' League, *A New Day*, p. 17.

37. Women's Bureau, *Negro Women in Industry*, pp. 34-35, 37-38; Haynes, *The Negro at Work*, pp. 126, 128.

38. Helen Ross, Freight House, Santa Fe RR, Topeka, Kansas, 28 October 1918, File 55, WSS, RG 14, NA, Washington, D.C.

39. Helen Ross, Warehouse Laborers, Pennsylvania RR, Pittsburgh, Pennsylvania, 8 March 1919, File 188b, WSS, RG 14, NA, Washington, D.C.; Edith Hall, Blockhouse, Pennsylvania RR, Kane, Pennsylvania, 22 November 1919, File 189, WSS, RG 14, NA, Washington, D.C.; Helen Ross, Office of Master Mechanic, Pennsylvania RR, Juniata, Pennsylvania, 10 February 1919, File 181b, WSS, RG 14, NA, Washington, D.C.; Helen Ross, Storeroom, Pennsylvania RR, 4 and 12 March 1919, File 188b, WSS, RG 14, NA, Washington, D.C.

40. Douglas, *Real Wages*, p. 178; Bing, *War-Time Strikes*, p. 204n.

41. National Industrial Conference Board, *Wartime Changes in Wages, September 1914 — March 1919*, Research Report no. 20 (Boston, 1919), pp. 100-106.

42. Consumers' League, *Colored Women as Industrial Workers*, p. 8.

43. Grosvenor B. Clarkson, *Industrial America in the World War: The Strategy Behind the Line, 1917-1918* (Boston, 1923); Benedict Crowell and Robert F. Wilson, *How America Went to War* (New Haven, 1921), vol. 1, *The Giant Hand: Our Mobilization and Control of Industry and National Resources, 1917-1918*; Robert Cuff, *The War Industries Board: Business-Government Relations During World War I* (Baltimore, 1973).

44. George Creel, *How We Advertised America* (New York, 1920); Harold Lasswell, *Propaganda Technique in the World War* (New York, 1927); James R. Mock and Cedric Larson, *Words that Won the War* (Princeton, 1939); Minna Lewinson and H. B. Hough, *A History of the Services Rendered by the American Press During the Year 1917* (New York, 1918).

45. Mary Barnett Gilson, *What's Past is Prologue: Reflections on My Industrial Experience* (New York, 1940), pp. 162-165; Captain C. R. Dickinson, Report on Work Done in Ordnance Plants for Industrial Stimulation, 18 July 1918, Box 58, File World War I—Labor, Mary van Kleeck Papers, Sophia Smith Collection, Smith College Library, Northampton, Massachusetts.

46. Newspapers such as the *Boston Herald, Cleveland Plain Dealer, Detroit Free Press*, and *New York Times* regularly reported women's paid and unpaid contributions to the war effort. See also Ida Clyde Clarke, *American Women and the World War* (New York, 1918); Harriet Stanton Blatch, *Mobilizing Woman-Power* (New York, 1918); Mabel Potter Daggett, *Women Wanted: The Story Written in Blood Letters on the Horizon of the Great World War* (New York, 1918); Emily Newell Blair, *The Woman's Committee, United States Council of National Defense, An Interpretative Report, April 21, 1917 to February 27, 1919* (Washington, D.C., 1920).

47. Ibid.

48. The Still Picture Branch in the Audiovisual Archives Division of the National Archives in Washington, D.C. has a superb slide collection of World War I posters.

49. Mrs. F. M. Huestis to W. B. Wilson, 23 August 1918, Industrial Arbitration, War Labor Policies Board, RG 1, NA, Washington, D.C.

50. Mrs. Simmons to Secretary of Labor, 31 May 1918, Chief Clerk's File 9/273-A, Department of Labor, RG 174, NA, Washington, D.C.

51. A Woman Clerk to the Secretary of Navy, 12 February 1919, Accession no. 55-A-485, File War 1918, WB, RG 86, NA, Washington, D.C.

52. Miss Morteson to Mr. Lowenthal, 12 July 1918, War Labor Policies Board, RG 1, NA, Washington, D.C.; New York, Department of Labor, Bureau of Women in Industry, *Report Submitted Relative to the Telephone Industry in New York State* (Albany, 1920), pp. 11-16, 41-43; Consumers' League, *Colored Women as Industrial Workers*, p. 38. See also Committee on Industrial Welfare of the Cleveland Chamber of Commerce, *A Report on the Problem of Women for Man Power in Industry* (Cleveland, July 17, 1918), p. 30.

53. Mary B. Cleveland, "Women Stenographers for Government Service," Committee on Labor, 10A-C3, Council of National Defense, RG 62, NA, Washington, D.C.

54. Bing, *War-Time Strikes*, pp. 1-13, 291-297; Gordon S. Watkins, *Labor Problems and Labor Administration in the United States During the War* (Urbana, Ill., 1920), pp. 17-117; Alexander Trachtenberg, ed., *American Labor Year Book, 1919-1920* (New York, 1920), pp. 161-166 on strikes and lockouts in the United States during 1917 and 1918.

55. Leo Wolman, *The Growth of American Trade Unions, 1880-1923* (New York, 1924), pp. 33, 98-99.

56. Annual Report of Executive Council, National Federation of Federal Employees, *Federal Employee* 3 (October 1918): 1010-1069; Harry Honig, *Brotherhood of Railway Clerks* (New York, 1937), pp. 37-65; Trachtenberg, ed., *American Labor Year Book*, pp. 188-189; for Lynn, Massachusetts clerical workers, see National Women's Trade Union League Convention Proceedings, 2-7 June 1919, Container 24: 252-254, NWTUL Papers, Library of Congress, Washington, D.C.

57. Brief Relative to Stenographers, Typists, and Bookkeepers' Wages and Conditions in Controversy between General Electric Company and Metal Trades Council of Schenectady, Docket 127, NWLB, RG 2, NA, Washington, D.C.

58. Julia O'Connor, "History of the Organized Telephone Operators' Movement," *Union Telephone Operator* 1 (June 1921): 14-20; (July 1921): 14-19.

59. International Association of Laundry Workers' Union Local 36 vs. Laundry Owners of Little Rock, Arkansas, Docket 233, NWLB, RG 2, NA, Washington, D.C.; "Girls Strike to See Liberty Celebration," *Seattle Union Record*, 27 April 1918; NWTUL Convention Proceedings, 2-7 June 1919, Container 24: 63, NWTUL Papers, LC, Washington, D.C.; Kansas City, Missouri Women's Trade Union League, *Report* (May 1917 to June 1919), pp. 8-8a can be found in the Cornelia Pinchot Papers, LC, Washing-

ton, D.C.; Elizabeth Ross Haynes, "Negroes in Domestic Service in the United States," *Journal of Negro History* 8 (October 1923): 435-436; "Women Conductors Strike," *Union Leader* 19 (June 15, 1918): 4; "Women Teachers Want War Bonus Same as Men," *SUR*, Weekly Edition, 12 October 1918. Other examples of women's militancy include "Department Store Waitresses Win Increase," *Life and Labor* 8 (July 1918): 141; Olive M. Sullivan, "The Women's Part in the Stockyards Organization Work," *Life and Labor* 8 (May 1918): 102-104; "Equal Pay for Women Clerks," *SUR*, Weekly Edition, 17 August 1918; Ethel M. Smith, "Low Wages Send Cigar Makers on Strike," *Life and Labor* 8 (May 1918): 92-93.

60. Women's Bureau, *Negro Women in Industry*, p. 8.

61. "Colored Girls Can Help," *CPD*, 4 November 1918.

62. Haynes, *Negro at Work*, p. 130.

63. Women's Bureau, *Negro Women in Industry*, p. 40.

64. Ibid., p. 46.

65. Consumers' League, *A New Day*, pp. 23-24.

66. Consumers' League, *Colored Women as Industrial Workers*, pp. 26-27.

67. "A Faithful Branch of Washington Local No. 2," *Federal Employee* 5 (May 8, 1920): 18; "Board of Representatives' Synopsis of Proceedings," *Federal Employee* 3 (September 1918): 956.

CHAPTER 2. THE TECHNICAL AND THE HUMAN: MANAGING WOMEN WORKERS

1. Ernest Fox Nichols, "The Employment Manager," *Annals of the American Academy of Political and Social Science* 65 (May 1916): 2.

2. These examples of new wartime work for women were drawn from the photographs of the Women's Bureau which are deposited in the Still Picture Branch in the Audiovisual Archives Division of the National Archives, Washington, D.C.

3. Samuel Haber, *Efficiency and Uplift: Scientific Management in the Progressive Era, 1890-1920* (Chicago, 1964), pp. ix, 61, 69n.

4. Frederick Winslow Taylor, *The Principles of Scientific Management* (New York, 1911), pp. 89-90.

5. Daniel Nelson, *Managers and Workers: Origins of the New Factory System in the United States, 1880-1920* (Madison, 1975), pp. 70-78. Nelson argues that scientific management increased the scope of the manager's duties, diminished those of the foreman, and only incidentally affected the craftsman's control over his work. In contrast, Harry Braverman con-

cludes that scientific management adversely affected skilled workers. Note the subtitle of his book *Labor and Monopoly Capital: The Degradation of Work in the Twentieth Century* (New York, 1974). David Montgomery is preparing an evaluation of scientific management which carefully examines the relationship of skilled, semiskilled, and unskilled workers' traditions, modes of thought, and reactions to the new business practices of the early twentieth century. Montgomery's view is complementary in many ways to Braverman's, but transcends it. See Montgomery's "The 'New Unionism' and the Transformation of the Workers' Consciousness in America, 1909-1922," *Journal of Social History* 7 (Summer 1974): 509-529; "Immigrant Workers and Scientific Management," (Paper delivered at the "Immigrants in Industry" Conference of the Eleutherian Mills Historical Library and the Balch Institute, Wilmington, Delaware, 2 November 1973); and "Workers' Control of Machine Production in the Nineteenth Century," *Labor History* 17 (Fall 1976): 485-509. Daniel T. Rodgers, *The Work Ethic in Industrial America, 1850-1920* (Chicago, 1978), pp. 30-64 includes a balanced and perceptive analysis of the intellectual and social origins of scientific management.

6. For a list of the textile, clothing, and metal-working firms which adopted scientific management, see Nelson, *Managers and Workers*, p. 71. Nelson did not include the American Telephone and Telegraph Company telephone exchanges in his list. See chapter 5 of this book for an analysis of scientific management in the Bell System.

7. Hugh Aitken, *Taylorism at Watertown* (Cambridge, Mass., 1960).

8. Braverman, *Labor and Monopoly Capital*, pp. 139-151; Loren Baritz, *The Servants of Power: A History of the Use of Social Science in American Industry* (Middletown, Conn., 1960), pp. 58-116; John Chynoweth Burnham, "Psychiatry, Psychology and the Progressive Movement," *American Quarterly.* 12 (Winter 1960): 457-465.

9. Herbert G. Gutman, "Work, Culture, and Society in Industrializing America, 1815-1919," *American Historical Review* 78 (June 1973): 531-588; Brandes, *American Welfare Capitalism*, pp. 17-19; Nelson, *Managers and Workers*, p. 115.

10. U.S., Department of Labor, Bureau of Labor Statistics, *Welfare Work for Employees in Industrial Establishments in the United States*, Bulletin no. 250 (Washington, D.C., 1919), p. 8. This study analyzes questionnaires collected in 1916 and 1917 from 431 establishments.

11. For an excellent discussion of management policies in department stores, see Susan Porter Benson, "'More Intelligent Acquiescence': The Drama of the American Department Store, 1900-1940" (Seminar paper, Boston University, 1975); Charles R. Henderson, *Citizens in Industry* (New

York, 1915) contains an appendix listing firms in several countries with welfare programs. Telephone exchanges and department stores are prominent among the American firms; Nelson, *Managers and Workers*, p. 116 lists firms with extensive welfare programs from 1905 to 1915.

12. Henderson, *Citizens*, pp. 273-276; Henry Eilbirt, "The Development of Personnel Management in the United States," *Business History Review* 33 (1959): 348-350; Bureau of Labor Statistics, *Welfare Work*, pp. 123-124; Frank B. Miller and Mary Ann Coghill, "Sex and the Personnel Manager," *Industrial and Labor Relations Review* 18 (October 1964): 32-34.

13. Robert C. Alberts, *The Good Provider: H. J. Heinz and His 57 Varieties* (Boston, 1973), pp. 135-148; Nelson, *Managers and Workers*, pp. 102, 106-107; Benson, "'More Intelligent Acquiescence,'"; Daniel Nelson and Stuart Campbell, "Taylorism Versus Welfare Work in American Industry: H. L. Gantt and the Bancrofts," *Business History Review* 46 (Spring 1972): 1-16; Nelson, *Managers and Workers*, pp. 112-114.

14. Lena Harvey Tracy, *How My Heart Sang: The Story of Pioneer Industrial Welfare Work* (New York, 1950), p. 112; U.S., Department of Labor, Bureau of Labor Statistics, *Proceedings of the Employment Managers' Conference*, Philadelphia, 2-3 April 1917, Bulletin no. 227 (Washington, D.C., 1917), pp. 153-154 on Hoskins; Nelson and Campbell, "Taylorism Versus Welfare Work," p. 9 on Briscoe.

15. Nelson, *Managers and Workers*, pp. 152-153.

16. The American Academy of Political and Social Science devoted the entire May 1916 issue of its organ to personnel and employment problems in industry. The articles include descriptions of personnel management in different economic settings. For one particularly noteworthy example, see Ernest Martin Hopkins, "A Functionalized Employment Department as a Factor in Industrial Efficiency," *Annals of the American Academy of Political and Social Science* 65 (May 1916): 67-75. See also Braverman, *Labor and Monopoly Capital*, pp. 139-151.

17. Nelson, *Managers and Workers*, p. 152.

18. Ibid., p. 151; Baritz, *The Servants of Power*, pp. 51-52; Eilbirt, "The Development of Personnel Management," p. 353; Eva Wechsler, "Uncle Sam's Employment Service," *Life and Labor* 8 (September 1918): 196-198; Mrs. M. A. Gadsby, "Provision for the Disabled and Vocational Education," *Monthly Labor Review* 6 (April 1918): 111-117.

19. Committee on Industrial Welfare of the Cleveland Chamber of Commerce, *A Report on the Problem of the Substitution of Woman for Man Power in Industry* (Cleveland, July 1918); National Industrial Conference Board, *Wartime Employment of Women in the Metal Trades*, Research Report no. 8 (Boston, July 1918).

20. See for example, "Women in Metal Trades," *Iron Age* 102 (August 1, 1918): 282; L. H. Butler, "Rest Rooms and Their Influence on Application to Work," *Industrial Management* 56 (July 1918): 63; Peter O'Shea, "A Shop Training School for Girls," *Industrial Management* 58 (September 1919): 213-215; W. L. Churchill, "Changing from Male to Female Help," *Industrial Management* 55 (April 1918): 322-324; Luther Burlingame, "War Work for Women," *Machinery* 24 (April 1918): 682-687.

21. Nelson, *Managers and Workers*, p. 109.

22. For a summary statement see Charles U. Carpenter, "How We Trained 5,000 Women," *Industrial Management* 55 (May 1918): 355-357. A longer version can be found in the Section on Industrial Training for the War Emergency, Form Letters and Publicity, 1918, U.S. Council of National Defense, RG 62, NA, Washington, D.C.

23. Carpenter, "How We Trained 5,000 Women," pp. 335-357.

24. The quotation is from the government's account of the wartime experiment at the Recording and Computing Machines Company.

25. F. L. Prentiss, "A Motor Company's Shop Training for Women," *Iron Age* (December 12, 1918): 1454-1455.

26. Ibid., p. 1455.

27. Ibid.

28. U.S., Department of Labor, Women's Bureau, *The New Position of Women in American Industry*, Bulletin no. 12 (Washington, D.C., 1920), p. 86.

29. William Crozier, *Ordnance and the World War: A Contribution to the History of American Preparedness* (New York, 1920), pp. 11-37.

30. L. P. Alford, "An Industrial Achievement of the War," *Industrial Management* 55 (February 1918): 97.

31. Mary van Kleeck, "Women in the Munition Industries," *Life and Labor* 8 (June 1918): 113-122.

32. Aitken, *Taylorism at Watertown*, p. 238; Milton Nadworny, *Scientific Management and the Unions, 1900-1932: A Historical Analysis* (Cambridge, Massachusetts, 1955), pp. 97-121.

33. Alford, "An Industrial Achievement," pp. 97-98 is the source historians have used to establish that the relationship between scientific management advocates and the Ordnance Department expanded dramatically during the war.

34. Nadworny, *Scientific Management*, p. 105; John M. Glenn, Lilian Brandt, and F. Emerson Andrews, *Russell Sage Foundation, 1907-1946*, 2 vols. (New York, 1947), 1: 256-257; Mary Anderson, *Woman at Work: The Autobiography of Mary Anderson as told to Mary N. Winslow* (Minneapolis, 1951), p. 88; van Kleeck, "Women in Munitions Industries," pp. 113-122.

35. W S. Carter, "Effect of Federal Control on Railway Labor," *Proceedings of the Academy of Political Science* 8 (1918-1920): 198-210; Walter Hines, *War History of American Railroads* (New Haven, 1928), pp. 152-191; Alexander M. Bing, *War-Time Strikes and Their Adjustment*, pp. 82-95; K. Austin Kerr, *American Railroad Politics, 1914-1920* (Pittsburgh, 1968), pp. 91-101.

36. "Work of Woman's Service Section, United States Railroad Administration," *Monthly Labor Review* 8 (March 1919): 209-212; Pauline Goldmark, "Women in the Railroad World," *Annals of the American Academy of Political and Social Science* 86 (November 1919): 214-221.

37. Female reformers were well read in the studies of their day on women wage earners. Some of the most famous prewar investigations of women's work include Mary van Kleeck, *Artificial Flower Makers* (New York, 1913); Mary van Kleeck, *A Seasonal Industry: A Study of the Millinery Trade in New York* (New York, 1917); Mary van Kleeck, *Women in the Bookbinding Trade* (New York, 1913); Edith Abbott, *Women in Industry: A Study in Economic History* (New York, 1910); Elizabeth Beardsley Butler, *Women and the Trades: Pittsburgh, 1907-1908*, The Pittsburgh Survey, ed. Paul Underwood Kellogg, vol. 1 (New York, 1909); Josephine Goldmark, *Fatigue and Efficiency: A Study in Industry* (New York, 1912); Elizabeth Beardsley Butler, *Saleswomen in Mercantile Stores: Baltimore, 1909* (New York, 1912); Louise Montgomery, *The American Girl in the Stockyards District*, A Study of Chicago's Stockyards Community, vol. 2 (Chicago, 1913); U.S., Congress, Senate, *Report on Condition of Women and Child Wage-Earners in the United States*, vol. 12; *Employment of Women in Laundries*, S. Doc. 645, 61st Cong., 2d sess. (Washington, D.C., 1911). See also Rodgers, *The Work Ethic*, pp. 201-209.

38. Louise C. Odencrantz, "The Irregularity of Employment of Women Factory Workers," *Survey* 22 (May 1, 1909): 196-210; Sue Ainslie Clark and Edith Wyatt, *Making Both Ends Meet: The Income and Outlay of New York Working Girls* (New York, 1911); Margaret F. Byington, *Homestead: Households of a Mill Town*, The Pittsburgh Survey, ed. Paul Underwood Kellogg, vol. 4 (New York, 1910); Annie Marion MacLean, *Wage-Earning Women* (New York, 1910); Alice Henry, *The Trade Union Woman* (New York, 1915); Louis D. Brandeis and Josephine Goldmark, *Women in Industry: Decision of the United States Supreme Court in Curt Muller vs. State of Oregon Upholding the Constitutionality of the Oregon Ten-Hour Law for Women, and Brief for the State of Oregon* (New York, n.d.).

39. Glenn et al., *Russell Sage*, 1: 61, 164-165; van Kleeck, *Artificial Flower Makers*; *Women in the Bookbinding Trade*; *A Seasonal Industry: A Study of the Millinery Trade in New York*.

40. van Kleeck, "Women in the Munitions Industries."

41. Glenn et al., *Russell Sage Foundation*, 1: 169.

42. Anderson, *Women at Work*, pp. 3-21.

43. Ibid., pp. 42-60.

44. Mary Anderson to Agnes Nestor, 19 August 1918, File Night Work, Women in Industry Service, RG 86, NA, Washington, D.C.

45. Biographical information about Pauline Goldmark is very difficult to find. The portrait of Josephine Goldmark in *Notable American Women* was used as the basic source of information about Pauline Goldmark's family. Edward and Janet Wilson James, eds., *Notable American Women, 1607-1950: A Biographical Dictionary*, 3 vols. (Cambridge, Mass., 1971), 1: 60-61. For information about Pauline Goldmark, see her obituary notice, *New York Times*, 20 October 1962. Also helpful is "Women in the Field of Railroading," *Southern Pacific, Western Pacific Bulletin* (August 1919): 11, which can be found in Railroad Administration, File 209a, WSS, RG 14, NA, Washington, D.C.

46. Louis Lee Athey, "The Consumers' League and Social Reform, 1890-1923" (Ph.D. diss., University of Delaware, 1965); Florence Kelley, "Twenty-five Years of Consumers' League Movement," *Survey* 35 (November 27, 1915): 212-214; Allis Rosenberg Wolfe, "Women, Consumerism, and the National Consumers' League in the Progressive Era, 1900-1923," *Labor History* 16 (Summer 1975): 378-392.

47. File 251, WSS, RG 14, NA, Washington, D.C.

48. Ibid.

49. "Federal Policy in the Employment of Women," *Monthly Labor Review* 7 (November 1918): 189; van Kleeck, "Women in the Munition Industries," pp. 113-122.

50. Glenn et al., *Russell Sage Foundation*, 1:257.

51. "Federal Policy," *Monthly Labor Review*, p. 189.

52. David Brody, *Steelworkers in America: The Nonunion Era* (Cambridge, Mass., 1960), pp. 214-230.

53. G. T. Fonda, Superintendent of the Bureau of Labor and Safety, Bethlehem Steel Company, to General Dickinson, U.S. Ordnance Department, 14 June 1918, File Bethlehem Steel, Women in the Industry Service, RG 86, NA, Washington, D.C.; Report from Lois B. Rantoul, Women's Branch, Industrial Service Section, to Major B. H. Gitchell, Chief Industrial Service Section, Washington, 2 September 1918, File Bethlehem Steel, Women in Industry Service, RG 86, NA, Washington, D.C.

54. Ibid.

55. Mrs. V. B. Turner, "Women in the Mechanical Trades in the United States," *Monthly Labor Review* 7 (September 1918): 210.

56. Report from Lois B. Rantoul to Major B. H. Gitchell.

57. Ibid.

58. Brody, *Steelworkers in America*, pp. 212-213; Memo from C. T. Clayton, Director of Training and Dilution, to Director, Women in Industry Service, 24 October 1918, File Bethlehem Steel, Women in Industry Service, RG 86, NA, Washington, D.C.

59. Paul H. Douglas, "Plant Administration of Labor," *Journal of Political Economy* 27 (July 1919): 550; Paul H. Douglas, "War Time Courses in Employment Management," *School and Society* (June 2, 1919): 692-695; Anderson, *Woman at Work*, pp. 88-89.

60. Mary Barnett Gilson, *The Past is Prologue* (New York, 1940), pp. 168-169.

61. "Training Women Begins," *Iron Age* 102 (July 25, 1918): 199; "Women Workers Make Good Showing," *Iron Age* 102 (August 1, 1918): 276-277; Nelson, *Managers and Workers*, pp. 110, 116.

62. Anderson, *Woman at Work*, p. 89.

63. Ibid., p. 90.

64. Ibid., pp. 89-90.

65. Clara Tead, Director Women's Branch to Mary van Kleeck, Director Woman in Industry Service, Report on Wages and Work of Women in U.S. Arsenals and Ordnance Plants, 21 December 1918, Accession no. 55-A-485, File War 1918, RG 86, NA, Washington, D.C. Women were often paid the same piece rates as men, but not the same hourly wage. It was often difficult to determine whether women performed the same work as men. This report summarizes the findings of many investigators.

66. Bing, *War-Time Strikes*, pp. 66-67 n. 4.

67. Memo from Helen Bryan to Colonel H.B. Jordan, 1 July 1919, Accession No. 55-A-485, File War 1918, RG 86, NA, Washington, D.C.

68. Bing, *War-Time Strikes*, p. 78.

69. Memo from Pauline Goldmark to Field Agents, 14 April 1919, File 239, WSS, RG 14, NA, Washington, D.C.; Report 42, Conference with Railroad Officials about Women Employees, Southern Pacific RR, 28 June 1919, File 239, WSS, RG 14, NA, Washington, D.C.

70. Florence Clark to Pauline Goldmark, 17 March 1919, File 241, WSS, RG 14, NA, Washington, D.C.

71. Complaint 41; File 232-234, WSS, RG 14, NA, Washington, D.C.

72. Report No. 39, 30 April 1919, Entry 1, File E-60, Division of Labor, Railroad Administration, RG 14, NA, Suitland, Maryland.

73. Memo from Pauline Goldmark to Field Agents, 14 April 1919, File 239, WSS, RG 14, NA, Washington, D.C.

74. Pauline Goldmark to Florence E. Clark, 11 July 1919, File 241, WSS, RG 14, NA, Washington, D.C.

75. Helen Ross, Ticket Accountant's Office, Santa Fe Railroad, Topeka, Kansas, 8 October 1918, File 55, WSS, RG 14, NA, Washington, D.C.; Edith Hall, Office of Auditor of Disbursements, General Office, B&O RR, Baltimore, 20 August 1919, File 75a, WSS, RG 14, NA, Washington, D.C.

76. Helen Ross, Report on Inquiry of Methods Used by the Railroads in Employing and Training Railroad Office Workers, Chicago and Northwestern RR, Ravenswood Station, n.d. Other reports on this road are dated 11-12 October 1919, File 105, WSS, RG 14, NA, Washington, D.C.

77. Edith Hall, Office of Auditor Merchandise Receipts, General Office, B&O RR, Baltimore, 20 August 1919, File 75b, WSS, RG 14, NA, Washington, D.C.

78. Digest of Discussion of Conference of Women's Service Section with Supervisors of Women Employees of the Railroads, Chicago, 20-21 October 1919, File 273, WSS, RG 14, NA, Washington, D.C.

79. Rose Yates, B&O RR, Wheeling, West Virginia, 23-25 January 1919, File 73, WSS, RG 14, NA, Washington, D.C.

80. Pauline Goldmark to Helen Ross, 7 April 1919, File 243, WSS, RG 14, NA, Washington, D.C.

81. Pauline Goldmark to Helen Ross, 8 March 1919, File 243, WSS, RG 14, NA, Washington, D.C.

82. Mary van Kleeck, "The Social Meaning of Good Management," *Bulletin of the Taylor Society* 9 (December 1924): 242; "The Interview as a Method of Research," *Bulletin of the Taylor Society* 11 (December 1926): 268-274; "Discussion of Financial Incentives," *Bulletin of the Taylor Society* 12 (June 1927): 440-441. The only information available concerning Goldmark's affiliation with AT&T is to be found in her obituary notice, *New York Times* 20 October 1962.

CHAPTER 3.   THE LIMITS OF OPPORTUNITY:
WORKING FOR THE RAILROADS

1. *U.S. Railroad Administration Order No. 8*, 8 February 1918.

2. K. Austin Kerr, *American Railroad Politics, 1914-1920* (Pittsburgh, 1968), pp. 6-72; William J. Cunningham, *American Railroads: Government Control and Reconstruction Policies* (Chicago, 1922), pp. 16-22.

3. Harry D. Wolf, *The Railroad Labor Board* (Chicago, 1927), p. 58. Class I carriers were those railroads with annual revenues above one million dollars.

4. Ibid., pp. 58-59; Harry Honig, *Brotherhood of Railway Clerks* (New York, 1937), app. D. The statistics were computed on the basis of voting strength at the American Federation of Labor conventions. Little information can be found on the number of women members in the railroad unions.

5. Leonard A. Lecht, *Experience under Railway Labor Legislation* (New York, 1955), pp. 33-34; Cunningham, *American Railroads*, pp. 106-108.

6. National Railroad Adjustment Board, *General Order No. 27 with Its Supplements, Addenda, Amendments and Interpretations* (Chicago, 1935), pp. 55-59, 78-81, 96-99, 110-113.

7. W. S. Carter, "Effect of Federal Control on Railway Labor," *Proceedings of the Academy of Political Science* 8 (1918-1920): 198-210; Walter Hines, *War History of American Railroads* (New Haven, 1928), pp. 152-191; Kerr, *American Railroad Politics*, pp. 91-101.

8. Cunningham, *American Railroads*, pp. 194-196.

9. U.S. Railroad Administration, *Annual Report of Walter B. Hines, Director General of Railroads, 1919* (Washington, D.C., 1920), pp. 77-79; File 273, WSS, U.S. Railroad Administration, RG 14, NA, Washington, D.C. Women's Service Section records are hereafter cited only by WSS file number.

10. *Annual Report, 1919*, p. 61.

11. Ibid., pp. 65, 71-72.

12. Ibid., p. 75.

13. Ibid., pp. 77-79.

14. Edith Hall, Baltimore Study of Employment and Training of Women Clerks, General Offices, B&O RR, 20 August 1919, File 75a, WSS; Florence Clark, General Offices, Great Northern RR, St. Paul, Minnesota, File 128, WSS.

15. Florence Clark, General Offices and Car Accountant's Office, Santa Fe RR, Topeka, Kansas, September 1919, File 61c, WSS.

16. Ibid.

17. Rose Yates, General Offices, B&O RR, Baltimore, 6 November 1918, File 74, WSS; Edith Hall, Office of Auditor of Disbursements, B&O RR, Baltimore, 20 August 1919, File 75a, WSS; Helen Ross, Santa Fe RR, Topeka, Kansas, 8 October 1918, File 55, WSS; Florence Clark, Car Accountant's Office, Santa Fe RR, Topeka, Kansas, September 1919, File 61c, WSS.

18. Rose Yates, General Offices, B&O RR, Baltimore, 6 November 1918, File 74, WSS.

19. For the Cincinnati situation, see Complaint 82, WSS. Other instances of sexual harassment are Florence Clark, Yardmaster's Office, Great Northern RR, Cut Bank, Montana, File 125, WSS and Revision Office, Chesapeake & Ohio Lines, Richmond, Virginia, 30 March 1919, File 239, WSS.

20. Digest of a WSS Discussion with Supervisors of Women Railroad Employees, Chicago, 21-22 October 1919, File 273, WSS; Edith Hall,

Office of Auditor of Merchandise Receipts, B&O RR, Baltimore, 22 August 1919, File 75b, WSS; Edith Hall, Auditor of Disbursements, B&O RR, Baltimore, 20 August 1919, File 75a, WSS; Florence Clark, Rest Room, Santa Fe RR, Topeka, Kansas, File 61c, WSS.

21. Florence Clark, Office of Ticket Auditor, Santa Fe RR, Topeka, Kansas, 13 September 1919, File 62, WSS.

22. Auditing Offices, Southern RR, Cincinnati, Ohio, 10 February 1920, File 239, WSS; Rose Yates, Mail & Express Department, B&O RR, Baltimore, 28 October 1918, File 74, WSS; Edith Hall to Pauline Goldmark, 3 March 1919, File 242, WSS; Complaint 64, WSS; Helen Ross to Pauline Goldmark, 9 April 1919, File 243, WSS; Complaint 82, WSS; Florence Clark, Office of Ticket Auditor, Santa Fe RR, Topeka, Kansas, 13 September 1919, File 62, WSS.

23. *Annual Report, 1919*, pp. 75-78.

24. Ibid., p. 77; Helen Ross, Office of Master Mechanic, Chicago, Milwaukee & St. Paul RR, Miles City, Montana, 9 December 1919, File 62, WSS; Complaint 58, WSS.

25. Florence Clark, General Offices, Wabash RR, St. Louis, Missouri, 28-30 October 1919, File 217, WSS.

26. Rose Yates, Mail and Express Department, B&O RR, Baltimore, 28 October 1918, File 74, WSS.

27. Complaint 58, WSS.

28. Helen Ross, Freight Claim Agents in Loss and Damage Department, Chicago, Burlington, and Quincy RR, Chicago, September 1919, File 86, WSS.

29. Ibid. See also *Annual Report, 1919*, p. 77.

30. For the official account of this training program, see *Annual Report, 1919*, pp. 76-77. Significantly, the conflict between the male and female workers is omitted from the published version of the WSS report. All of the WSS publications offer the brighter side of the women railroad workers' experience.

31. Edith Hall to Pauline Goldmark, DuBois, Pennsylvania, 20 November 1919, File 242, WSS; Rose Yates, Master Mechanic's Office, B&O RR, Keyser, West Virginia, 6 December 1918, File 70, WSS; Helen Ross, Office of Car Accountant, Belt Railway, Chicago, 11 April 1919, File 77, WSS; Florence Clark to Pauline Goldmark, 22 August 1919, File 241, WSS concerns the Cleveland, Ohio situation of the New York Central RR; Florence Clark to Pauline Goldmark, 20 September 1919, File 241, WSS concerns Topeka, Kansas.

32. Leo Wolman, *The Growth of American Trade Unions, 1880-1923* (New York, 1924), pp. 22-23; Theresa Wolfson, *The Woman Worker and the Trade Unions* (New York, 1926), p. 214; Honig, *Brotherhood of Railway Clerks*, p. 284.

33. Rose Yates, General Offices, B&O RR, Baltimore, 6 November 1918, File 74, WSS; Complaint 87, WSS; Florence Clark, Office of Ticket Auditor, Santa Fe RR, Topeka, Kansas, 13 September 1919, File 62, WSS; Rose Yates, Inspection of Clerks, B&O RR, Cumberland, Maryland, 16 November 1918, File 69, WSS.

34. Complaints involving the aid of the Brotherhood of Railway Clerks include numbers 14, 19, 20, 22, 23, 28, 34, 40, 45, 60, 63, 65, 67, 73, 74, 77, 78, 87, 99, WSS. For the case of Mayme Hayes, see Complaint 82, WSS.

35. U.S. Railroad Administration, *Annual Report of W.G. McAdoo, Director General of Railroads, 1918* (Washington, D.C., 1919), pp. 17, 25.

36. Helen Ross, Supply Department, Missouri Pacific RR, Kansas City, Missouri, 29 October 1918, File 148, WSS.

37. Ibid.

38. *Annual Report, 1918*, p. 21.

39. Florence Clark, Collingwood Shops, New York Central RR, Cleveland, Ohio, 10-11 June 1919, File 152a, WSS. See also Helen Ross, Freight House, Santa Fe RR, Topeka, Kansas, 28 October 1918, File 55, WSS.

40. Florence Clark, Women Truckers, Minnesota Transfer Company, St. Paul, Minnesota, 2 December 1918, File 147, WSS.

41. Helen Ross, Yard Employees, Santa Fe RR, Topeka, Kansas, 17 October 1918, File 55, WSS. See also Edith Hall, Memo on Moral Situation in Regard to Women Operators, Pennsylvania RR, Allegheny Division, 6 November 1919, File 174b, WSS.

42. Complaint 59, WSS.

43. Florence Clark, Pullman Company, Chicago, Milwaukee and St. Paul RR, St. Paul, Minnesota, 21 November 1919, File 93, WSS; Helen Ross, Coach Cleaners, Chicago, Minneapolis, Columbus, Pittsburgh and Pitcairn Yards, File 82b, WSS.

44. *Annual Report, 1918*, pp. 18, 27.

45. Florence Clark, Electric Welders, Mt. Clare Shops, B&O RR, Baltimore, 31 October 1918, File 66b, WSS.

46. U.S., Department of Labor, Women's Bureau, *The New Position of Women in American Industry*, Bulletin no. 12 (Washington, D.C., 1920), pp. 108-109.

47. David Montgomery, "Workers' Control of Machine Production in the Nineteenth Century," *Labor History* 17 (Fall 1976): 491.

48. Ibid., pp. 491-494. For an analysis of the craft tradition among British machinists during the First World War, see James Hinton, *The First Shop Stewards' Movement* (London, 1973).

49. An excellent description of such work practices can be found in Elizabeth Beardsley Butler, *Women and the Trades: Pittsburgh, 1907-1908*, The Pittsburgh Survey, ed. Paul Underwood Kellogg, vol. 1 (New York, 1909), pp. 95-96.

50. National Industrial Conference Board, *Wartime Employment of Women in the Metal Trades*, Research Report no. 8 (Boston, 1918), pp. 32-34. Examples of unrestricted output among women can be found in Women's Bureau, *The New Position of Women*, pp. 102, 103, 109.

51. Helen Ross, Plumbing Shop, Pennsylvania RR, Pitcairn, Pennsylvania, 10 March 1919, File 188b, WSS.

52. The cartoon was captioned "Another Military Expediency?" and published in *Machinists' Monthly Journal* 29 (July 1917): 703.

53. "Annual Report," *Machinists' Monthly Journal* 30 (April 1918): 3; Mrs. May Peake, "The Woman Machinist: Her Accomplishments and Her Possibilities," *Life and Labor* 9 (December 1919): 326-329. For reports on union drives in different places, see the April, May, and June 1918 issues of *Machinists' Monthly Journal*. A chart showing the number of members of the International Association of Machinists over the course of fifty-three years can be found in Mark Perlman, *The Machinists: A New Study in American Trade Unionism* (Cambridge, Mass., 1961), p. 206.

54. Helen Ross, Plumbing Shop, Pennsylvania RR, Pitcairn, Pennsylvania, 10 March 1919, File 188b, WSS; Florence Clark, Riverside Yards, B&O RR, Baltimore, 17 October 1918, File 66a, WSS.

55. Florence Clark, Electric Welders, Mt. Clare Shops, B&O RR, Baltimore, 31 October 1918, File 66b, WSS.

56. Women's Bureau, *The New Position of Women*, pp. 108-109, 158.

57. "O.F. of L.," *Cleveland Citizen*, 1 February 1919; Patricia Kendrick Brito, "Protective Legislation in Ohio, 1918-1939" (Paper delivered at the College of St. Catherine's Conference on Women's History, St. Paul, Minnesota, 22 October 1977).

58. Floyd W. Parsons, "Employment of Women in Mining," *Coal Age* 13 (May 11, 1918); R. Dawson Hall, "The Labor Situation," *Coal Age* 13 (May 11, 1918), p. 886.

59. *Springfield Reporter*, 28 November 1917 and 5 December 1917. These poems can also be found in Wayne G. Boehl, Jr., *Precision Valley; The Machine Tool Companies of Springfield, Vermont: Jones and Lamson Machine Company, Fellows Gears Shaper Company [and] Bryant Chucking Grinder Company* (Englewood, New Jersey, 1959), pp. 98-100.

60. Florence Clark, Supervisor of Women, Pennsylvania RR, Harrisburg, Pennsylvania, 21 January 1919, 27 January 1919, 18 February 1919, File 180a, WSS.

61. Florence Clark, Memorandum of Conversation with L.B. Jones, Pennsylvania RR, Harrisburg, Pennsylvania, 7 February 1919, File 187e, WSS.

62. L.B. Jones to Mrs. Westbrook, 10 February 1919, Pennsylvania RR, Harrisburg, Pennsylvania, File 187h, WSS.

63. Helen Ross, Altoona Yards, Pennsylvania RR, Harrisburg, Pennsylvania, 4 February 1919, File 181b, WSS and 29 January 1919, File 180a, WSS.

64. Helen Ross, Office of Car Accountant, Pennsylvania RR, Altoona, Pennsylvania, 30 January 1919, File 181b, WSS; Edith Hall to Pauline Goldmark, 8 February 1919, File 242, WSS.

65. Florence Clark, General Office and Office of Car Accountant, Santa Fe RR, Topeka, Kansas, 8-9 September 1919, File 61c, WSS.

66. Edith Hall, Erecting Shop, Erie Railroad, Jersey City, New Jersey, 30 December 1918, File 118, WSS.

67. Florence Clark, Auditor of Disbursement, Voucher Department, General Office, Wabash RR, St. Louis, Missouri, 28-30 October 1919, File 217, WSS.

68. Some Employees to Mr. William Elmer, Pennsylvania RR, File 187e, WSS.

69. Complaints involving the aid of the Brotherhood of Railway Clerks are 14, 19, 20, 22, 23, 28, 34, 40, 45, 60, 63, 65, 67, 73, 74, 77, 78, 87, 99, WSS.

70. Complaint 99, WSS.

71. Anna Crosson to Miss Clark, 4 April 1919, File 193c, WSS. See also File 187e, WSS.

72. Edith Hall, Clerks and Storeroom Attendants, Pennsylvania RR, Harrisburg, Pennsylvania, April 1919, File 187e, WSS; Cora Knisely to Miss Clark, 11 May 1919, File 193, WSS; Anna Crosson to Miss Clark, 20 May 1919, File 193, WSS.

73. Complaint 75, WSS.

74. William Cunningham, *American Railroads*, pp. 186-193.

75. *Annual Report, 1919*, p. 73.

76. Carrie Fearing to Director General Hines, 28 January 1919, File 193a, WSS.

77. Edith Hall, Enginehouse, Pennsylvania RR, Oil City, Pennsylvania RR, 29 March 1919, File 174a, WSS.

78. Helen Ross, Warehouse Laborers, Pennsylvania RR, Pitcairn, Pennsylvania, 8 March 1919, File 188b, WSS.

79. *Annual Report, 1919*, pp. 62-64.

CHAPTER 4.   THE RIGHT TO WAGE LABOR: WOMEN AS STREETCAR CONDUCTORS

1. U.S., Department of Labor, Women's Bureau. *Women Street Car Conductors*, Bulletin no. 11 (Washington D.C., 1921), p. 34.

2. It is very difficult to determine the precise number of cities where women conductors were introduced. According to reports in *Motorman and Conductor*, the national organ of the Amalgamated Association of Street and Electric Railway Employees, *Union Leader*, the local Chicago transit union newspaper, *Survey*, a middle-class reformers' journal, and *Electric Railway Journal*, the municipal railway trade organ, women were introduced into Kenosha, Brooklyn, New York City, St. Louis, Camden and Elizabeth, Baltimore, Detroit, Cleveland, Kansas City, Duluth, Little Rock, Milwaukee, and Los Angeles.

3. *Motorman and Conductor* 26 (August 1918): 28.

4. On the early history of street railways, see U.S., Bureau of the Census, *Street and Electric Railways: 1902* (Washington, D.C., 1905), pp. 159-171; George W. Hilton and John F. Due, *The Electric Interurban Railways in America* (Stanford, 1960), p. 7; Edward S. Mason, *The Street Railway in Massachusetts: The Rise and Decline of an Industry* (Cambridge, 1932), p. 5.

5. Delos Franklin Wilcox, *Analysis of the Electric Railway Problem: Report to the Federal Electric Railways Commission with Summary and Recommendations, Supplemented by Special Studies of Transportation Issues in the State of New Jersey and the City of Denver, with Notes on Recent Developments in the Electric Railway Field* (New York, 1921), pp. 36-45.

6. Ibid., pp. 61-66; Mason, *The Street Railway*, p. 12.

7. Wilcox, *Analysis of the Electric Railway Problem*, pp. 75-77; Mason, *The Street Railway*, pp. 118-122.

8. Wilcox, *Analysis of the Electric Railway Problem*, pp. 78-87; Delos Franklin Wilcox, *Municipal Franchises: A Description of the Terms and Conditions Upon Which Private Corporations Enjoy Special Privileges in the Streets of American Cities*, 2 vols. (New York, 1910-1911) contains a detailed examination of transportation franchises; Mason, *The Street Railway*, pp. 110-113.

9. Emerson Peter Schmidt, *Industrial Relations in Urban Transportation* (Minneapolis, 1937), p. 45; Wilcox, *Analysis of the Electric Railway Problem*, pp. 99-113; Mason, *The Street Railway*, pp. 127-132.

10. Schmidt, *Industrial Relations*, pp. 115, 121, 208n; Kent Healy, *The Economics of Transportation in America: The Dynamic Forces in Development, Organization, Functioning and Regulation* (New York, 1940), p. 364; Wilcox, *Analysis of the Electric Railway Problem*, p. 534.

11. U.S., Department of Labor, Bureau of Labor Statistics, *National War Labor Board*, Bulletin no. 287 (Washington, D.C., 1922), pp. 85-87, 105-115; Paul H. Douglas, *Real Wages in the United States, 1890-1926* (New York, 1930), pp. 324-329.

12. "Cleveland Railway Shows Deficit for 1917," *Electric Railway Journal* 52 (August 10, 1918): 255; "Facts Must Be Faced," *ERJ* 52 (August 31, 1918): 379-380; "Cleveland Body Will Investigate," *ERJ* 51 (May 25, 1918): 1031.

13. "Detroit and Cleveland Wages Under Advisement," *ERJ* 51 (June 1, 1918): 1064; "DUR Attitude Stated," *ERJ* 51 (June 8, 1918): 1107; Charles William to Attorney General of the United States, 4 February 1919, File 16-114-29, Records of the Department of Justice, RG 60, NA, Washington, D.C.; "Let the City Try It," *ERJ* 52 (October 19, 1918): 683.

14. "The Sacrifices of Habit," *ERJ* 49 (June 30, 1917): 1173; "Employment of Women Is Inevitable," *ERJ* 49 (June 23, 1917): 1125; "Latest Attack on the Amalgamated: Let's Get Rid of Men," *Union Leader* 19 (March 1918): 1; Carey D. Ferguson, "Women as Street Car Conductors," *M&C* 26 (November 1918): 32-33.

15. Col. T. S. Williams, "Women Successful as Conductors," *ERJ* 51 (March 2, 1918): 416-417; "Women Conductors in Kansas City, Kenosha and Camden," *ERJ* 51 (June 15, 1918): 1147-1148; "Women Conductors for St. Louis," *ERJ* 51 (January 26, 1918): 202n; "Duluth Has Women Car and Shop Workers," *ERJ* 52 (September 7, 1918): 414.

16. "Conductresses for Detroit," *ERJ* 52 (September 21, 1918): 521; "Women Prove Highly Satisfactory," *ERJ* 52 (October 5, 1918): 637.

17. Howard Barton Myers, "The Policing of Labor Disputes in Chicago: A Case Study," (Ph.D. diss., University of Chicago, 1929), chapter 7. Graham Adams, *Age of Industrial Violence* (New York, 1966), pp. 181-188; Edward Levinson, *I Break Strikes! The Technique of Pearl L. Bergoff* (New York, 1935), pp. 89-104; "Kansas City 'Carries On,'" *ERJ* 52 (December 21, 1918): 1112; "Women Conductors in Kansas City, Kenosha and Camden," *ERJ* (June 15, 1918): 1148; "Women Conductors Strike," *UL* 19 (June 15, 1918): 4.

18. In St. Louis women were given preference in assignments over older male employees. Men's seniority rights were being violated. "Strikes and Lockouts," *M&C* 26 (February 1918): 14; "How St. Louis Corporation Tried to Kill New Union," *Cleveland Citizen*, 24 August 1918. For the New York situation see Benjamin Squires, "Women Street Railway Employees," *Monthly Labor Review* 6 (May 1918): 1049-1070.

19. Margaret Hobbs, "Moral Menace and Danger to Health," *UL* 19 (June 15, 1918): 5; "Presentment of the Grand Jury of Kings County, New York, June 18, 1918," Employment Service, War Labor Policies Board, RG 1, NA, Washington, D.C.; Pauline Goldmark, "Women Conductors," *Survey* 40 (June 29, 1918): 369.

20. "Latest Attack on the Amalgamated: Let's Get Rid of Men," *UL* 19 (March 1918): 1; "Fifteenth Convention Resolution of Principles, Policies

and Endorsements," *M&C* 26 (December 1917): 35; "Demand Higher Wages," *M&C* 26 (April 1918): 30 on Utica, New York; "Momentous Question," *M&C* 26 (October 1919): 24 on Cleveland; "Oppose Commercializing Womanhood," *M&C* 25 (November 1917): 21 on Worcester; "Men Object to Women on Cars," *ERJ* 51 (May 18, 1918): 983 on Ontario.

21. "Strikes and Lockouts," *M&C* 26 (February 1918): 14; "Men Object to Women on Cars," *ERJ* 51 (May 18, 1918): 983; "Distatsefil *[sic]* Results from Employment of Women as Street Car Conductors," *M&C* 26 (November 1918): 29-31. For a broader discussion of the relationship between the introduction of women and technological and operating changes in different industries, see U.S., Department of Labor, Women's Bureau, *Technological Changes in Relation to Women's Employment*, Bulletin no. 107 (Washington, D.C., 1935).

22. "Harnessing Women," *UL* 19 (December 21, 1918): 4.

23. "Conducting of Street Cars An Inadvisable Occupation for Women," *M&C* 26 (August 1918): 7; Schmidt, *Industrial Relations*, p. 81.

24. P. F. Sheehan, "Keep the Girls Off the Cars," *M&C* 26 (August 1918): 28.

25. "The Amalgamated Association and Its' *[sic]* Lady Members," *M&C* 26 (November 1918): 33-34; "Chicago Women Workers of the Amalgamated Association," *M&C* 27 (December 1918): 4-5.

26. "Proceeding of Semi-Annual Meeting of General Executive Board," *M&C* 26 (September 1918): 3-8; "Los Angeles in Line," *M&C* 27 (December 1918): 21. For the Washington situation see "Commission against Women," *ERJ* 51 (January 26, 1918): 202; "Exploitation of Women Treason," *SUR*, Weekly Edition, 29 December 1917; "Introduction of Women Is Merely to Keep Wages Low," *SUR*, Weekly Edition, 12 January 1918; Fred Tuite, Building Employees Union, to Editor, *SUR*, Weekly Edition, 12 January 1918. The Wisconsin and New York legislation is described in U.S., Department of Labor, Women's Bureau, *The Effects of Labor Legislation on the Employment Opportunities of Women*, Bulletin no. 65 (Washington, D.C., 1928): 269-270, 273-274. The role of the New York Central Labor Union in pressuring for the New York law is described in "Use of Women Protested," *ERJ* 51 (February 5, 1918): 253.

27. "Proceedings of the Semi-Annual Meeting of General Executive Board," *M&C* 26 (September 1918): 31.

28. "Reports by Medical Inspector of State Industrial Commission," *ERJ* 51 (May 25, 1918): 1008-1013; Women's Bureau, *The Effect of Labor Legislation*, p. 33; "Duluth Has Women Car and Shop Workers," *ERJ* 52 (September 7, 1918): 414; Col. T.S. Williams, "Women Successful as Conductors," *ERJ* 51 (March 2, 1918): 416-417; Estelle Levy, "A Glimpse of

Women in Transportation," unpub. mss., 18 December 1918, Box 60, Folder Women in Industry Investigations, 1914-1922, Mary van Kleeck Papers, Sophia Smith Collection, Smith College Library, Northampton, Mass.

29. Schmidt, *Industrial Relations*, p. 81; Wilcox, *Municipal Franchises*, p. 16; "Women Conductors Success at Kansas City," *ERJ* 52 (October 5, 1918): 617-618; "Street Railway Men," *Cleveland Citizen*, 7 December 1918.

30. Women's Bureau, *The Effects of Labor Legislation*, p. 33; "Women and War Work," *ERJ* 51 (March 9, 1918): 466; "Reports by Medical Inspector," *ERJ* 51 (May 25, 1918): 1008-1013.

31. Women's Bureau, *The Effects of Labor Legislation*, p. 33.

32. Ibid.

33. Employees of Detroit United Railway, Members of the Amalgamated Association of Street and Electric Railway Employees of America vs. Detroit United Railway, and Women Conductor's Association vs. Amalgamated Association of Street and Electric Railway Employees of America, Transcript of 13 December 1918 Hearing, Docket 444, NWLB, RG 2, NA, Washington, D.C.

34. Report from Agnes Peterson and Ethel Best to Mary van Kleeck, 22 July 1919, Accession no. 51-101, WB, RG 86, NA, Washington, D.C.; Employees vs. Detroit United Railway, Transcript of 13 December 1918 Hearing, p. 30, Docket 444, NWLB, RG 2, NA, Washington, D.C.; "The Woman Street Car Conductor—Shall She Have Fair Play?" *Life and Labor* 9 (January 1919): 15-16.

35. "Car Women Hear Stand Applauded," *Cleveland Plain Dealer*, 25 September 1918; "Women Conductors' Association," Survey Materials, Bulletins nos. 11, 15, 18, File Streetcar Conductors, WB, RG 86, NA, Washington, D.C.

36. "Women Conductors' Association," Survey Materials, Bulletins nos. 11, 15, 18, File Streetcar Conductors, WB, RG 86, NA, Washington, D.C.

37. Employees vs. Detroit United Railway, Transcript of 13 December 1918 Hearing, pp. 25-26, Docket 444, NWLB, RG 2, NA, Washington, D.C.; "Car Women Hear Stand Applauded," *CPD*, 25 September 1918.

38. Schmidt, *Industrial Relations*, pp. 82-84.

39. Philip Taft and Philip Ross, "American Labor Violence: Its Causes, Character, and Outcome," in *The History of Violence in America: Historical and Comparative Perspectives*, eds. Hugh Davis Graham and Ted Robert Gurr (New York: Bantam Books, 1969), pp. 311-314.

40. Interview with Mr. Ward, former secretary of the Detroit Amalgamated, 1 July 1919, Survey Materials, Bulletins nos. 11, 15, 18, File Streetcar Conductors, WB, RG 86, NA, Washington, D.C.

41. W. M. Rea to William B. Wilson, 26 September 1918, Docket 491, NWLB, RG 2, NA, Washington, D.C.; Employees of Cleveland Railway Company, Members of Amalgamated Association of Street and Railway Employees of America, vs. Cleveland Railway Company, and Women Conductors' Association vs. Amalgamated Association of Street and Electric Railway Employees of America, Transcript of 8 November 1918 Hearing, pp. 55-60, Docket 491, NWLB, RG 2, NA, Washington, D.C.

42. Henry B. Dielmann and Margaret Russanowska to Fred Telschow, 9 September 1918, Docket 491, NWLB, RG 2, NA, Washington, D.C.; Federal investigators' decision, 21 September 1918, Docket 491, NWLB, RG 2, NA, Washington, D.C.; Preliminary Report of Commissioner of Conciliation, 4 September 1918, Docket 491, NWLB, RG 2, NA, Washington, D.C.

43. "Cleveland Women Appeal," *ERJ* 52 (October 26, 1918): 753; Florence Allen to William B. Wilson, 1 October 1918, Docket 491, RG 2, NA, Washington, D.C.

44. Elizabeth Hauser to the President of the United States, 26 September 1918; Edna Perkins to William B. Wilson, 26 September 1918; Telegram from the Cleveland Federation of Women's Clubs to William B. Wilson, 26 September 1918; Telegram from Harriet Taylor Upton to the White House, 26 September 1918, Docket 491, NWLB, RG 2, NA, Washington, D.C.

45. "Reconsiders Car Ruling, Is Report," *CPD* (September 28, 1918): 15; Committee on Industrial Welfare of the Cleveland Chamber of Commerce, *A Report on the Problem of Woman for Man Power in Industry* (Cleveland, July 17, 1918).

46. Telegram from William B. Wilson to A. L. Faulkner, 26 October 1918; A. L. Faulkner to William B. Wilson, 30 October 1918; J. A. Groves to William B. Wilson, 27 September 1918; John T. Bishop to William B. Wilson, 2 October 1918; William Rea to William B. Wilson, 26 September 1918, Docket 491, NWLB, RG 2, NA, Washington, D.C.

47. Employees vs. Cleveland Street Railway Company, Transcript of 8 November 1918 Hearing, pp. 55-85, Docket 491, NWLB, RG 2, NA, Washington, D.C.

48. Ibid., pp. 13-30.

49. Bureau of Labor Statistics, *National War Labor Board*, p. 305; "U.S. Asks Dismissal of Car Women; Service May Resume This Afternoon" and "Carless Traffic Jams in Rainfall," *CPD*, 4 December 1918.

50. William C. Liller to Hugh L. Kerwin, 21 January 1919, File 33-1950, FMCS, RG 280, NA, Washington, D.C.

51. "Confer to Find Car Women Jobs," *CPD*, 8 December 1918; "Strike May Set Women's Status," *CPD*, 12 December 1918; "Car Women Hear Stand Applauded," *CPD*, 25 September 1918; "Carmen Agree to Work Again, Women to Go," *CPD*, 6 December 1918.

52. "Carmen Agree to Work Again, Women to Go," *CPD*, 6 December 1918; "Car Fares Won't Go Above 5 Cents," *CPD*, 10 December 1918.

53. "Car Women Fight Dusting at Gathering," *CPD*, 24 September 1918; *CPD*, 25 September 1918; "Car Women May Ask National Aid," *CPD*, 7 December 1918; *CPD*, 12 December 1918; "Cleveland Strike Settled," *ERJ* 52 (December 14, 1918): 1061.

54. Margaret Dreier Robins et al. to NWLB, 11 December 1918; Florence Simms to NWLB, 21 December 1918; Florence T. Perkins to NWLB, 3 January 1919; Telegram from Cornelia B. Pinchot to NWLB, 22 December 1918; Florence King to NWLB, 14 December 1918, Docket 491, NWLB, RG 2, NA, Washington, D.C.

55. Mary van Kleeck and Mary Anderson to W. Jett Lauck, 10 December 1918, Docket 491, NWLB, RG 2, NA, Washington, D.C. For Lauck's response see W. Jett Lauck to Mary van Kleeck and Mary Anderson, 19 December 1918, Accession no. 55-A-485, File War 1918, WB, RG 86, NA, Washington, D.C.

56. Rose Moriarty to Frank P. Walsh, 23 December 1918, General Correspondence, Box 26, Frank P. Walsh Papers, New York Public Library, New York City.

57. "Harnessing Women," *UL* 19 (December 21, 1918): 4.

58. President Gompers' Conference, 16 December 1918, Reel no. 4, Conference 4, American Federation of Labor Archives, Washington, D.C.

59. Graeme O'Geran, *A History of Detroit Railways* (Detroit, 1931), pp. 318-319; Bureau of Labor Statistics, *National War Labor Board*, pp. 150-151; Employees of Detroit United Railway, Members of the Amalgamated Association of Street and Electric Railway Employees of America, vs. Detroit United Railway, and Women Conductors' Association vs. Amalgamated Association of Street and Electric Railway Employees of America, Transcript of 13 December 1918 Hearing, pp. 11, 28, Docket 444, NWLB, RG 2, NA, Washington, D.C.

60. Employees of Detroit United Railway vs. Detroit United Railway and Women Conductors' Association, Transcript of 13 December 1918 Hearing, pp. 1-10, Docket 444, NWLB, RG 2, NA, Washington, D.C. The percentage of women conductors was computed from the evidence offered at the January 17, 1919 NWLB hearing in the case. On December 9, 1918, the company employed 2,359 motormen and conductors. At that time the women conductors numbered 260.

61. David Allan Levine, *Internal Combustion: The Races in Detroit 1915-1926* (Westport, Conn., 1976), pp. 28-29; "Coercion of Labor in Detroit Charged," *Christian Science Monitor*, 5 October 1918; *Detroit Labor News*, 20 September 1918.

62. Bureau of Labor Statistics, *National War Labor Board*, pp. 298-300.

63. See "Executive Minutes," 19 December 1918, NWLB, RG 2, NA, Washington, D.C. for an illuminating debate on the matter of reopening the Cleveland case. The meeting clearly reveals the differing attitudes of the board members toward women.

64. Frank P. Walsh to Victor A. Olander, 4 December 1918; Ethel M. Smith to Frank P. Walsh, 11 January 1919; Ethel M. Smith to Frank P. Walsh, 14 January 1919; Frank P. Walsh to Rose Moriarty, 27 January 1919; Telegram from Ethel M. Smith to Frank P. Walsh, 10 March 1919, General Correspondence, Boxes 26-29, 1918-1919, Walsh Papers, New York Public Library, New York City.

65. Employees vs. Cleveland Railway Company, Transcript of 13 March 1919 Hearing, pp. 25-28, Docket 491, NWLB, RG 2, NA, Washington, D.C.

66. Basil M. Manly to Frank P. Walsh, 19 March 1919, General Correspondence, Box 29, Walsh Papers, New York Public Library, New York City.

67. Bureau of Labor Statistics, *National War Labor Board*, pp. 304-306.

68. Frank P. Walsh to Rose Moriarty, 21 March 1919 and Rose Moriarty to Frank P. Walsh, 20 March 1919, General Correspondence, Box 29, Walsh Papers, New York Public Library, New York City.

69. Telegram from Ethel M. Smith to Frank P. Walsh, 19 March 1919 and Ethel M. Smith to Frank P. Walsh, 21 March 1919, General Correspondence, Box 29, Walsh Papers, New York Public Library, New York City.

70. "History of Cleveland Street Car Case," Accession no. 51-101, WB, RG 86, NA, Washington, D.C.; "Union Women Protest Action of Labor Board in Cleveland," *SUR*, 26 December 1918.

71. "Women Conductors' Association" and Interview with Mr. Brooks of the Detroit United Railways, 30 June 1919, Survey Materials, Bulletins nos. 11, 15, 18, File Streetcar Conductors, WB, RG 86, NA, Washington, D.C.

72. Kansas City, Missouri Women's Trade Union League, *Report* (May 1917 to June 1919), pp. 9-10. This report can be found in the Cornelia Pinchot Papers, LC, Washington, D.C. F.J. Rohde to William B. Wilson, 10 February 1919, File 33/2965, FMCS, RG 280, NA, Washington, D.C.; Mrs. G.W. Addison to William B. Wilson, 13 March 1918, File 33-993, FMCS, RG 280, NA, Washington, D.C.

73. F.W. Porter to William B. Wilson, 16 March 1918, File 33-993, FMCS, RG 280, NA, Washington, D.C.

74. Addison to Wilson, 13 March 1918, File 33-993, FMCS, RG 280, NA, Washington, D.C.

75. Telegram from Joseph H. Anderson, Frank Peterson, and J.C. Snyder to the President of the United States, 15 March 1918 and Addison to Wilson, 13 March 1918, File 33-993, FMCS, RG 280, NA, Washington, D.C.

76. Alexander Bing, *War-Time Strikes and Their Adjustment* (New York, 1921), p. 30 n. 1.

77. Kansas City, Missouri Women's Trade Union League, *Report*, p. 8d.

78. "Sarah Lloyd Green," *Life and Labor Bulletin* 7 (October 1929): 3.

79. Kansas City, Missouri Women's Trade Union League, *Report*, p. 8h.

80. "The International Field," *UL* 19 (March 16, 1918): 5.

81. "Minutes of Meeting of the National Executive Board, New York City, 17-19 April 1912, Box 19, File Historical Data 1912-1919, NWTUL Papers, LC, Washington, D.C.; Alice Henry, *The Trade Union Woman* (New York, 1915), p. 84; Kansas City, Missouri Women's Trade Union League, *Report*, pp. 2-8a.

82. Kansas City, Missouri Women's Trade Union League, *Report*, p. 9; Ethel M. Smith, "The Woman's Labor Movement, *Federal Employee* 4 (April 1919): 214-217.

83. Amalgamated Association of Street and Electric Railway Employees of America, Division 764 vs. The Kansas City Railways Company, Transcript of 16 September 1918 and 1 October 1918 Hearings, Docket 265, NWLB, RG 2, NA, Washington, D.C.; Bureau of Labor Statistics, *National War Labor Board*, pp. 250-252.

84. Bureau of Labor Statistics, *National War Labor Board*, p. 253.

85. Kansas City, Missouri Women's Trade Union League, *Report*, pp. 8h and 9; Women's Bureau, *Women Street Car Conductors*, p. 38; Employees vs. Kansas City Railways, Transcript of 3 January 1919 and 18 January 1919 Hearings, Docket 265, NWLB, RG 2, NA, Washington, D.C.

86. Bureau of Labor Statistics, *National War Labor Board*, pp. 254-255; Kansas City, Missouri Women's Trade Union League, *Report*, p. 9.

87. Kansas City, Missouri Women's Trade Union League, *Report*, p. 9-10; "Strikes and Lockouts," *M&C* 27 (May 1919): 14; Women's Bureau, *Women Street Car Conductors*, p. 38.

88. Wilcox, *Analysis of the Electrical Railway Problem*, pp. 534-535; F. Robertson to Attorney General of the United States, 30 October 1920, File 16-114-29 Section II, Department of Justice, RG 60, NA, Washington, D.C.

89. U.S., Department of Commerce, Bureau of the Census, *Fifteenth Census of the United States: 1930*, vol. 4: *Population: Occupations, by States* (Washington, D.C., 1933), Table 13: 30.

90. C. C. Arbuthnot, Western Reserve University, to the Editor, *CPD*, 10 December 1918.

CHAPTER 5.   NO SERVICE, NO SMILE:
TELEPHONE OPERATING AND THE WAR

1. N. R. Danielian, *AT&T: The Story of Industrial Conquest* (New York, 1939), p. 235.

2. The term "industrial conquest" is taken from N.R. Danielian's book, *AT&T*, which critically examines the growth of the Bell System from the 1870s to the 1930s.

3. Danielian, *AT&T*, pp. 39-46; J. Warren Stehman, *The Financial History of the American Telephone and Telegraph Company* (Boston, 1925), pp. 1-21, 32-36, 65, 74, 132-136; Joseph Leigh Walsh, *Connecticut Pioneers in Telephone: The Origin and Growth of the Telephone Industry in Connecticut* (New Haven, 1950), pp. 84, 87-88, 99, 110, 135, 143-144, 200.

4. Stehman, *Financial History*, pp. 51-59, 96, 129-130; Danielian, *AT&T*, pp. 46-50, 58.

5. Albert Bigelow Paine, *Theodore N. Vail, A Biography* (New York, 1929), pp. 2-308; Danielian, *AT&T*, pp. 70-71; Stehman, *Financial History*, pp. 124-126; Walsh, *Connecticut Pioneers*, pp. 368-369; John Nixon Brooks, *Telephone, The First Hundred Years: The Wondrous Invention that Changed a World and Spawned a Corporate Giant* (New York, 1975), pp. 67-72; Alfred D. Chandler, Jr., *The Visible Hand: The Managerial Revolution in American Business* (Cambridge, Mass., 1977), pp. 201-203.

6. Stehman, *Financial History*, pp. 68, 145; Marion May Dilts, *The Telephone in a Changing World* (New York, 1941), pp. 32-35, 67; Brooks, *Telephone*, pp. 112, 114. The history of one telephone company which succeeded in remaining independent from the Bell System is told in William D. Torrence, "Great Independent: The Lincoln Telephone Company, 1903-1908," *Business History Review* 33 (1959): 359-382.

7. U.S., Bureau of the Census, *Census of Electrical Industries: 1917, Telephones* (Washington, D.C., 1920), pp. 30-32.

8. Danielian, *AT&T*, p. 27.

9. Cecil W. Mackenzie, "Early Days of the Telephone in Buffalo: An Autobiographical Retrospect of Fifty Years with the Bell Telephone Company," typescript, September 1936 (New York, AT&T Archives), p. 29; Dilts, *Telephone*, pp. 98-99, 105; Walsh, *Connecticut Pioneers*, p. 26.

10. Mackenzie, "Early Days of the Telephone," p. 22; Nathaniel W. Lillie, "Reminiscences of the Telephone in Boston, 1877-1914," typescript, 1932 (New York, AT&T Archives), pp. 31-32; Angus Hibbard, *Hello, Goodbye; My Story of Telephone Pioneering* (Chicago, 1941), pp. 23-25; "First Lady of the Switchboards," *Long Line Magazine* (April 1959); "First Woman Telephone Operator Dies," *Boston Globe*, 4 June 1926;

Katherine M. Schmitt, "I Was Your Old 'Hello' Girl," *Saturday Evening Post* (July 12, 1930): 18-19, 120; Walsh, *Connecticut Pioneers*, pp. 73-75, 103, 129.

11. U.S., Bureau of the Census, *Statistics of Women at Work: 1900* (Washington, D.C., 1907), p. 34. The accurate numerical breakdown of telephone operators in 1900 shows 54.6 percent native-born white with both parents native-born white; 39.1 percent native-born white with one or more parents foreign-born; 6.2 percent foreign-born white; 0.1 percent Negro, Indian or Mongolian.

12. Dilts, *Telephone*, pp. 101-105; Kingsbury, *The Telephone and Telephone Exchanges: Their Invention and Development* (New York, 1915), p. 318.

13. U.S., Bureau of the Census, *Census of Electrical Industries: 1922, Telephones* (Washington, D.C., 1922), p. 52.

14. Dilts, *Telephone*, p. 100.

15. Ibid., p. 107; Walsh, *Connecticut Pioneers*, pp. 132-133, 206; U.S., Congress, Senate, *Investigation of Telephone Companies*, 61st Cong., 2d sess., S. Doc. 380, February 1910, pp. 76-77. Schmitt, "I Was Your Old 'Hello' Girl," p. 121; Mackenzie, "Early Days of the Telephone," pp. 47, 66; Brooks, *Telephone*, p. 117.

16. Walsh, *Connecticut Pioneers*, p. 133.

17. Ibid., pp. 167-169. See also Mackenzie, "Early Days of the Telephone," p. 100.

18. "First Woman Telephone Operator," *Boston Globe*, 4 June 1926; Schmitt, "I Was Your Old 'Hello' Girl," pp. 18-19, 120-122; Walsh, *Connecticut Pioneers*, pp. 377-380. See also Mackenzie, "Early Days of the Telephone," pp. 99-100.

19. Elizabeth Beardsley Butler, *Women and the Trades: Pittsburgh 1907-1908*, The Pittsburgh Survey, ed. Paul Underwood Kellogg, vol. 1 (New York, 1909), pp. 282-285; Dilts, *Telephone*, p. 109; Walsh, *Connecticut Pioneers*, p. 251.

20. Senate, *Investigation of Telephone Companies*, 1910, pp. 19-20, 21n. 22-23; Chicago Commission on Race Relations, *The Negro in Chicago: A Study of Race Relations and a Race Riot* (Chicago, 1922), p. 392.

21. Sadie Cameron, "Sadie, The Switchboard Girl, Speaks Her Mind," *Journal of Electrical Workers and Operators* (May 1926): 12; "Good Points and Bad of Telephone Operating as a Trade for Philadelphia Girls," *Survey* 31 (February 7, 1914): 542-543.

22. Lesson number one of the 1910 Chicago telephone operator's manual is reprinted in Senate, *Investigation of Telephone Companies*, 1910, p. 333. See app. B, Specimens of First Lessons in Telephone Operating, for a fuller description of one company's training program. The ex-

pression telephone service "with a smile" was a familiar slogan according to U.S., Department of Labor, Women's Bureau, *The Woman Telephone Worker*, Bulletin no. 207 (Washington, D.C., 1946), p. 2. Information about other training schools for telephone operators can be found in "New England Telephone and Telegraph Company," *Labor Bulletin of the Commonwealth of Massachusetts* 10 (December 1906): 462; Schmitt, "I Was Your Old 'Hello' Girl," pp. 121-122; "American Public Just Mumbles Now, but Spoke Well in '80's, Says Original 'Hello Girl,' in Charge of 600 Phones Here Then," *New York World-Telegram*, 29 January 1938.

23. Cameron, "Sadie," pp. 13-14, 49; "Good Points and Bad," *Survey* 31 (February 7, 1914): 543; Butler, *Women and the Trades*, pp. 288-289; Julia O'Connor, "History of the Organized Telephone Operators' Movement," *UTO* 1 (January 1921): 14.

24. "Telephone Girls and Laundry Workers," *Survey* 36 (April 8, 1916): 57; Senate, *Investigation of Telephone Companies*, 1910, pp. 45-48, 60; Butler, *Women and the Trades*, pp. 285-288; Cameron, "Sadie," p. 13; Josephine Goldmark, *Fatigue and Efficiency: A Study in Industry* (New York, 1913), pp. 43-52; "'Hello, Central!' What It Means to Be a Telephone Girl as Told by the Central Labor Council's Woman Organizer to Gale," *SUR*, 27 April 1918.

25. Cameron, "Sadie," p. 14.

26. Senate, *Investigation of Telephone Companies*, 1910, pp. 54-55; Butler, *Women and the Trades*, pp. 287-288.

27. Cameron, "Sadie," p. 12; Senate, *Investigation of Telephone Companies*, 1910, p. 17. Stress and strict surveillance still characterize telephone operating according to Janet Bertinuson, "CWA Pickets Pacific Telephone over Job Pressures, Stress," *Monitor* (September-October 1978): 14-15. Thanks is due Judy Hilkey for this reference.

28. Senate, *Investigation of Telephone Companies*, 1910, p. 97; Butler, *Women and the Trades*, p. 285; Anne Withington, "The Telephone Strike," *Survey* 42 (April 26, 1919): 146; "Hurry, Girls, Hurry!" *Survey* 44 (June 12, 1920): 367; John N. Schacht, "Toward Industrial Unionism: Bell Telephone Workers and Company Unions, 1919-1937," *Labor History* 16 (Winter 1975): 14.

29. New York, Department of Labor, Bureau of Women in Industry, *Report Submitted Relative to the Telephone Industry in New York State* (Albany, 1920), pp. 38-39; Senate, *Investigation of Telephone Companies*, 1910, pp. 48-49; Butler, *Women and the Trades*, pp. 291-292; Michael Mulcaire, *The International Brotherhood of Electrical Workers* (Washington, D.C., 1923), p. 35n.

30. See Louise Odencrantz, "The Irregularity of Employment of Women Factory Workers," *Survey* 22 (May 1, 1909): 196-210 for an excellent discussion of women's industrial work. According to this report, the single most important reason for unemployment was the seasonal or temporary nature of women's industrial work. When women voluntarily left their jobs, low pay and limited advancement ranked first on the list of reasons.

31. Montgomery, "The 'New Unionism' and the Transformation of Workers' Consciousness in America, 1909-1922," *Journal of Social History* 7 (Summer 1974): 518. Montgomery used the term "submerged, impenetrable obstacle to management's sovereignty" to describe the strategy that skilled workers were forced to use after the introduction of scientific management destroyed their traditional methods for controlling their work; the term also aptly describes the technique employed by unskilled and semiskilled workers in manufacturing to subvert production quotas set by management.

32. Bureau of Women in Industry, *Report*, pp. 38-39.

33. O'Connor, "History," *UTO* 1 (March 1921): 14-15. See also Emily Barrows, "Trade Union Organization Among Women in Chicago" (M.A. Thesis: University of Chicago, 1927), p. 136.

34. Montgomery, "The 'New Unionism,'" pp. 512, 519.

35. Cameron, "Sadie," pp. 13-14; Walsh, *Connecticut Pioneers*, pp. 250-252; Schacht, "Toward Industrial Unionism," pp. 8-13.

36. "Historic Gavel for Hello Girl," *SUR*, Weekly Edition, 5 January 1918; National Women's Trade Union League, *Proceedings of the Seventh Biennial Convention*, Philadelphia, 2-7 June 1919, Container 24: 25-26, NWTUL Papers, LC, Washington, D.C.

37. *Who's Who in Labor: The Authorized Biographies of the Men and Women Who Lead Labor in the United States and Canada and of Those Who Deal With Labor* (New York, 1946), pp. 272-273; "The Beating of Burleson as Told by Julia O'Connor to Anise," *SUR*, 27 May 1919; National Women's Trade Union League, *Newsletter* 1917, Box 19, File Historical Data 1912-1919, NWTUL Papers, LC, Washington, D.C.; *Boston Herald*, 17 April 1919; "Tumulty Wires Pleas to Telephone Strikers," *Boston Herald*, 16 April 1919.

38. Minutes of Meeting of National Executive Board, New York City, 17-19 April 1912, Box 19, File Historical Data, 1912-1919, NWTUL Papers, LC, Washington, D.C.; O'Connor, "History," *UTO* 1 (February 1921): 15-17; Anne Withington, "When the Telephone Girls Organized," *Survey* 30 (August 16, 1913): 621-623; "The Beating of Burleson," *SUR*, 27 May 1919.

39. Ibid.

40. O'Connor, "History," *UTO* 1 (February 1921): 16-17.

41. Danielian, *AT&T*, pp. 223-224. Although Danielian comments on Bell's labor policies during the 1920s and 1930s, his evaluations are valid for the prewar period as well. For the precise terms of Bell's employee benefits, see Arthur W. Page, *The Bell Telephone System* (New York, 1941), app. II, pp. 217-243. The meagerness of benefits to women is confirmed in Women's Bureau, *The Woman Telephone Worker*, p. 36.

42. Stehman, *Financial History*, p. 45; *Annual Report of the Directors of American Telephone and Telegraph Company to the Stockholders for the Year Ending December 31, 1916* (New York, 1917), pp. 20-22, 26-27.

43. Withington, "When the Telephone Operators Organized," p. 623; O'Connor, "History," *UTO* 1 (February 1921): 16.

44. Stehman, *Financial History*, pp. 169-175; Walsh, *Connecticut Pioneers*, pp. 259-260.

45. Stehman, *Financial History*, pp. 176, 181-186. On the one hand, Stehman argued that telephone companies appeared better able to meet the financial demands of the wartime emergency than railroad companies. On the other hand, he argued that Bell began to feel the pinch of inflation before the government assumed economic responsibility for the telephone wires.

46. *Annual Report of AT&T, 1916*, pp. 20-22, 26-27.

47. Bureau of Women in Industry, *Report*, pp. 11-12, 14-16.

48. Ibid., pp. 13, 41-43. In 1910, at the time of the federal investigation of telephone companies, the average service of an operator was about three years. The lower the age of an operator, the longer she stayed with a company. Senate, *Investigation of Telephone Companies*, 1910, p. 48. The longer length of prewar service can probably be attributed to the girls' lack of work experience and job options. The wartime work opportunities disrupted this pattern as females of all ages deliberately chose to change their jobs frequently.

49. "Telephone Dispute, Pacific Coast," n.d., Chief Clerk's File 20/473, U.S. Department of Labor, RG 174, NA, Washington, D.C.

50. Ibid.

51. G.E. McFarland, Major D.P. Fullerton, H.D. Allsbury of the Pacific Telephone and Telegraph to Vernon Z. Reed, President's Mediation Commission, 2 November 1917, Chief Clerk's File 20/473, DL, RG 174, NA, Washington, D.C.

52. "Summary of Report of President's Mediation Commission," n.d., Chief Clerk's File 20/473, DL, RG 174, NA, Washington, D.C.

53. One of the girls who *favors* a union to Vernon Z. Reed, Los Angeles, 8 November 1917, File 33-758, FMCS, RG 280, NA, Washington, D.C.; "Administration of the Telephone Agreement," Chief Clerk's File 20/473, DL, RG 174, NA, Washington, D.C.; "Girls Accept Settlement," *SUR*, Weekly Edition, 8 December 1917, "Phone Workers Get New Wage," *SUR*, Weekly Edition, 29 December 1917; "Phone Operators Eagerly Waiting on the Government," *SUR*, 16 March 1918; "Phone Girls Are Wanted by Company," *SUR*, Weekly Edition, 18 May 1918; "Phone People Ask Fair Trial," *SUR*, Weekly Edition, 25 May 1918.

54. K. Austin Kerr, *American Railroad Politics, 1914-1920* (Pittsburgh, 1968), pp. 72-127; Danielian, *AT&T*, pp. 243-270.

55. Danielian, *AT&T*, p. 252.

56. Ibid.

57. Albert Burleson to David F. Houston, Sec. of the Treasury, 1 May 1920, Container 25, Albert Burleson Papers, LC, Washington, D.C.; Danielian, *AT&T*, pp. 254-270.

58. Kerr, *American Politics*, pp. 72-100; O'Connor, "History," *UTO* 1 (May 1921): 15; J. H. Walker to William B. Wilson, 15 July 1919, File 170-562, FMCS, RG 280, NA, Washington, D.C.

59. *The National Cyclopaedia of American Biography*, vol. 28 (New York, 1940), pp. 386-387.

60. Alexander M. Bing, *War-Time Strikes and Their Adjustment* (New York, 1921), p. 108 n. 3; "A.F. of L. Hits at Burleson," *SUR*, Weekly Edition, 24 November 1917.

61. William Preston, Jr., *Aliens and Dissenters: Federal Suppression of Radicals, 1903-1933* (New York, 1966), pp. 144-151; "Progress and Development of the Postal Service under Postmaster Burleson," mimeograph, Container 22, Burleson Papers, LC, Washington, D.C.

62. Albert Burleson, Address to the Annual Convention of the National Hardware Association of the United States, 15 October 1919, Container 24, LC, Washington, D.C.

63. Preston, *Aliens and Dissenters*, pp. 181-272; Robert K. Murray, *Red Scare: A Study in National Hysteria* (New York, 1964), pp. 203-204.

64. Post Office Order 2005, 13 September 1918, Office of the Solicitor, Records on Federal Control, U.S. Post Office Department, RG 28, NA, Washington, D.C.; "Problems and Activities of Women," *Federal Employee* 4 (March 1919): 146.

65. "Minutes of the Wire Control Board," 24 October 1918, Chief Clerk's File 20/473, DL, RG 174, NA, Washington, D.C.

66. The Post Office Department records in the National Archives contain numerous reports about labor disputes during the period of federal control. The reports include the evaluations of department inspectors, correspondence from IBEW leaders and telephone officials as well as newspaper clippings. Of particular interest is Office of the Solicitor, Records on Federal Control, Box 268, Record Group 28 which pertains to employment conditions.

67. Ethel Smith, "Government Control and Industrial Rights," *Life and Labor* 9 (April 1919): 86; W. F. Allmon, Post Office Inspector, "Report on Wichita Kansas Case," 8 January 1919, Office of the Solicitor, PO, RG 28, NA, Washington, D.C.

68. Memo from Louis Post, Assistant Secretary of Labor, to William B. Wilson, Secretary of Labor, 23 December 1918, Chief Clerk's File 20/473, DL, RG 174, NA, Washington, D.C.; A. S. Burleson to W. B. Wilson, 15 March 1919, Office of the Solicitor, PO, RG 28, NA, Washington, D.C.; Linna E. Bressette, Secretary of the Industrial Commission of Kansas, to Mary Anderson, 2 January 1919, Chief Clerk's File 20/473, DL, RG 174, NA, Washington, D.C.; "Report of Women in Industry Service," 28 December 1918, War Labor Policies Board, Box 19, RG 1, NA, Washington, D.C.; *Wichita Eagle*, 7-8 January 1919.

69. Allmon, "Report."

70. Ibid.

71. Julia O'Connor, "The Blight of Company Unionism," *American Federationist* 33 (May 1926); 544-549.

72. O'Connor, "The Truth about the New England Phone Strike," *Life and Labor* 9 (June 1919): 131-133; H. J. Skeffington to H. L. Kerwin, 5 June 1919, File 170-338, RG, FMCS, 280, NA, Washington, D.C.

73. National Women's Trade Union League, *Proceedings of the Seventh Biennial Convention 1919*, pp. 113-116.

74. Ibid. See also "Probe Complaint of W.U. Office at Hingham," *Boston Herald*, 17 April 1919 for another account of operator-soldier unity.

75. National Women's Trade Union League, *Proceedings, 1919*, pp. 114-115; Stephen H. Norwood, "The New England Telephone Operators' Union, 1912-1923" (Paper delivered at the New England Historical Association Meeting, Boston, Massachusetts, 3 May 1975).

76. "Telegraphers' Union Asks Strike Sanction," *Boston Herald*, 19 April 1919; "Operators Joyous as They Wait for Reports," *Boston Herald*, 21 April 1919; "Koons Coming Here for Parley with Strikers," *Boston Herald*, 17 April 1919; "Arrest Sailors in Strike Disorders," *Boston Herald*, 19 April 1919.

77. "Strips Uniform from Boy Scout," *Boston Herald*, 21 April 1919; "Brockton Mayor Demands Action," *Boston Herald*, 19 April 1919; "Telephone Clerks May Join Strikers," *Boston Herald*, 19 April 1919; "Society Girls at Switchboards," *Boston Herald*, 18 April 1919; "Smith Girls Run the Gantlet [*sic*]," *Boston Herald*, 19 April 1919; National Women's Trade Union League, *Proceedings, 1919*, p. 115.

78. National Women's Trade Union League, *Proceedings, 1919*, p. 115; "Society Girls at Switchboards," *Boston Herald*, 18 April 1919; "Nashua Merchants Treat Strikers," *Boston Herald*, 19 April 1919.

79. O'Connor, "History," *UTO* 1 (June 1921): 16.

80. O'Connor, "The Truth about the New England Phone Strike," *Life and Labor* 9 (June 1919): 133; "Must Raise Telephone Rates, Koons Declares," *Boston Herald*, 22 April 1919.

81. O'Connor, "History," *UTO* 1 (July 1921): 19; Edith Simpson, "Trade Union Organization among the Telephone Operators in the United States," *UTO* 1 (November 1921): 14-15; O'Connor, "History," *UTO* 1 (March 1921): 19; File 16-125-30, Department of Justice, RG 60, NA, Washington, D.C., on the Lousville, Kentucky strike; File 16-125-67, RG 60, NA, Washington, D.C., on the Columbia, South Carolina strike; File 16-125-58, RG 60, NA, Washington, D.C., on the Cleveland, Ohio strike; File 16-119, RG 60, NA, Washington, D.C., on the Linton, Indiana strike.

82. Albert Burleson, *Government Control and Operation of the Telephone and Telegraph Systems* (Washington, D.C., 1921).

83. J. H. Walker to William B. Wilson, 15 July 1919, File 170-562, FMCS, RG 280, NA, Washington, D.C.

84. Testimony by Mildred Luebbers to M. B. Lanney, Chief Inspector, 29 June 1919, Office of the Solicitor, PO, RG 28, NA, Washington, D.C.

85. O'Connor, "History," *UTO* 1 (June 1921): 17-19; Hawley to Department of Labor, 30 August 1919, File 170-668, FMCS, RG 280, NA, Washington, D.C.

86. O'Connor, "History," *UTO* 1 (July 1921): 16-18; Telephone Operators' Department of the International Brotherhood of Electrical Workers, *Proceedings of the Second Biennial Convention, 1921*, p. 9.

87. Simpson, "Trade Union Organization," *UTO* 1 (November 1921): 14-16.

88. Theresa Wolfson, *The Woman Worker and the Trade Unions* (New York, 1926), p. 214.

89. O'Connor, "History," *UTO* 1 (March 1921): 14-19; Jack Barbash, *Unions and Telephones* (New York, 1952), pp. 3-4; Mulcaire, *International Brotherhood of Electrical Workers*, pp. 30-37.

90. Wolfson, *Woman Worker*, pp. 80-81; International Brotherhood of

Electrical Workers, *Proceedings of the Fifteenth Convention, 1919.* See Resolution 17 granting IBEW money to the telephone operators' organization, Telephone Operators' Department, *Report of the Officers, 1921,* p. 5. See also Simpson, "Trade Union Organization," *UTO* 1 (November 1921): 14-16.

91. Telephone Operators' Department, *Report of the Officers, 1921,* p. 13; "Bell Trust Refuses to Co-operate with Unions," *Journal of Electrical Workers and Operators* (May 1926): 15, 50.

92. O'Connor, "The Blight of Company Unionism," *American Federationist* 33 (May 1926): 544-549.

93. E. K. Hall, "What is Employee Representation?" *Personnel* 4 (February 1928): 78-79. See also *Annual Report of the Directors of American Telephone and Telegraph Company to the Stockholders for the Year Ending December 31, 1919,* (New York, 1920), pp. 29-31.

94. Ibid., p. 82.

95. Ibid., p. 77; Barbash, *Union and Telephones,* pp. 12-13; Schacht, "Toward Industrial Unionism," pp. 18-20.

96. Howard Fitch, "Technique of Holding Employee Representation Council or Committee Meetings: Where Female and Often Young Workers Predominate," *Personnel* 4 (February 1928): 150.

97. Danielian, *AT&T,* pp. 281-285; Report on Bell System Outside Contacts of the Bell System, Exhibit 228, Investigation Case File 1, Records of the Office of Secretary, Federal Communications Commission, RG 173, NA, Suitland, Maryland.

98. Simpson, "Trade Union Organization," *UTO* 1 (November 1921): 14-16.

99. E. K. Hall, "To Get the Best From Each," *System* 57 (April 1930): 374.

100. Schacht, "Toward Industrial Unionism," pp. 22-27.

101. Women's Bureau, *The Change from Manual to Dial,* Bulletin no. 110 (Washington, D.C., 1933), p. 3; Women's Bureau, *The Woman Telephone Worker,* pp. 36-37.

Bibliography

MANUSCRIPT COLLECTIONS

American Telephone and Telegraph Company Archives, New York City, New York

Arthur and Elizabeth Schlesinger Library on the History of Women in America, Cambridge, Massachusetts
Mary Anderson Papers
Alice Hamilton Papers
National Women's Trade Union League Papers
Anna Howard Shaw Papers

Library of Congress, Washington, D.C.
Albert Sidney Burleson Papers
Pauline Goldmark Papers
National Consumers' League Papers
National Women's Trade Union League Papers
Cornelia Pinchot Papers

National Archives, Washington, D.C.
Record Group 1. Records of the War Labor Policies Board
Record Group 2. Records of the National War Labor Board (World War I)
Record Group 14. Records of the United States Railroad Administration
Record Group 28. Records of the Post Office Department
Record Group 60. Records of the Department of Justice
Record Group 62. Records of the Council of National Defense
Record Group 80. Records of the Department of the Navy

Record Group 86. Records of the Women's Bureau
Record Group 174. General Records of the Department of Labor
Record Group 183. Records of the Bureau of Employment Security
Record Group 280. Records of the Federal Mediation and Conciliation Service

National Archives, Suitland, Maryland
Record Group 156. Records of the Office of the Chief of Ordnance
Record Group 173. Records of the Federal Communications Commission

New York Public Library, New York City, New York
Frank P. Walsh Papers

Sophia Smith Collection, Smith College Library, Northampton, Massachusetts
Florence Allen Papers
Mary van Kleeck Papers

BOOKS AND DISSERTATIONS

Adams, Elizabeth Kemper. *Women Professional Workers: A Study Made for the Women's Educational and Industrial Union.* New York: Macmillan, 1921.

Adams, Graham. *Age of Industrial Violence, 1910-1915: The Activities and Findings of the United States Commission on Industrial Relations.* New York: Columbia University Press, 1966.

Aitken, Hugh. *Taylorism at Watertown: Scientific Management in Action, 1908-1915.* Cambridge: Harvard University Press, 1960.

Alberts, Robert C. *The Good Provider: H.J. Heinz and His 57 Varieties.* Boston: Houghton Mifflin, 1973.

Anderson, Dewey H., and Davidson, Percy E. *Occupational Trends in the United States.* Stanford: Stanford University Press, 1940.

Anderson, Mary. *Woman at Work: Autobiography of Mary Anderson as Told to Mary N. Winslow.* Minneapolis: University of Minnesota Press, 1951.

Athey, Louis Lee. "The Consumers' League and Social Reform, 1890-1923." Ph.D. dissertation, University of Delaware, 1965.

Banner, Lois W. *Women in Modern America: A Brief History.* New York: Harcourt Brace Jovanovich, Inc., 1974.

Barbash, Jack. *Unions and Telephones: The Story of the Communications Workers of America.* New York: Harper & Bros., 1952.

Baritz, Loren. *The Servants of Power: A History of the Use of Social Science in American Industry.* Middletown, Connecticut: Wesleyan University, 1960.

Bing, Alexander M. *War-Time Strikes and Their Adjustment.* New York: E.P. Dutton, 1921.

Blair, Emily Newell. *The Woman's Committee, United States Council of National Defense, An Interpretative Report, April 21, 1917 to February 27, 1919.* Washington, D.C.: Government Printing Office, 1920.

Blatch, Harriet Stanton. *Mobilizing Woman-Power.* New York: The Woman's Press, 1918.

Blaxall, Martha, and Reagan, Barbara B., eds. *Women and the Workplace: The Implications of Occupational Segregation.* Published as *Signs: Journal of Women in Culture and Society,* vol. 1, no. 3, pt. 2 (Spring 1976 Supplement).

Brandeis, Louis D., and Goldmark, Josephine. *Women in Industry: Decision of the United States Supreme Court in Curt Muller vs. State of Oregon Upholding the Constitutionality of the Oregon Ten-Hour Law for Women, and Brief for the State of Oregon.* New York: National Consumers' League, n.d.

Brandes, Stuart D. *American Welfare Capitalism.* Chicago: University of Chicago Press, 1976.

Braverman, Harry. *Labor and Monopoly Capital: The Degradation of Work in the Twentieth Century.* New York: Monthly Review Press, 1974.

Brody, David. *Steelworkers in America: The Nonunion Era.* Cambridge: Harvard University Press, 1960.

Broehl, Wayne G. Jr. *Precision Valley; the Machine Tool Companies of Springfield, Vermont: Jones and Lamson Machine Company, Fellows Gears Shaper Company [and] Bryant Chucking Grinder Company.* Englewood, N.J.: Prentice-Hall, 1959.

Brooks, John Nixon. *Telephone, The First Hundred Years: The Wondrous Invention that Changed a World and Spawned a Corporate Giant.* New York: Harper & Row, 1975.

Butler, Elizabeth Beardsley. *Saleswomen in Mercantile Stores: Baltimore, 1909.* New York: Russell Sage Foundation, Charities Publication Committee, 1912.

————. *Women and the Trades: Pittsburgh, 1907-1908.* The Pittsburgh Survey, edited by Paul Underwood Kellogg, vol. 1. New York: Russell Sage Foundation, Charities Publication Committee, 1909.

Byington, Margaret F. *Homestead: Households of a Mill Town.* The Pittsburgh Survey, edited by Paul Underwood Kellogg, vol. 4. New York: Russell Sage Foundation, Charities Publication Committee, 1910.

Catlin, George. *The Story of Detroit.* Detroit: The Detroit News, 1923.

Chafe, William H. *The American Woman: Her Changing Social, Economic, and Political Roles, 1920-1970.* New York: Oxford University Press, 1972.

Chandler, Alfred Jr. *Strategy and Structure: Chapters in the History of Industrial Enterprise.* Cambridge: M.I.T. Press, 1962.

_____. *The Visible Hand: The Managerial Revolution in American Business.* Cambridge: Harvard University Press, Belknap Press, 1977.

Chicago Commission on Race Relations. *The Negro in Chicago: A Study of Race Relations and a Race Riot.* Chicago: University of Chicago Press, 1922.

Clark, Sue Ainslie, and Wyatt, Edith. *Making Both Ends Meet: The Income and Outlay of New York Working Girls.* New York: Macmillan Company, 1911.

Clarke, Ida Clyde. *American Women and the World War.* New York: D. Appleton, 1918.

Clarkson, Grosvenor B. *Industrial America in the World War: The Strategy Behind the Line, 1917-1918.* Boston: Houghton Mifflin, 1923.

Cleveland Chamber of Commerce. *A Report on the Substitution of Woman for Man Power in Industry.* Cleveland, 1918.

Cochran, Thomas. *The American Business System: A Historical Perspective, 1900-1955.* New York: Harper & Row, 1962.

Consumers' League of Eastern Pennsylvania. *Colored Women as Industrial Workers in Philadelphia.* Philadelphia, 1920.

Consumers' League of the City of New York. *A New Day for the Colored Woman Worker: A Study of Colored Women in Industry in New York City.* New York, 1919.

Coyle, Grace. *Present Trends in Clerical Occupations.* New York: Women's Press, 1928.

Creel, George. *How We Advertised America.* New York: Harper & Bros., 1920.

Crowell, Benedict, and Wilson, Robert F. *How America Went to War.* 6 vols. New Haven: Yale University Press, 1921.

Crozier, Michel. *The World of the Office Worker.* Translated by David Landau. New York: Schocken Books, 1973.

Crozier, William. *Ordnance and the World War: A Contribution to the History of American Preparedness.* New York: Scribner's, 1920.

Cuff, Robert D. *The War Industries Board: Business-Government Relations During World War I.* Baltimore: Johns Hopkins University Press, 1973.

Cunningham, William J. *American Railroads: Government Control and Reconstruction Policies.* Chicago: A. W. Shaw, 1922.

Daggett, Mabel Potter. *Women Wanted: The Story Written in Blood Letters on the Horizon of the Great World War.* New York: George H. Doran Co., 1918.

Danielian, N.R. *AT&T: The Story of Industrial Conquest.* New York: Vanguard Press, 1939.

Dilts, Marion May. *The Telephone in a Changing World.* New York: Longmans, Green and Co., 1941.

Douglas, Paul H. *Real Wages in the United States, 1890-1926.* New York: Houghton Mifflin, 1930.

Dublin, Thomas. *Women at Work: The Transformation of Work and Community in Lowell, Massachusetts, 1826-1860.* New York: Columbia University Press, 1979.

Filene, Peter Gabriel. *Him/Her/Self: Sex Roles in Modern America.* New York: Harcourt Brace Jovanovich, Inc., 1974.

Gilbert, James B. *Work Without Salvation: America's Intellectuals and Industrial Alienation, 1880-1910.* Baltimore: Johns Hopkins University Press, 1977.

Gilson, Mary Barnett. *What's Past Is Prologue: Reflections on My Industrial Experience.* New York: Harper, 1940.

Glenn, John M.; Brandt, Lilian; and Andrews, F. Emerson. *Russell Sage Foundation, 1907-1946.* 2 vols. New York: Russell Sage Foundation, 1947.

Goldmark, Josephine. *Fatigue and Efficiency: A Study in Industry.* New York: Survey Associates, Inc., 1913.

Gottlieb, Peter. "Making Their Own Way: Southern Blacks' Migration to Pittsburgh, 1916-1930." Ph.D. dissertation, University of Pittsburgh, 1977.

Graham, Hugh Davis, and Gurr, Ted Roberts, eds. *The History of Violence in America.* New York: Bantam Books, Inc., 1969.

Grubbs, Frank. *The Struggle for Labor Loyalty: Gompers, the AF of L, and the Pacifists, 1917-1920.* Durham: Duke University Press, 1968.

Haber, Samuel. *Efficiency and Uplift: Scientific Management in the Progressive Era, 1890-1920.* Chicago: University of Chicago Press, 1964.

Haynes, George E. *The Negro at Work During the World War and Reconstruction: Statistics, Problems, and Policies Relating to the Greater Inclusion of Negro Wage Earners in American Industry and Agriculture.* Washington, D.C.: Government Printing Office, 1921.

Healy, Kent. *The Economics of Transportation in America: The Dynamic Forces in Development, Organization, Functioning and Regulation.* New York: The Ronald Press Company, 1940.

Henderson, Charles. *Citizens in Industry*. New York: D. Appleton and Company, 1915.

Henry, Alice. *The Trade Union Woman*. New York: D. Appleton and Company, 1915.

_____. *Women and the Labor Movement*. New York: George H. Doran Co., 1923.

Hewes, Amy. *Women as Munitions Workers: A Study of Conditions in Bridgeport*. New York: Russell Sage Foundation, 1917.

Hibbard, Angus. *Hello, Goodbye; My Story of Telephone Pioneering*. Chicago: A.C. McClurg & Company, 1941.

Hilton, George W., and Due, John F. *The Electric Interurban Railways in America*. Stanford: Stanford University Press, 1960.

Hines, Walter. *War History of American Railroads*. New Haven: Yale University Press, 1928.

Hinton, James. *The First Shop Stewards' Movement*. London: George Allen & Unwin, Ltd., 1973.

Holcombe, Lee. *Victorian Ladies at Work*. Hamden, Conn.: Archon Books, 1973.

Hollander, Herbert. *Quest for Excellence*. Washington, D.C.: Current Publications, Inc., 1968.

Honig, Harry. *Brotherhood of Railway Clerks*. New York: Columbia University Press, 1937.

Hughes, Gwendolyn Salisbury. *Mothers in Industry: Wage-Earning by Mothers in Philadelphia*. New York: New Republic, Inc., 1925.

Hymowitz, Carol, and Weissman, Michaele. *A History of Women in America*. New York: Bantam Books, Inc., 1978.

James, Edward, and James, Janet Wilson, eds. *Notable American Women, 1607-1950: A Biographical Dictionary*. 3 vols. Cambridge: Harvard University Press, 1971.

Kerr, K. Austin. *American Railroad Politics, 1914-1920: Rates, Wages, and Efficiency*. Pittsburgh: University of Pittsburgh Press, 1968.

Kingsbury, John E. *The Telephone and Telephone Exchanges: Their Invention and Development*. New York: Longmans, Green and Co., 1915.

Kirkland, Edward Chase. *Industry Comes of Age: Business, Labor and Public Policy, 1860-1897*. New York: Holt, Rinehart & Winston, 1961.

Kolko, Gabriel. *The Triumph of Conservatism: A Reinterpretation of American History, 1900-1916*. New York: Free Press, 1963.

Kraditor, Aileen. *The Ideas of the Woman Suffrage Movement, 1890-1920*. New York: Columbia University Press, 1965.

Lasswell, Harold. *Propaganda Technique in the World War.* New York: Alfred Knopf, 1927.

Lecht, Leonard. *Experience under Railway Labor Legislation.* New York: Columbia University Press, 1955.

Lemons, J. Stanley. *The Woman Citizen: Social Feminism in the 1920's.* Urbana: University of Illinois Press, 1973.

Levine, David Allan. *International Combustion: The Races in Detroit.* Westport, Conn.: Greenwood Press, 1976.

Levinson, Edward. *I Break Strikes! The Technique of Pearl L. Bergoff.* New York: Robert M. McBride & Company, 1935.

Lewinson, Minna, and Hough, H.B. *A History of the Services Rendered by the American Press During the Year 1917.* New York: Columbia University Press, 1918.

Lieberman, Joseph Andrew. "Their Sisters' Keepers: The Women's Hours and Wages Movement in the United States, 1890-1925." Ph.D. dissertation, Columbia University, 1971.

MacLean, Annie Marion. *Wage-Earning Women.* New York: Macmillan, 1910.

Mason, Edward S. *The Street Railway in Massachusetts: The Rise and Decline of an Industry.* Cambridge: Harvard University Press, 1932.

Melosh, Barbara. "'Skilled Hands, Cool Heads, and Warm Hearts': Nurses and Nursing, 1920-1960." Ph.D. dissertation, Brown University, 1979.

Mock, James R., and Larson, Cedric. *Words that Won the War: The Story of the Committee on Public Information, 1917-1919.* Princeton: Princeton University Press, 1939.

Montgomery, Louise. *The American Girl in the Stockyards District.* A Study of Chicago's Stockyards Community, vol. 2. Chicago: University of Chicago Press, 1913.

Mulcaire, Michael. *The International Brotherhood of Electrical Workers: A Study in Trade Union Structure and Functions.* Washington, D.C.: Catholic University Press, 1923.

Murray, Robert K. *Red Scare: A Study in National Hysteria.* New York: McGraw-Hill, 1964.

Myers, Howard Barton. "The Policing of Labor Disputes in Chicago: A Case Study." Ph.D. dissertation, University of Chicago, 1929.

Nadworny, Milton. *Scientific Management and the Unions, 1900-1932.* Cambridge: Harvard University Press, 1955.

National Industrial Conference Board. *Wartime Changes in Wages, September 1914 — March 1919.* Research Report no. 20. Boston, 1919.

———. *Wartime Employment of Women in the Metal Trades.* Research Report no. 8. Boston, 1918.

Nelson, Daniel. *Managers and Workers: Origins of the New Factory System in the United States, 1880-1920.* Madison: University of Wisconsin Press, 1975.

Nelson, Ralph. *Merger Movements in American Industry, 1895-1956.* Princeton: Princeton University Press, 1959.

O'Geran, Graeme. *A History of Detroit Street Railways.* Detroit: The Conover Press, 1931.

O'Neill, William. *Everyone Was Brave: The Rise and Fall of Feminism in America.* Chicago: Quadrangle, 1969.

Page, Arthur W. *The Bell Telephone System.* New York: Harper & Bros., 1941.

Paine, Albert Bigelow. *Theodore N. Vail, A Biography.* New York and London: Harper & Bros., 1921.

Perlman, Mark. *The Machinists: A New Study in American Trade Unionism.* Cambridge: Harvard University Press, 1961.

Peterson, H.D., and Fite, Gilbert. *Opponents of War, 1917-1918.* Madison: University of Wisconsin Press, 1957.

Preston, William. *Aliens and Dissenters: Federal Suppression of Radicals, 1903-1933.* New York: Harper & Row, Harper Torchbook, 1966.

Radosh, Ronald. *American Labor and United States Foreign Policy.* New York: Random House, 1969.

Rodgers, Daniel T. *The Work Ethic in Industrial America, 1850-1920.* Chicago: University of Chicago Press, 1978.

Schmidt, Emerson Peter. *Industrial Relations in Urban Transportation.* Minneapolis: University of Minnesota Press, 1937.

Slosson, Preston William. *The Great Crusade and After, 1914-1928.* New York: Macmillan, 1930.

Stehman, J. Warren. *The Financial History of the American Telephone and Telegraph Company.* Boston: Houghton Mifflin, 1925.

Stigler, George. *Domestic Servants in the United States, 1900-1940.* New York: National Bureau of Economic Research, 1946.

Taylor, Frederick Winslow. *The Principles of Scientific Management.* New York: Harper & Bros., 1911.

Terrell, Mary Church. *A Colored Woman in a White World.* Washington, D.C.: Ransdell, Inc., 1940.

Titmuss, Richard. *Essays on "The Welfare State."* 2d ed. Boston: Beacon Press, 1969.

Trachtenberg, Alexander, ed. *American Labor Year Book, 1919-1920.* New York: The Rand School of Social Science, 1920.

Tracy, Lena Harvey. *How My Heart Sang: The Story of Pioneer Industrial Welfare Work.* New York: Richard R. Smith, 1950.

Urofsky, Melvin. *Big Steel and the Wilson Administration.* Columbus: Ohio State University Press, 1969.

van Kleeck, Mary. *Artificial Flower Makers.* New York: Survey Associates, 1913.

_____. *A Seasonal Industry: A Study of the Millinery Trade in New York.* New York: Russell Sage Foundation, 1917.

_____. *Women in the Bookbinding Trade.* New York: Survey Associates, 1913.

Walsh, Joseph Leigh. *Connecticut Pioneers in Telephone: The Origin and Growth of the Telephone Industry in Connecticut.* New Haven: Morris F. Tyler Chapter, Telephone Pioneers of America, 1950.

Watkins, Gordon S. *Labor Problems and Labor Administration in the United States During the World War.* Urbana: University of Illinois Press, 1920.

Weinstein, James. *The Corporate Ideal in the Liberal State.* Boston: Beacon Press, 1963.

Wiebe, Robert F. *Businessmen and Reform: A Study of the Progressive Movement.* Cambridge: Harvard University Press, 1962.

_____. *The Search for Order, 1877-1920.* New York: Hill and Wang, 1967.

Wilcox, Delos Franklin. *Analysis of the Electric Railway Problem: Report to the Federal Electric Railways Commission with Summary and Recommendations Supplemented by Special Studies of Local Transportation Issues in the State of New Jersey and the City of Denver, with Notes on Recent Developments in the Electric Railway Field.* New York: The Author, 1921.

_____. *Municipal Franchises: A Description of the Terms and Conditions Upon Which Private Corporations Enjoy Special Privileges in the Streets of American Cities.* 2 vols. New York: McGraw Hill, 1910-1911.

Wolf, Harry. *The Railroad Labor Board.* Chicago: University of Chicago Press, 1927.

Wolman, Leo. *The Growth of American Trade Unions, 1880-1923.* New York: National Bureau of Economic Research, 1924.

Wolfson, Theresa. *The Woman Worker and the Trade Unions.* New York: International Publishers, 1926.

ARTICLES AND CONFERENCE PAPERS

Specific citations for unsigned articles can be found in the notes to individual chapters. The journals in which these articles appear are collectively listed in the bibliography under "Newspapers and Periodicals."

Alford, A.L. "An Industrial Achievement of the War." *Industrial Management* 55 (February 1918): 97-100.

Benson, Susan Porter. "'The Clerking Sisterhood': Rationalization and the Work Culture of Saleswomen." *Radical America* 12 (March-April 1978): 15-32.

_____. "'More Intelligent Acquiescence': The Drama of the American Department Store, 1900-1940." Seminar paper, Boston University, 1975.

Bertinson, Janet. "CWA Pickets Pacific Telephone over Job Pressures, Stress." *The Monitor* (September-October 1978): 14-15.

Brito, Patricia Kendrick. "Protective Legislation in Ohio, 1918-1939." Paper delivered at the College of St. Catherine's Conference on Women's History, St. Paul, Minnesota, 22 October 1977.

Carpenter, Charles U. "How We Trained 5,000 Women." *Industrial Management* 55 (May 1918): 355-357.

Carter, W.S. "Effect of Federal Control on Railway Labor." *Proceedings of the Academy of Political Science* 8 (1918-1920): 198-210.

Churchill, W.L. "Changing from Male to Female Help." *Industrial Management* 55 (April 1918): 322-324.

Davies, Margery. "Woman's Place Is at the Typewriter: The Feminization of the Clerical Labor Force." *Radical America* 8 (July-August 1974): 1-28.

Douglas, Paul. "Plant Administration of Labor." *Journal of Political Economy* 27 (July 1919): 544-560.

Douglas, Paul H. "War Time Courses in Employment Management." *School and Society* (June 2, 1919): 692-695.

Eilbirt, Henry. "The Development of Personnel Management in the United States." *Business History Review* 33 (1959): 345-64.

Ferguson, Carey D. "Women as Street Car Conductors." *Motorman and Conductor* 26 (November 1918): 32-33.

Fitch, Howard. "Technique of Holding Employee Representation Council or Committee Meetings: Where Female and Often Young Workers Predominate." *Personnel* 4 (February 1928): 147-151.

Gadsby, Mrs. M.A. "Provision for the Disabled and Vocational Education." *Monthly Labor Review* 6 (April 1918): 111-117.

Goldmark, Pauline, "Women Conductors." *Survey* 40 (June 29, 1918): 369.

_____. "Women in the Railroad World." *The Annals of the American Academy of Political and Social Sciences* 86 (November 1919): 214-221.

Greenwald, Maurine Weiner. "Women Workers and World War I: The American Railroad Industry, A Case Study." *Journal of Social History* 9 (Winter 1975): 154-177.

Gutman, Herbert. "Work, Culture, and Society in Industrializing America, 1815-1919." *American Historical Review* 78 (June 1973): 531-588.

Hall, E. K. "To Get the Best from Each." *System* 57 (April 1930): 374.

_____. "What is Employee Representation?" *Personnel* 4 (February 1928): 71-84.

Hall, R. Dawson. "The Labor Situation." *Coal Age* 13 (May 11, 1918): 886.

Haynes, Elizabeth Ross. "Negroes in Domestic Service in the United States." *Journal of Negro History* 8 (October 1923): 384-442.

Hobbs, Margaret. "Moral Menace and Danger to Health." *Union Leader* 19 (June 15, 1918): 5.

Hopkins, Ernest Martin. "A Functionalized Employment Department as a Factor in Industrial Efficiency." *Annals of the American Academy of Political and Social Science* 65 (May 1916): 67-75.

Jackson, M. D. "The Colored Woman in Industry." *Crisis* (November 1918): 12-17.

Kelley, Florence. "Twenty-five Years of the Consumers' League Movement." *Survey* 35 (November 27, 1915): 212-214.

Lynch, Margaret C. "Women's Work in Iron, Steel, and Metal Industries." *Iron Trade Review* 62 (January 17, 1918): 205-212.

Meier, August, and Elliot, Rudwick. "The Rise of Segregation in the Federal Bureaucracy." *Phylon* 28 (Summer 1967): 178-185.

Miller, Frank B., and Coghill, Mary Ann. "Sex and the Personnel Manager." *Industrial and Labor Relations Review* 18 (October 1964): 32-44.

Montgomery, David. "Immigrant Workers and Scientific Management." Paper delivered at the "Immigrants in Industry" Conference of the Eleutherian Mills Historical Library and the Balch Institute, Wilmington, Delaware, 2 November 1973.

_____. "The 'New Unionism' and the Transformation of Workers' Consciousness in America, 1909-1922." *Journal of Social History* 7 (Summer 1974): 509-529.

_____. "Quel standards? Les ouvriers et la réorganisation de la production aux Etats-Unis (1900-1920)." *Le Mouvement Social* 102 (Janvier-Mars 1978): 101-127.

_____. "Workers' Control of Machine Production in the Nineteenth Century." *Labor History* 17 (Fall 1976): 485-509.

Nelson, Daniel, and Campbell, Stuart. "Taylorism Versus Welfare Work in American Industry: H.L. Gantt and the Bancrofts." *Business History Review* 46 (Spring 1972): 1-16.

Nichols, Ernest Fox. "The Employment Manager." *Annals of the American Academy of Political and Social Science* 65 (May 1916): 1-8.

Norwood, Stephen. "The New England Telephone Operators' Union, 1912-1923." Paper delivered at the New England Historical Association, Boston, Massachusetts, 3 May 1975.

O'Connor, Julia. "Before and After Taking Unionism." *The Boiler Makers' and Iron Ship Builders' Journal* 28 (January 1926): 42-44.

_____. "The Blight of Company Unionism." *American Federationist* 33 (May 1926): 544-549.

_____. "History of the Organized Telephone Operators' Movement." *The Union Telephone Operator* 1 (January-March, May-July 1921).

_____. "The Truth about the New England Phone Strike." *Life and Labor* 9 (June 1919): 131-133.

Odencrantz, Louise. "The Irregularity of Employment of Women Factory Workers." *Survey* 22 (May 1, 1909): 196-210.

O'Shea, Peter F. "A Shop Training School for Girls." *Industrial Management* 58 (September 1919): 213-215.

Parsons, Floyd W. "Employment of Women in Mining." *Coal Age* 13 (May 11, 1918): n.p.

Peake, Mrs. May. "The Woman Machinist: Her Accomplishments and Her Possibilities." *Life and Labor* 9 (December 1919): 326-329.

Prentiss, F.L. "A Motor Company's Shop Training for Women." *The Iron Age* 102 (December 12, 1918): 1453-1455.

Reverby, Susan. "The Search for the Hospital Yardstick: Nursing and the Rationalization of Hospital Work." In *Health Care in America: Essays in Social History*, edited by Susan Reverby and David Rosner. Philadelphia: Temple University Press, 1979.

Schacht, John N. "Toward Industrial Unionism: Bell Telephone Workers and Company Unions, 1919-1937." *Labor History* 16 (Winter 1975): 5-36.

Sheehan, P.F. "Keep the Girls Off the Cars." *Motorman and Conductor* 26 (August 1918): 28.

Simpson, Edith. "Trade Union Organization among the Telephone Operators in the United States." *Union Telephone Operator* 1 (November 1921): 14-16.

Smith, Ethel. "Government Control and Industrial Rights." *Life and Labor* 9 (April 1919): 85-88.

_____. "The Woman's Labor Movement." *Federal Employee* 4 (April 1919): 214-217.

Smith, Mary Roberts. "The Negro Woman as an Industrial Factor." *Life and Labor* 8 (January 1918): 7-8.

Squires, Benjamin. "Women Street Railway Employees." *Monthly Labor Review* 6 (May 1918): 1049-1070.

Sullivan, Olive M. "The Women's Part in the Stockyards Organization Work." *Life and Labor* 8 (May 1918): 102-104.

Torrence, William D. "Great Independent: The Lincoln Telephone Company, 1903-1908." *Business History Review* 33 (1959): 365-382.

Turner, Mrs. V. B. "Women in Mechanical Trades in the United States." *Monthly Labor Review* 7 (September 1918): 206-215.

van Kleeck, Mary. "Discussion of Financial Incentives." *Bulletin of the Taylor Society* 11 (December 1926): 440-441.

_____. "The Interview as a Method of Research." *Bulletin of the Taylor Society* 11 (December 1926): 268-274.

_____. "The Social Meaning of Good Management." *Bulletin of the Taylor Society* 9 (December 1924): 242.

_____. "Women in the Munition Industries." *Life and Labor* 8 (June 1918): 113-122.

Viall, William A. "Women in Machine Tool Industry." *Iron Trade Review* 62 (May 9, 1918): 1190-1191.

Washington, Forrester B. "Reconstruction and the Colored Woman." *Life and Labor* 9 (Januay 1919): 3-9.

Wechsler, Eva. "Uncle Sam's Employment Service." *Life and Labor* 8 (September 1918): 196-198.

Withington, Anne. "The Telephone Strike." *Survey* 42 (April 26, 1919): 146.

_____. "When the Telephone Girls Organized." *Survey* 30 (August 16, 1913): 621-623.

Wolfe, Allis Rosenberg. "Women, Consumerism, and the National Consumers' League in the Progressive Era, 1900-1923." *Labor History* 16 (Summer 1975): 378-392.

Wolfe, H. B., and Olson, Helen. "Wartime Industrial Employment of Women in the United States." *Journal of Political Economy* 27 (October 1919): 639-669.

GOVERNMENT DOCUMENTS

Burleson, Albert. *Government Control and Operation of the Telephone and Telegraph Systems.* Washington, D.C.: Government Printing Office, 1921.

Edwards, Alba M. *Sixteenth Census of the United States: 1940. Population. Comparative Occupation Statistics for the United States, 1870-1940.* Washington, D.C.: Government Printing Office, 1943.

Hill, Joseph A. *Women in Gainful Occupations, 1870-1920.* U.S. Bureau of the Census. Census Monographs no. 9. Washington, D.C.: Government Printing Office, 1929.

Hooks, Janet M. *Women's Occupations through Seven Decades*. U.S. Department of Labor. Women's Bureau. Bulletin no. 218. Washington, D.C.: Government Printing Office, 1947.

Manning, Caroline. *The Immigrant Woman and Her Job*. U.S. Department of Labor. Women's Bureau. Bulletin no. 74. Washington, D.C.: Government Printing Office, 1930.

National Railroad Adjustment Board. *General Order No. 27 with Its Supplements, Addenda, Amendments and Interpretations*. Chicago, 1935.

New York Department of Labor. Bureau of Women in Industry. *Report Submitted Relative to the Telephone Industry in New York State*. Albany: J.B. Lyon Co., 1920.

New York State Industrial Commission. *The Industrial Replacement of Men by Women in the State of New York*. Bulletin no. 93. Albany, 1919.

U.S. Bureau of the Census. *Census of Electrical Industries: 1917. Telephones*. Washington, D.C.: Government Printing Office, 1920.

_____. *Census of Electrical Industries: 1922. Telephones*. Washington, D.C.: Government Printing Office, 1924.

_____. *Fifteenth Census of the United States: 1930*. Vol. 4: *Population: Occupations, by States*. Washington, D.C.: Government Printing Office, 1933.

_____. *Fifteenth Census of the United States: 1930*. Vol. 5: *Population: General Report on Occupations*. Washington, D.C.: Government Printing Office, 1933.

_____. *Fourteenth Census of the United States: 1920*. Vol. 4: *Population: Occupations*. Washington, D.C.: Government Printing Office, 1923.

_____. *Statistics of Women at Work: 1900*. Washington, D.C.: Government Printing Office, 1907.

_____. *Street and Electric Railways: 1902*. Washington, D.C.: Government Printing Office, 1905.

U.S. Congress. Senate. *Investigation of Telephone Companies*. S. Doc. 380, 61st Cong., 2d sess. Washington, D.C.: Government Printing Office, 1910.

_____. *Report on Condition of Women and Child Wage-Earners in the United States*. Vol. 12: *Employment of Women in Laundries*. S. Doc. 645, 61st Cong., 2d sess. Washington, D.C.: Government Printing Office, 1911.

U.S. Department of Labor. Bureau of Labor Statistics. *National War Labor Board*. Bulletin no. 287. Washington, D.C.: Government Printing Office, 1922.

_____. *Proceedings of the Employment Managers' Conference, 2-3 April 1917.* Bulletin no. 227. Washington, D.C.: Government Printing Office, 1917.

_____. *Proceedings of the Employment Managers' Conference, 9-11 May 1918.* Bulletin no. 247. Washington, D.C.: Government Printing Office, 1919.

_____. *Welfare Work for Employees in Industrial Establishments in the United States.* Bulletin no. 250. Washington, D.C.: Government Printing Office, 1919.

U.S. Department of Labor. Women's Bureau. *The Change from Manual to Dial Operation in the Telephone Industry.* Bulletin no. 110. Washington, D.C.: Government Printing Office, 1933.

_____. *The Effects of Labor Legislation on the Employment Opportunities of Women.* Bulletin no. 65. Washington, D.C.: Government Printing Office, 1928.

_____. *Negro Women in Industry.* Bulletin no. 20. Washington, D.C.: Government Printing Office, 1922.

_____. *The New Position of Women in American Industry.* Bulletin no. 12. Washington, D.C.: Government Printing Office, 1920.

_____. *The Occupational Progress of Women, 1910-1930.* Bulletin no. 104. Washington, D.C.: Government Printing Office, 1933.

_____. *The Share of Wage-Earning Women in Family Support.* Bulletin no. 30. Washington, D.C.: Government Printing Office, 1933.

_____. *Technological Changes in Relation to Women's Employment.* Bulletin no. 107. Washington, D.C.: Government Printing Office, 1935.

_____. *The Woman Telephone Operator.* Bulletin no. 207. Washington, D.C.: Government Printing Office, 1946.

_____. *Women Street Car Conductors.* Bulletin no. 11. Washington, D.C.: Government Printing Office, 1921.

U.S. Railroad Administration. *Annual Report of W. G. McAdoo, Director General of Railroads, 1918.* Washington, D.C.: Government Printing Office, 1919.

_____. *Annual Report of Walter B. Hines, Director General of Railroads, 1919.* Washington, D.C.: Government Printing Office, 1920.

_____. *U.S. Railroad Administration Order No. 8.* 8 February 1918.

NEWSPAPERS AND PERIODICALS

Annals of the American Academy of Political and Social Science. 1916-1920.

Annual Report of the Directors of American Telephone and Telegraph Company to the Stockholders. 1912-1924.

Boston Herald. 1918-1919.

Cleveland Citizen. 1918-1919.

Cleveland Plain Dealer. 1918-1919.

The Crisis: A Record of the Darker Races. 1917-1920.

Detroit Labor News. 1918-1919.

Electric Railway Journal. 1917-1919.

Federal Employee. 1917-1920.

General Electric Review. 1917-1920.

Industrial Management. 1917-1920.

Iron Age. 1917-1920.

Iron Trade Review. 1917-1920.

Journal of Political Economy. 1917-1920.

Life and Labor. 1917-1919.

Machinery. 1917-1920.

Machinists' Monthly Journal. 1917-1920.

Monthly Labor Review. 1916-1920.

Motorman and Conductor. 1917-1920.

Personnel. 1928.

Proceedings of the American Academy of Political Science. 1919.

Seattle Union Record. Daily Edition. 1918-1922.

Seattle Union Record. Weekly Edition. 1917-1920.

School and Society. 1919.

Survey. 1916-1920.

Union Leader. 1917-1920.

Union Telephone Operator. 1921.

Index

Abbott, Edith, 68
Addison, Mrs. G. W., 174
Adler, Felix, 67
Allen, Florence (suffragist and lawyer), 160, 162
Alliance Employment Bureau, 65
Amalgamated Association of Street and Electric Railway Employees of America (AASRE): resistance to the hiring of women conductors, 141, 146-47, 149-53, 158, 180; history, 144-45; Cleveland local, 159, 161-64, 166, 171, 180-81; Detroit local, 167-68, 172, 180-81; Kansas City local, 172, 176-78, 182
Amalgamated Clothing Workers of America, 43
American Federation of Labor, 115, 149, 166, 215
American Locomotive Works, 40
American Management Association Conference, 227
American Telephone and Telegraph Company, 85; postwar strikes against, 40, 216-22, 224-25; scientific management proponent, 50, 196-200; welfare work proponent, 51, 207; history, 186-89; wartime

strikes against, 210-11; reaction to labor militancy, 223-24, 227-31; employee representation program, 227-30; technological innovation, 230-31
Anderson, Mary: biography, 67; role as wartime administrator, 75-76; supports Cleveland women streetcar conductors, 165-66; supports Wichita telephone operators, 217
Armour, J. Ogden, 172
Association of Women Street Railway Employees (Cleveland), 160, 163-65. See also Detroit Women Conductors' Association

Baltimore and Ohio Railroad, 82, 83, 98, 102, 117, 120, 123
Barnett, Ella (railroad office worker), 101, 102-03
Bell, Alexander Graham, 188
Bell System. See American Telephone and Telegraph Company
Bell Telephone Company, 187, 189
Bell Telephone Company of Philadelphia, 189
Bethlehem Steel Company, 71-73

Black women wage earners: wartime changes in employment, 20, 22-27, 107; and racial discrimination, 24, 26-27, 41-43, 88, 114-15, 137, 197; and trade unions, 43-45; reaction to protective legislation, 113

Borden, Gail, 5

Boston Women's Trade Union League, 204

Brandeis, Louis, 67

Breckinridge, Sophonisba, 68

Briscoe, Elizabeth F. (welfare secretary), 52

Brooklyn Rapid Transit Company, 147, 148

Brotherhood of Boilermakers, Iron Ship Builders, and Helpers, 217

Brotherhood of Railway Carmen: wartime growth, 90; and sex and racial discrimination, 115, 133, 137

Brotherhood of Railway Clerks, 40, 69, 217; wartime growth, 90; and sex discrimination, 99, 102, 105-06; 131-32; compared to the Brotherhood of Railway Carmen, 133

Bryant Chucking Grinder Company, 125

Bryn Mawr College, 68

Bulletin of the Taylor Society, 85

Burleson, Albert: postmaster general, 208; head of Wire Administration, 212-13; labor policies, 213-16, 218-20; biography, 214-15; and 1919 New England telephone operators' strike, 221-23; and company unionism, 227

Business: impact of organizational revolution on women's employment patterns, 4-12, 94, 234, 242

Carpenter, Charles, U. (personnel manager), 55

Carter, W. S. (president of the Brotherhood of Firemen and Enginemen and Director of Labor for the United States Railroad Administration), 60

Case School of Applied Science, 74

Central Union Telephone Company, 189

Chesapeake and Ohio Railroad, 99

Chicago, Burlington, and Quincy Railroad, 103

Chicago Federation of Labor, 67

Clark, Florence (Women's Service Section field agent), 68, 79, 97, 98

Clerical occupations: feminization of, 8-10; for women in railroad offices, 22, 87, 88, 92, 93-106; wartime trade union organization of women in, 39-40, 105-06, 235; and sex discrimination in the railroad industry, 79, 88, 97-99, 131-33; wartime promotions for women in, 100-04; conflicts between men and women wage earners in, 102-05, 129, 130. *See also* Demobilization of women in the railroad industry; Sexual harrassment

Cleveland Building Trades Council, 161

Cleveland Chamber of Commerce: Industrial Welfare Committee, 54; supports women streetcar conductors, 161

Cleveland Federation of Women's Clubs, 160

Cleveland Plain Dealer, 160, 164

Cleveland Railway Company: financial condition, 145; open-shop drive, 159; and dispute over employment of women conductors, 159-64, 171. *See also* Detroit United Railway Company; Kansas City Railways Company

Cleveland Telephone Company, 223

Cleveland Waitresses' Union, 157, 172
Coal miners: attitudes towards women's employment in mining, 124
Commercial Telegraphers' International Union, 225
Commission of Inquiry. *See* Unitea States Wire Administration
Considine, Ellen (pioneer telephone operator), 195, 196
Cooke, Morris, L. (scientific management expert), 58
Council of Churches, 217
Council of National Defense: Industrial Training for the War Emergency, 54. *See also* Ohio Women in Industry Committee
Crosson, Anna (railroad office worker), 132
Curley, Mary (trade union leader), 203

Danielian, N. R., 212-13
Davis, Harry L. (mayor of Cleveland), 162
DeLaney, Irene (trade union leader), 203
Delaware, Lackawanna and Western Railroad, 79-80
Demobilization of women in the railroad industry: violations of seniority during, 129-31; union responses to, 131-34; women's reactions to, 134-35; statistics on, 135-36
Detroit United Railway Company (DUR): financial condition, 145; and dispute over employment of women conductors, 167, 168. *See also* Cleveland Railways Company; Kansas City Railways Company
Detroit Women Conductors' Association, 156. *See also* Association of Women Street Railway Employees (Cleveland)

Dickey, Walter (Kansas City businessman), 173
Dilution of skilled labor: effect on women's pre-World War I employment patterns, 6-10, 234; effect on women's wages, 8, 77; effect on women's wartime opportunities, 13, 15, 116-20, 123-28, 242; reaction of machinists and molders to, 116-20, 123-28, 133-34, 136-37, 237-38
Domestic service: decline as an occupation, 11-13, 21-24; concentration of black women in, 22-24; wartime organization of women in, 40-41
Duffy, Mary (trade union leader), 203
Dunn, "Mother" (welfare secretary), 52

Electric Review, 54
Employee representation: at AT&T, 227-30
Employers' Association of Detroit, 168
Employers' associations, 168, 173
Employment, women's: wartime job changes in, 3-4, 13-32, 38, 44, 92-93, 116-17, 139, 185; gender segregation in, 4, 7-10, 88, 93-94, 97-98; pre-World War I patterns of, 5-12; racial segregation in, 22-23, 26-27, 41-43, 88, 114-15 (*see also* Black women wage earners). *See also* Demobilization of women in the railroad industry; Strikes; Union organization
Erie Railroad, 130

Fancy Leather Goods Union, 43
Federal Vocational Board, 54
Fellows Gears Shaper Company, 125
Feminism: and female social reformers, 48, 69, 84; effect on women streetcar conductors, 156, 164-65; effect on women telephone operators, 203

Foley, Maud (trade union leader), 203
Forrester, J. J. (president of the Brotherhood of Railway Clerks), 106
Frankford Arsenal, 44
Frankfurter, Felix, 217
Freiss, Adrianna (railroad office worker), 101

Gantt, Henry L., 72
General Electric Company, 38, 40
Gessner, Mabel T. (railroad office worker), 102
Goldmark, Pauline (head of Women's Service Section of the United States Railroad Administration), 60, 79-80, 81, 82; biography, 67-68, 85
Gompers, Samuel, 166
Grand Trunk Railroad, 132
Green, Sarah (trade unionist), 176, 177
Guernsey, N. T. (lawyer for AT&T), 212

Hadley, Jennie (railroad elevator operator), 80
Hall, E. K. (ATT&T executive), 227
Hall, Edith (Women's Service Section field agent), 68, 82-83, 98
Hayes, Mayme (railroad office worker), 106
Heim, J. J. (Kansas City businessman), 173
H. J. Heinz Company: welfare work, 51-52
Hoskins, Jean (Welfare secretary), 52

Industrial Management, 54
International Association of Machinists (IAM): and wartime organization of women, 120, 123; postwar national agreement in the railroad industry, 133-34. *See also* Dilution of skilled labor
International Boot and Shoe Workers' Union, 67

International Brotherhood of Electrical Workers (IBEW): Cleveland local opposes hiring of women streetcar conductors, 161; strength compared with railroad brotherhoods, 214; supports New England telephone operators' 1919 strike, 220; organizes telephone operators' union, 222, 225-27; demise following 1919 telephone strike wave, 224-26. *See also* Strikes; Telephone industry
International Ladies' Garment Workers' Union, 43
International Molders' and Foundry Workers' Union: opposes employment of women in railroad shops, 117, 123-24. *See also* Dilution of skilled labor
Interstate Commerce Commission, 89
Iron Age, 54
Iron Trade Review, 54

Johnson, Blanche (trade union leader), 203
Jones and Lamson Machine Tool Company, 125
Joseph Bancroft & Sons Company: and welfare work, 52
June, Mary E. (trade union leader), 203

Kansas City Railways Company: financial condition, 145, 180; and women conductors, 175-76, 178, 175-76, 178, 179. *See also* Cleveland Railways Company; Detroit United Railway Company
Kansas City Women's Trade Union League, 175-76, 177, 182
Kealy, P. J. (president of Kansas City Railways), 145
Kemper, W. T. (Kansas City businessman), 173
Kerr, Rhoda (trade union leader), 203
Kingsbury, Susan, 68

Labor militancy: women's wartime, 4-5, 38-45, 99, 113, 131, 132, 134, 156, 160, 164-65, 173-74, 210-11, 216-18. *See also* Strikes; Union organization

Labor turnover, 38, 201, 202, 208-09

Lane Commission, 90-91

Lane, Franklin K., 90

Lehigh Coal and Navigation Company, 124

Leland, Henry M. (president of Lincoln Motor Company), 56

Lincoln Motor Company: wartime training program for women, 54, 56-57

Long, R. A. (Kansas City businessman), 173

McGovern, Kathryn (trade union leader), 203

Machinery, 54

Machinists' Monthly Journal, 120

Manufacturing: trends in women's prewar work, 6-8; trends in women's wartime work, 15-22, 72-73. *See also* Railroad industry

Married women workers: minority in labor force, 5; labor force participation among blacks, 23; and demobilization, 139; as streetcar conductors, 157

Massachusetts Anti-Suffrage Association, 221

Matthews, May (trade union leader), 203

Metropolitan Railways, 145

Miller, Jeannette (railroad office worker, 132

Minnesota Transfer Company, 113

Missouri Pacific Railroad, 107

Mix, Jessie (pioneer telephone operator), 194, 195

Montgomery, David, 118, 202

Moran, Helen (trade union leader), 203

Moriarty, Rose (suffragist), 164, 166, 170, 171

Motorman and Conductor, 149

Mountain States Telephone and Telegraph Company, 189

National American Woman Suffrage Association, 165

National Cash Register Company: welfare work, 52

National Consumers' League, 68; Ohio branch, 124

National Federation of Federal Employees: and wartime organization of clerical workers, 40; wartime responses from black women wage earners to, 44

National Industrial Conference Board, 54, 119

National Industrial Recovery Act (1933), 230

National War Labor Board (NWLB), 40, 240; and Cleveland streetcar dispute, 161, 162-63, 169-71, 182-83; and Detroit streetcar dispute, 166, 168-69, 182-84; and Kansas City streetcar dispute, 178, 184

National Women's Trade Union League: and Cleveland streetcar dispute, 164, 166. *See also* Boston Women's Trade Union League; Kansas City Women's Trade Union League

New England Bell Telephone Company, 189, 218-19, 222

New England Union of Telephone Operators, 218

New York Central Railroad, 101, 102, 113

New York Railways Company, 147, 148

New York School of Social Philanthropy, 66, 68

New York Telephone Company, 189, 209

Nichols, Ernest Fox, 46
Nutt, Emma N. (first female tele-
    phone operator), 195

O'Connor, Julia (trade union leader),
    202, 203-04, 215-16, 221, 222, 230
Odlin, Margaret (trade union leader),
    203
Ohio Industrial Commission, 124
Ohio State Federation of Labor,
    124, 161
Ohio Woman Suffrage Association,
    160
Ohio Women in Industry Committee
    of the Council of National Defense,
    160
Ordnance Department of the United
    States Army, 57-59; Women's
    Branch of, 47-48, 58-60, 70-78, 85

Pacific Telephone and Telegraph Com-
    pany, 189, 210-11, 224-25
Pennsylvania Department of Mines,
    124
Pennsylvania Railroad, 79, 80, 123,
    129-30, 131, 132, 133
Personnel management, 53, 73-75, 86
Phipps, Waity Lela (telephone
    operator), 216-17
Pin-money theory of women's em-
    ployment, 131; disputed, 155
Polland, Laura (trade union leader),
    203
Porter, F. W. (Kansas City business-
    man), 174
Post Office Department: Order No.
    3209, 223
Powers, Birdie (trade union leader),
    203
President's Mediation Commission,
    210-11
Prince, Laura (streetcar conductor),
    156, 157, 163, 171-72

Protective legislation for women: and
    National Consumers' League, 68;
    and Women's Branch of the Ord-
    nance Department of the United
    States Army, 70; and Women's Ser-
    vice Section of the United States
    Railway Administration, 78, 84,
    107, 113, 137; and railroad
    shopmen, 116, 123-24; and coal
    miners, 124; and streetcar men, 149,
    152
Providence Telephone Company, 222
Public Service Commission of
    Washington, 152

Quinn, Mary: trade union leader, 203

Railroad Brotherhoods, 90
Railroad industry: under federal
    control, 60, 87-92, 212, 214, 215;
    women office workers employed in,
    93-106; women common laborers
    employed in, 106-16; women
    machine shop workers employed in,
    116-28. See also Women's Service
    Section of the United States
    Railroad Administration
Recording & Computing Machines
    Company: wartime training
    program for women, 54-56
Restriction of output: union machin-
    ists' attitude towards, 118; women
    operatives' attitudes towards, 118,
    235; employers' interest in, 119. See
    also Dilution of skilled labor
Rockefeller, John D., 5
Rock Island Arsenal, 77
Rocky Mountain Telephone Com-
    pany, 189
Ross, Helen (Women's Service Section
    field agent), 68, 98, 101, 104
Round Table (Kansas City women's
    club), 175-76
Russell Sage Foundation, 65-66, 68

Sales occupations: trends in women's prewar work, 10-11; wartime increase in women's jobs, 13-14

Santa Fe Railroad, 98, 114, 130

Schacht, John, 230

Schmitt, Katherine M. (pioneer telephone operator), 195

Scientific management: principles of, 47-50; in the telephone industry, 50, 184, 196-200, 228, 231; reaction of molders at Watertown Arsenal to, 58; and the Women's Branch of the Ordnance Department of the United States Army, 70-72

Scott, Walter Dill (industrial psychologist), 54

Scribner, Grace (trade union leader), 203

Seniority: effect on women's wartime railroad work, 100-03; disregard of during demobilization, 128-33

Sexual harassment, 98-100

Shaw, Anna Howard (minister and suffragist), 169, 170

Smith College, 65

Smith, Ethel (labor reformer), 169, 170

Southern Bell Telephone Company, 189

Southern New England Telephone Company, 194

Southern Railroad, 98

Southwestern Bell Telephone Company, 218

Stanley, John (president of the Cleveland Railway Company), 159, 164

Streetcar industry: relations between male and female employees in, 139, 141-42, 146-84; economic conditions in, 142-46, 180; hiring of women conductors in, 145-46; profile of women and men employees in, 153-58

Strikebreakers: among women railroad workers, 104; imported by New England Bell (in 1912), 205; treatment by community during 1919 New England telephone operators' strike, 220-21

Strikes: Cleveland streetcar (1918), 162-63; Detroit streetcar (1919), 172; Kansas City street railway and packing-house (1917), 173; Kansas City laundry workers (1917), 173-75; Kansas City general strike (1918), 174-75; Kansas City streetcar strike (1918), 179; Pacific Coast telephone (1917), 210-11; Wichita telephone (1918), 216-18; New England telephone (1919), 218-22; Southwestern telephone (1919), 224; Pacific Coast telephone (1919), 224-25

Sullivan, Rose (trade union leader), 203

Swift, Gustavus F., 5

Taylor, Clyde (Kansas City businessman), 175-76

Taylor, Frederick Winslow, 48-50, 58

Taylorism. *See* Scientific management

Taylor Society, 58

Telephone industry: under federal control, 185-86, 212-16; development of corporate telephone operating, 190, 194-202; trade union organization in, 202-05, 210-11, 222, 225; effect of World War I on, 207-11. *See also* American Telephone and Telegraph Company; Strikes; Telephone operating

Telephone operating: shift from males to females in, 10-11; nature of in the 1880s and 1890s, 190, 194-96; scientific management in, 196-200; training for, 197-98; surveillance system in, 199-200; pay scales for, 200; pro-

motion within, 201; labor turnover,
202, 208-09; trade union organization of, 202-07, 210-11, 222, 225;
trade union leaders of, 205-06. *See
also* American Telephone and
Telegraph Company; Strikes
Thorne, Florence (trade unionist), 166
Tracy, Lena Harvey (welfare
secretary), 52

Union Leader, 149, 150
Union organization: of women in
the clothing, textile, and shoe industries, 39; of women railroad and
clerical workers, 39-40, 105; of
black women, 43-44; of women in
metal-working firms, 120; women's
attitudes towards, 156-57, 172,
202-05, 217, 219, 226-27, 235-36; of
telephone operators, 202-05, 222,
224. *See also* Labor militancy
United States Department of Labor:
investigation of Cleveland streetcar
dispute, 159-60; investigation of
Kansas City streetcar dispute, 176
United States Employment Service, 54
United States Railroad Administration
(USRA): Women's Service Section,
47-48, 59-61, 78-84, 85; Division of
Labor, 60-61; Lane Commission,
90-91; General Order No. *27*, 91;
Board of Railroad Wages and
Working Conditions, 91; and
women's wartime wages, 93; and
seniority principle, 130; compared
with United States Wire Administra-
tion, 212, 213-16. *See also* Women's
Service Section of the United States
Railroad Administration
United States Wire Administration,
212-16; compared with United
States Railroad Administration,
212, 213-16
University of Chicago, 68

Vahey, James (labor lawyer), 162
Vail, Theodore N. (ATT&T executive),
188-89, 207, 215
van Kleeck, Mary (head of the
Women's Branch of the Ordnance
Department of the United States Ar-
my),58, 74; biography, 65-66, 85;
supports Cleveland women streetcar
conductors, 165-66. *See also*
Women's Branch of the Ordnance
Department of the United States
Army

Wabash Railroad, 101, 130
Walsh, Frank P. (labor lawyer), 169-71
War Industries Board, 54
Watertown Arsenal, 58
Welding: as a new occupation for
women, 117, 123. *See also* Dilution
of skilled labor
Welfare work, 47, 50-53, 73, 78
Western Electric Manufacturing
Company, 187
Western Telegraph Company, 187
William Filene & Sons Company:
welfare work, 52
Wilson, William B. (secretary of
labor), 160, 161, 217
Wilson, Woodrow: administration,
32-35. *See also* United States
Railroad Administration; United
States Wire Administration
Wire Control Board, 215-16
Wisconsin Gas and Electric Com-
pany, 148
Wisconsin Industrial Commission, 152
Woman's Committee of the Council of
National Defense: Kansas City, 174
Woman Suffrage Party of Cleveland,
160
Women in Industry Service of the
Department of Labor, 165, 166

Women reformers: profile of those employed in wartime government work, 61-70; support Cleveland women streetcar conductors, 160, 165-66; and Kansas City streetcar dispute, 175-76, 182; aid telephone operators in organizing a union, 204; assessment of wartime role, 240-42. *See also* Women's Branch of the Ordnance Department of the United States Army; Women's Service Section of the United States Railroad Administration

Women's Association of Commerce of U.S.A., 165

Women's Branch of the Ordnance Department of the United States Army: origin, 47-48, 58-60; operation, 70-78; and Bethlehem Steel Company, 71-73; and personnel management, 74-75; ineffectiveness, 75-77. *See also* Women's Service Section of the United States Railroad Administration

Women's Bureau of the Department of Labor, 57

Women's Service Section of the United States Railroad Administration (WSS): origin, 47-48, 59-61; operation, 78-84, 88; and protective legislation, 78, 84, 106, 107, 113, 137; and sex discrimination, 79-80; conservative theory of labor relations, 80-84; and moral supervision of women wage earners, 83-84, 114; and sexual harassment, 100; and demobilization, 133, 134; complaints submitted to, 134. *See also* Women's Branch of the Ordnance Department of the United States Army

World War, First: effect on women's self-image, 4-5, 32-38, 41-42, 126-27, 134-35, 141, 156, 180; labor shortage during, 4, 15, 20, 72, 208-09; effect on immigration, 15; effect on women's wages, 25-26, 32, 93, 155, 208; patriotic involvement of labor, 32-35, 220; propaganda, 32-37; effect on union growth, 39-41, 43-45, 90, 105, 222; strikes during, 39-41 (*see also* Strikes); effect on labor management, 53-61, 209 (*see also* Women's Branch of the Ordnance Department of the United States Army; Women's Service Section of the United States Railroad Administration; Employee representation); conflicts between male and female wage earners during, 102-15, 116, 117-28, 131, 133, 136-37, 141, 149-72, 180-81, 237-38; cooperation between male and female wage earners during, 172-80, 220-21, 236-37, 239; as historical prism, 233, 242-43. *See also* Black women wage earners; Employment, women's

Yates, Rose (Women's Service Section field agent), 69, 83, 98

Young Women's Christian Association, 165

About the Author

MAURINE WEINER GREENWALD is Associate Professor of History at the University of Pittsburgh. Her articles have appeared in the *Journal of Social History, International Labor and Working Class History*, and *American Women and American Studies*, edited by Betty E. Chmaj.

CPSIA information can be obtained at www.ICGtesting.com
Printed in the USA
LVOW011111261111

256543LV00004B/5/P

OWENS COMMUNITY COLLEGE
P.O. Box 10,000
Toledo, OH 43699-1947